HEINEMANN SECONDARY HISTORY PROJECT

THE MODERN WORLD

FOUNDATION EDITION

Rosemary Rees

CONTENTS

CHAPTER 1 — THE FIRST WORLD WAR

- 1.1 Why did war break out in 1914? 4
- 1.2 What was the fighting like on the Western Front? 9
- 1.3 What was it like to serve on the Western Front? 12
- 1.4 Where else did fighting take place? 14
- 1.5 What did the navy and air force do during the war? 16
- 1.6 What was the war like for civilians? 18
- 1.7 Did attitudes to war change between 1914 and 1918? 19
- 1.8 How did the war end? 21
- 1.9 Exercise 22

CHAPTER 2 — INTERNATIONAL RELATIONS 1919–39

- 2.1 How was peace restored after the First World War? 23
- 2.2 What was the League of Nations? 28
- 2.3 How did the countries try to avoid war after 1919? 32
- 2.4 The road to war: the League discredited 34
- 2.5 Hitler and the expansion of Germany 38
- 2.6 Exercise 47

CHAPTER 3 — THE UNITED STATES OF AMERICA 1918–41

- 3.1 Why did the USA decide to follow a policy of isolationism? 49
- 3.2 How did the policy of isolationism work? 51
- 3.3 The USA in the 1920s – was there a 'Golden Age'? 52
- 3.4 Why did government policy towards immigration change in the 1920s? 57
- 3.5 How were the immigrants treated? 58
- 3.6 What was prohibition? 59
- 3.7 What were the effects of the Wall Street Crash? 61
- 3.8 How successful was President Hoover in dealing with the Depression? 65
- 3.9 What steps did President Roosevelt take to end the Great Depression? 67
- 3.10 What opposition was there to the New Deal? 72
- 3.11 War – the end of isolationism and the end of the Depression 74
- 3.12 Exercise 75

CHAPTER 4 — GERMANY 1919–39

- 4.1 How did Germany react to The Treaty of Versailles? 78
- 4.2 What problems faced the Weimar Republic 1919–24? 80
- 4.3 The Stresemann era 1924–9 84
- 4.4 The beginnings of the Nazi Party 1919–29 86
- 4.5 How did the Nazis achieve power? 88
- 4.6 How did Hitler become dictator of Germany? 90
- 4.7 What did Hitler believe in? 92
- 4.8 How did Hitler and the Nazi Party control Germany? 94
- 4.9 How did the Nazi Party use the German economy? 96
- 4.10 What was everyday life like for young people? 98
- 4.11 The persecution of the Jews 100
- 4.12 Exercise 101

CHAPTER 5 — RUSSIA 1905–39

- 5.1 What was Russia like in 1905? 102
- 5.2 Who opposed the Tsar's government? 104
- 5.3 The Revolution of 1905 106
- 5.4 Two important men: Peter Stolypin and Grigori Rasputin 110
- 5.5 What was the impact of the First World War on Russia? 112
- 5.6 Why was there a Revolution in March 1917? 114
- 5.7 How did the Bolsheviks gain power? 115

5.8	How did the Bolsheviks establish themselves in power?	118
5.9	Who will succeed Lenin?	121
5.10	The collectivization of agriculture	124
5.11	Five Year Plans for Industry	126
5.12	What was life like in Stalin's USSR?	128
5.13	Exercise	131

CHAPTER 6   BRITAIN 1901–51

6.1	What was Britain like in 1901	132
6.2	How did the Liberal Governments attack poverty 1906–14?	136
6.3	How did the government intend to pay for the reforms?	138
6.4	How did the Labour Party begin?	140
6.5	Votes for Women?	142
6.6	Why was there a General Strike in 1926?	147
6.7	The Depression: How did industry and government cope?	151
6.8	The Depression: How did people cope?	154
6.9	How did the government plan for peacetime Britain?	156
6.10	Why did the Labour Party win the General Election of 1945?	158
6.11	How did the Labour government begin rebuilding Britain?	159
6.12	Exercise	162

CHAPTER 7   THE SECOND WORLD WAR 1939–45

7.1	What was the war like in the early years?	163
7.2	How important was the fighting in North Africa?	167
7.3	Why did war break out in the Pacific in 1941?	168
7.4	What was it like for civilians during the war?	170
7.5	The Holocaust	172
7.6	How did the Allies defeat Hitler?	174
7.7	How was Japan defeated?	177
7.8	Exercise	180

CHAPTER 8   THE COLD WAR

8.1	The origins of the Cold War	182
8.2	The Berlin crisis and the formation of NATO	185
8.3	War in Korea 1950–53	188
8.4	Hungary and Suez: two crises in one year	191
8.5	Why was the Berlin Wall built?	194
8.6	The Cuban missile crisis 1962	196
8.7	Czechoslovakia: The 'Prague Spring' 1968	198
8.8	Vietnam: A struggle for power	200
8.9	From arms race to détente 1945–80	204
8.10	The United Nations: another way of keeping the peace?	207
8.11	The end of the Cold War	209
8.12	Exercise	211

CHAPTER 9   SOUTH AFRICA

9.1	How did the Whites first settle in South Africa?	213
9.2	The Second World War	215
9.3	How was the policy of apartheid established in South Africa?	216
9.4	Who opposed apartheid?	218
9.5	How did the rest of the world react to apartheid?	221
9.6	Apartheid under pressure	223
9.7	Why did the reforms of P.W. Botha fail?	226
9.8	The end of apartheid	231
9.9	Exercise	234

INDEX	235

CHAPTER 1

THE FIRST WORLD WAR 1914–18

In August 1914, Britain, France and Russia (the **Allies**) went to war against Germany and Austria-Hungary (the **Central Powers**). Soon other smaller countries joined in. In 1917, the USA joined the Allies.

Most of the fighting during the war took place in northern France and Belgium. By 1918, both sides were worn out. Germany asked for peace. The Allies had won, but 8.5 million people were dead and over 21 million wounded.

Source A

This is a dark day and a dark hour . . . This war will demand of us enormous sacrifice in life and money, but we will show our enemy what it is to provoke Germany.

▲ Kaiser Wilhelm II talking about the outbreak of war in August 1914.

1.1 Why did war break out in 1914?

Source B

▲ A British cartoon printed in 1914. The Kaiser is reaching for his Europe-shaped soap.

The major European countries were great **rivals**. By 1914, their rivalry was so great that they were ready to go to war. All they needed was an excuse. This came in June 1914 when **Archduke Franz Ferdinand**, the heir to the throne of Austria, was killed by a gunman.

In 1914 Europe was divided into two groups. Britain, France and Russia joined together in the **Triple Entente**. Germany, Austria-Hungary and Italy made up the **Triple Alliance**.

▲ Europe and the Balkans in 1914. This map shows how Europe was divided in 1914. The two rival groups argued over the Balkans. Romania, Bosnia, Bulgaria and Serbia were countries in the area known as the Balkans.

Economic rivalry

In the 19th century, Britain produced more industrial goods than any other country in the world. These goods were sold throughout the world. Britain became the richest country in the world. But by 1914, Germany was producing more iron, steel and coal than Britain. Because of this, British politicians thought that Germany was threatening Britain's wealth.

Colonial rivalry

When one country rules over many other countries you can say it has an **empire**. Britain and France had huge overseas empires in Africa, India and the Far East where the lands they ruled were called **colonies**. The German **Kaiser** began to talk about Germany 'having a place in the sun'. He wanted Germany to have more land in Europe, and he wanted Germany to rule over some colonies. Germany had a large and powerful army. So Britain and France were afraid that Germany would try to capture parts of their empires.

QUESTIONS

1. Look at the map. Make a list of who was in:

   The Triple Alliance
   The Triple Entente

2. Read pages 4–6. Make a list of the reasons why members of the Triple Entente were suspicious of members of the Triple Alliance.

Source C

▲ Franz Ferdinand and his wife pictured shortly before they were assassinated.

Rivalry at sea

The British navy was the most powerful in the world. This was important because Britain was an island and had a huge empire to defend. But in 1908, the Kaiser said that he was going to enlarge the German navy. The British were worried that Germany was going to build **dreadnoughts**. These were powerful battleships. Then Germany would threaten Britain's navy.

Rivalry in the Balkans

The Balkans is an area of south-east Europe. Serbia, Bulgaria and Romania were countries in the Balkans. Serbia was made up mostly of people of the Slav race. Serbia wanted to bring all Slavs together into one large country. This was called **Panslavism**.

Austria-Hungary

Many Slavs lived in Austria-Hungary. The rulers of Austria-Hungary were afraid that the idea of Panslavism would lead to the break up of their empire.

Russia

Russia supported Serbia. This was because the Russian rulers wanted to limit the influence of Austria-Hungary in the Balkans. They also hoped to be allowed to use some Mediterranean ports because their own were iced up in the winter.

Assassination!

Some Slavs who supported Panslavism became terrorists. One group of Slav terrorists was called the **Black Hand**.

Source D

ASSASSINAT DE L'ARCHIDUC HÉRITIER D'AUTRICHE ET DE LA DUCHESSE SA FEMME A SARAJEVO

◀ A painting of the assassination of the Archduke Franz Ferdinand published on 12 July 1914.

On 28 June 1914, **Archduke Franz Ferdinand**, who would have been the next Emperor of Austria-Hungary, and his wife Sophie were visiting Sarajevo. At that time Sarajevo was a town in Austria-Hungary, close to the border with Serbia. A member of the Black Hand gang called **Gavrilo Princip** shot the Archduke and his wife.

After the assassination

This action by one man was the spark that really started the war. First, the government of Austria-Hungary ordered its troops to invade Serbia. The German government promised to support Austria-Hungary. Then Russia promised to support Serbia, and so Germany declared war on Russia as well. France joined in support of its ally, Russia. What would Britain do?

The Schlieffen Plan

In 1908, the German War Minister, **Count von Schlieffen**, drew up a plan to show how Germany could win a war in Europe. The plan said that Germany should first defeat France in a quick knock-out blow. Then the German army could turn and defeat the Russians. Von Schlieffen said the Russian army would take so long to get ready that Germany would have plenty of time to defeat the French.

SUMMARY

From peace to war

- **28 June** Archduke Franz Ferdinand assassinated.
- **28 July** Austria-Hungary declared war on Serbia.
- **1 August** Germany declared war on Russia.
- **3 August** Germany declared war on France.
- **4 August** Britain declared war on Germany.
- **6 August** Austria-Hungary declared war on Russia.

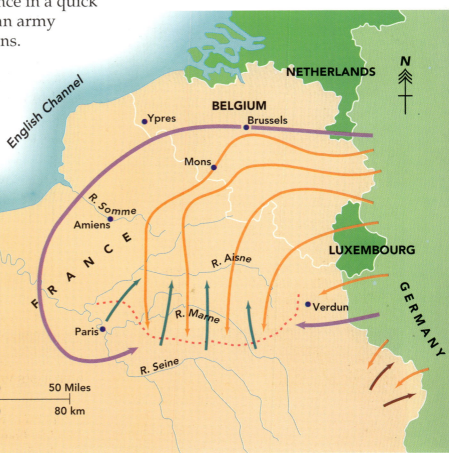

▶ The Schlieffen Plan to defeat France, and the actual route taken by the German army in 1914.

Did the Schlieffen Plan work?

It did not quite work out like that. On 3 August 1914, a German army of more than one million men marched into Belgium on its way to France. But the Belgian army fought fiercely, and this held up the German advance. The French had time to rush troops northwards to meet the invading Germans. And in the east, the Russian army was ready much more quickly than expected.

What did Great Britain do?

Many years before Britain had promised to defend Belgium against any invasion. Now Britain could use this promise as an excuse to join the war against Germany.

Source E

We felt that to stand aside would mean ... that Germany would wield total power in the continent. How would Germany use that power as regards Britain?

▲ Adapted from a speech made by the British Foreign Secretary, Sir Edward Grey, to the House of Commons in August 1914.

Source F

▲ Published in *Punch* on 12 August 1914, this cartoon shows the Kaiser bullying Belgium.

Source G

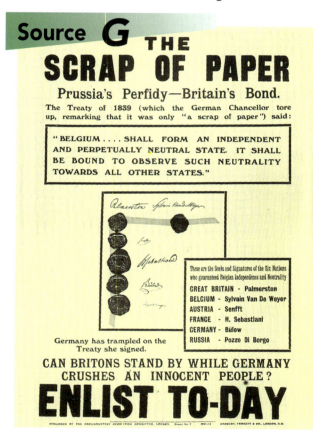

▶ A British poster.

QUESTIONS

1. **a** What did Serbia want in the Balkans?
   b Why did problems in the Balkans involve the Great Powers?

2. **a** Look at Sources E and G. Use them to help explain why Britain went to war in 1914.

1.2 What was the fighting like on the Western Front?

The British Expeditionary Force

The British government sent the **British Expeditionary Force** (BEF) to help the Belgians fight against the Germans. The BEF could not stop the German troops in northern France. But together with the French, they managed to slow the Germans down at the **Battle of the Marne**.

Digging trenches

The German troops began to dig trenches to protect themselves from attack. So did the Allied troops. Before long a line of trenches stretched all the way from Switzerland to the English Channel. This chain of trenches, over 600 kilometres long, was called the **Western Front**. It was along this line that the worst fighting of the war took place.

Trench warfare

One way of destroying enemy trenches was to dig tunnels under them and blow them up. Another way was to **bombard** enemy trenches with **artillery** shells. The idea was that the enemy trenches would be destroyed before the attacking troops advanced. But often, the shells went off on the ground in front of the trenches. It turned this area, called **No-Man's-Land**, into a sea of mud. So the artillery shells often made things worse for the soldiers going 'over the top' to attack.

Source A

For almost a month the Germans had pushed forward, often marching up to 80 kilometres a day. Now . . . the Germans had retreated 60 kilometres. The great advance had been stopped. The German commander told the Kaiser 'Your Majesty, we have lost the war.'

▲ This source explains how important the battle of the Marne was.

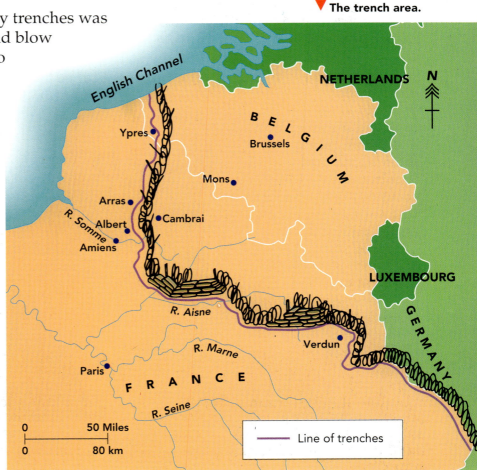

▼ The trench area.

Source B

▶ Victims of a gas attack at Béthune in northern France in April 1918.

Source C

Imagine a bright May morning and men busy washing and cooking. Suddenly a tremendous explosion, a deathly silence. Then fearful screams and groans and death gasps.
The sight of the wounded shedding their blood from gaping wounds, and their agonised cries – would convince any humane man that war is an impossible way of settling national questions.
The trench after the dead and wounded were removed presented a ghastly sight – it was red with blood like a room papered in crimson.

▲ Lance-Sergeant Elmer Cotton, of the Northumberland Fusiliers, describes the effects of a German shell on British trenches near Ypres in May 1915.

Gas

In April 1915, the Germans used a new weapon, **gas**. This burned men's lungs and blinded them. Soon both sides were using gas.

Tanks

In August 1916, the British used **tanks** for the first time. They were useful because they could smash right through the enemy trenches. Tanks became important at the end of the war when they became more reliable.

Source D

▲ Huge Crater cemetery on the Ypres-Menin road in Belgium. The cemetery is on the site of a huge mine explosion and contains 5,923 graves.

Source E

Gas! Gas! Quick boys – an ecstasy of fumbling,
Fitting the clumsy helmets just in time;
But someone still was yelling out and stumbling
And floundring like a man in fire or lime…

▲ Extract from the poem *Dulce et Decorum Est*, by Wilfred Owen. It describes a gas attack on front-line soldiers. Owen was killed on 4 November 1918.

Source F

▲ 'The Harvest of Battle', a painting by C.R.W. Nevison. It was finished in 1921.

Wearing down the enemy

Neither side seemed able to break through the **stalemate** on the Western Front. The generals began a policy of **attrition**. This meant that they planned battles with the idea of wearing down the enemy. They thought if the enemy lost more men than you, then your side had won. This is one of the reasons why so many men were killed.

The Battle of the Somme 1916

On 1 July 1916, the British started to attack German troops along the River Somme. They bombarded the German trenches for seven days. Then the soldiers were ordered to go 'over the top' and capture the German positions. But the Germans had sheltered in specially built deep trenches, and mowed down the British soldiers as they moved across No-Man's-Land. There were over 55,000 British casualties on just the first day. By November the British had advanced only 15 kilometres and lost 620,000 men.

Source G

The officers were in front. When we started firing we just had to load and reload.
They went down in their hundreds.
You didn't have to aim; just fire into them.

▲ A German machine gunner describing how easy it was to shoot down British soldiers on the first day of the Battle of the Somme.

QUESTIONS

1. a What does 'stalemate' mean?
   b Why was there stalemate on the Western Front?
   c How did both sides try to break the stalemate?
2. Look at Source F. Which parts of the painting would the artist have had to check up on before he began painting? Which parts do you think he made up? Give reasons for your answer.

1.3 What was it like to serve on the Western Front?

Who went to fight?

In August 1914, when Britain joined the war in support of Belgium, most British people were glad. Soon 500,000 men had volunteered to fight. They were aged between 19 and 35. They did not know what they were letting themselves in for. They had been told that the war would be over by Christmas and wanted to fight for their country before it was too late. The same thing happened in Germany and France. Thousands of young men rushed to join their country's army.

After a short training, the British **volunteers** were sent to the trenches. In the trenches, they fought alongside professional soldiers who were already in the **regular army**.

What were the trenches like?

The front line trenches were two metres deep. They had **sandbags** in the front along the top. These made a **parapet**. The parapet was supposed to protect the soldiers from enemy fire. Enemy snipers were waiting to shoot anyone foolish enough to stick his head over the parapet. The soldiers used **periscopes** to look out of their trenches. There were wooden **duckboards** along the bottom of the trenches. These kept soldiers' feet out of the mud. Along the front edge that faced the enemy trenches were lines of coiled barbed wire. These were supposed to make it difficult for enemy soldiers to attack. Beyond this barbed wire was No-Man's-Land. And beyond No-Man's-Land were the enemy trenches.

Dirt and disease

Life in the trenches was harsh. Soldiers found it difficult to keep clean. Huge rats became fat by feeding off the bodies in No-Man's-Land. Manure from all the army horses attracted thousands of flies. Dirt led to disease, which was spread by the rats, flies and lice.

Source A

▲ A famous recruiting poster: Lord Kitchener, the Minister of War, calls Britons to arms.

Source B

It was marvellous being accepted. My mother said I was a fool and she'd give me a good hiding: I told her 'I'm a man now, you can't hit a man.'

▲ Private George Morgan remembers joining up in 1914 at the age of sixteen.

All this meant that soldiers were often ill. They stood for hours in cold mud and got **trench foot**, which made their feet swell to three times their size.

Food

Food in the trenches was pretty awful. Soldiers mostly ate tinned beef with bread or biscuits. Sometimes the soldiers had treats like bacon, cheese or jam. Soldiers only had proper hot meals when they were safely behind the front line.

Water

Soldiers had to carry all the water they needed in tins. Often the water tasted bad because empty petrol tins were used.

Boredom

Life in the trenches was dull when there were no battles being fought. Some soldiers were on sentry duty. Some brought in supplies or repaired the trenches. In some parts of the front line, there were no battles for the whole war.

Source D

... troop-filled trains hurrying their way to the west, shouts of enthusiasm, fluttering of handkerchiefs, bursts of song, flushed faces of eager soldiers ... And of all of this which might be some great national festival, means but death and foul disaster.

▲ Princess Blücher, describing German troops leaving for the advance into Belgium.

Source C

Daddy, what did YOU do in the Great War?

▲ A British poster encouraging married men to join the armed forces during the First World War.

QUESTIONS

1. What made life so hard in the trenches? Make a list.
2. If conditions were so bad on the Western Front, why do you think men were so keen to join the army?
3. What point is being made in the poster (Source C).

SUMMARY

Trench warfare
- German advance stopped in 1914.
- Trenches dug for protection.
- Strong defences caused stalemate.
- Policy of attrition.
- Hardship of trench life.
- Heavy casualties.

1.4 Where else did fighting take place?

Source A

Thousands of Russians were driven into two huge lakes and the dying shrieks of men and horses were terrible.
To shorten their agony the Germans turned the machine guns on them. But in spite of that, we could see movement among them for a week afterwards.

▲ General von Moltke, writing in his memoirs about the German slaughter of Russian troops at the Masurian Lakes in 1914.

The Eastern Front

There were battles on the Eastern Front which were mainly in Germany, Poland, Austria and Russia. In August 1914, a Russian army of 800,000 men smashed into Germany. The German army fought back, and defeated the Russians at **Tannenberg** and the **Masurian Lakes**. The slaughter was terrible. About 300,000 Russians were killed or wounded. By 1917, over two million Russian soldiers were dead. Millions more Russian peasants had died from starvation. In March 1918, the new Russian Bolshevik government (see pages 114–119) wanted to make peace with Germany. So Russia signed the **Treaty of Brest-Litovsk**.

The Italian Front

In 1915, Italy joined the war on the side of the Allies. They were badly defeated by the Germans at **Caporetto** in 1917. But a year later, the Italian army crushed the Austrians at **Vittorio Veneto**.

▼ The First World War was fought all over the World.

14 CHAPTER 1 THE FIRST WORLD WAR

Gallipoli

In April 1915, the Allies attacked Turkey at **Gallipoli**. The Allies wanted to control the area so that they could get supplies to Russia. An army of **Anzacs** (soldiers from Australia and New Zealand) landed at Gallipoli. But their attack was a disaster. The Anzacs on the beaches were fired at from the cliff tops by Turkish soldiers. In December 1915, the 135,000 Allied troops left in Turkey were rescued from Gallipoli by the navy.

The Middle East

The **Suez Canal** was very important to the Allies. Oil tankers carried fuel from the Persian Gulf through the Suez Canal to Britain and France. The Allies had to protect the Suez route. They sent troops to fight the Turks in Mesopotamia. They backed **Colonel T. E. Lawrence**, who led gangs of Arabs in raiding parties against the Turks. Finally, in September 1918, General Allenby defeated the Turkish army.

Africa

In Africa, the Allies captured the German colonies of Togoland, German South-West Africa and the Cameroons. Japanese troops invaded China and seized German colonies there. The Japanese also captured the Caroline and Marshall Islands in the Pacific Ocean.

So the war, which started as a quarrel between Austria-Hungary and Serbia, ended by becoming a general European war which then spread throughout the world.

Source B

No plan was prepared for an attack on the Gallipoli peninsular and Kitchener ought to have seen that this was done.

 From a British government report about the failure of the Gallipoli campaign, published in 1917.

Source C

I looked at the place where
  my legs used to be
And thanked Christ there was
  nobody waiting for me
To grieve, to mourn and to
  pity
And the band played
  Waltzing Matilda
As they carried us down the
  gangway
But nobody cheered, they
  just stood there and stared
And they turned their faces
  away.

▲ Part of an Australian folk song describing Australian wounded arriving home after the Gallipoli campaign.

SUMMARY

War world-wide

- **1914** Major defeats for Russia on the Eastern Front.
- **1915** Allied failure at Gallipoli.
- **1916** German defeats in the Pacific and Africa.
- **1917** Russia left the war.
- **1918** (March) Russia signed treaty of Brest-Litovsk with Germany.
- **1918** (September) Turkish army defeated.

QUESTIONS

1 Why did fighting in the war spread to so many different parts of the world?
2 Why did the attack on Gallipoli fail?
3 What point was the songwriter (Source C) trying to make?

1.5 What did the navy and air force do during the war?

Source A

> London has become the night battlefield in which seven million harmless men, women and children live.
>
> Here is war at the very heart of civilisation, threatening all the millions of things that human hearts and human minds have created in past centuries.

▲ An American journalist writing about the bombing of London by German Zeppelins in 1914.

In 1914, few people thought planes would be important. They were flimsy, made of wood and canvas, and held together by piano wire. The cockpits were open. The pilots had to wear warm clothes to survive.

Planes

In 1914, the **Royal Flying Corps** (RFC) sent 41 planes to France. They flew over enemy trenches and reported back on troop movements. The pilots dropped bombs out of the planes by hand. Then both sides in the war developed a machine gun that could fire through the propeller blades without shooting them off.

Flying aces

Some pilots who were good at fighting in the skies were called 'aces'. The German **Baron von Richthofen**, who was nicknamed the 'Red Baron', shot down 80 Allied planes before he was killed. Over 50,000 pilots were killed in the war.

Source B

> **I am the bit left over: the slice eaten absent mindedly when really I wasn't needed: I am the waste crust.**
>
> If you collected me and my companions for a whole week you would find that we amounted to 9,380 tons of good bread -
>
> **WASTED!**
> Nine shiploads of good bread.
> **Save me and I will save you!**

Airships

The Germans had airships called **Zeppelins**. They used these Zeppelins to drop bombs on Great Yarmouth, King's Lynn and London. The British used airships to protect their navy and report on enemy movements at sea.

Bombers

In 1917, the Germans used a **Gotha bomber** to make raids on Folkestone and then on London. In the London raid, 162 men, women and children were killed. In 1918, the British began building **Handley-Page bombers**. These were used to bomb German towns.

◄ Part of a British government leaflet issued in 1916.

The Battle of Jutland 1916

In May 1916, the German High Seas Fleet clashed with the British Royal Navy at the **Battle of Jutland**. Britain lost more ships and sailors than the Germans. But the German Fleet stopped fighting first, and sailed for the safety of German ports. Both sides said they had won.

U-boats

The Germans built a lot of submarines, called **U-boats**. They used them to sink merchant ships bringing supplies to Britain. The German U-boats brought Britain close to defeat. In April 1917, Britain only had enough food for six weeks. The Prime Minister, David Lloyd George, decided that merchant ships should travel together in **convoys**. The convoys could then be protected by destroyers. This worked. Far fewer ships were sunk, and Britain survived.

The *Lusitania*

German submarines helped bring the USA into the war. In May 1915, a German submarine sank a passenger ship called the *Lusitania*. Over 1,000 people drowned, including 124 Americans. Many Americans felt their country should join the war on the side of the Allies.

Blockades

German submarines brought Britain close to starvation. But it was the German people who suffered most from food shortages. The British navy stopped supply ships getting into German ports. Many German people nearly starved. Some historians say that food shortages made the German people want to give up fighting the war. They believe it was partly because of the food shortages that the German government asked for peace in November 1918.

Source C

▲ A German couple nursing their 'baby' as a smiling Kaiser looks on.

QUESTIONS

1. What use was the Royal Flying Corps at the beginning of the war?
2. Were airships of more use than planes? (Remember to back up your answer with facts.)
3. What was a U-boat?
4. What point is being made in the poster (Source B)?

1.6 What was the war like for civilians?

The First World War had a greater effect on the lives of British people than any earlier war. Ordinary people were involved. They went to fight, and they were bombed in their own homes. The British government brought in special laws, taking more power than any other government before.

Internment
At the start of the war, the British government put all foreign men into camps. They had to stay there until the war was over. This was called **internment**.

DORA
At the end of 1914, Parliament passed the **Defence of the Realm Act** (DORA). This gave the government power to control factories, mines and transport. The government also told newspaper editors what they could, and could not, print.

Conscription
By 1916, thousands of the young men who had volunteered to fight were already dead. Parliament needed to pass the **Military Service Act**. Any unmarried man aged between 18 and 41 could be forced to fight for his country. This is called **conscription**.

Source A

If we are lucky, we are given one egg every three weeks.

Our bread is mixed with turnips before it is baked because there isn't enough flour.

▲ Princess Blücher describes conditions in Germany in 1917.

Source B

▲ Women munition workers in a British factory painted in 1917 by E. F. Skinner. The government gave the artist the job of painting pictures of the war.

Rationing

In 1917, the government introduced **rationing**. This meant that people could only buy set amounts of goods that were in short supply like tea, sugar and butter.

Women at work

Many men were away from home fighting. They left their everyday jobs. Women took over these jobs and became bus drivers and chimney sweeps, factory workers and lab technicians. Women went out to France and Belgium, where the fighting was worst. They became nurses and drivers, cooks and clerks.

Many people were so impressed with the work women had done in the war that they came to accept that women should be allowed to vote. After the war, in 1918, the government gave women the vote, though they had to be aged 30 or over. It was not for another ten years that they were given the vote at 21, the same age as men.

1.7 Did attitudes to war change between 1914 and 1918?

Why did people change their minds?

In 1914, most people were enthusiastic about the war. Men wanted the chance to fight. Many people wanted the chance to show how much they supported their country. But as the war dragged on, they lost heart. Thousands of young men were being killed. The generals did not seem to know what to do. The politicians did not seem to know what to do. To many people it seemed as if the war would go on for ever.

Men against the war

Some men were **conscientious objectors**. This meant that their beliefs would not allow them to fight. They had to convince a **tribunal** that they were not cowards. Some conscientious objectors went to the Front and worked as stretcher bearers and cooks. Other men were **absolutists**, who refused to have anything at all to do with the war. They were sent to prison.

Source A

▲ A British cartoon postcard. It is making fun of the prison life of a conscientious objector.

Women against the war

The **Women's Peace Crusade** (WPC) held rallies in Britain. They wanted the war to end. Some people said these women were not supporting Britain and were **unpatriotic**. But by 1918, there were 120 branches of the WPC in England alone.

Protests in France and Russia

People protested about the war in France, Germany and Russia. In France in 1917, workers in the giant Renault factory went on strike. They were protesting against the war. In Russia the effects of the war were so great that they helped bring down the Tsar's government in a bloody revolution (see pages 114–119).

▼ A street party in a London street to celebrate the end of the First World War, July 1919.

Source B

1.8 How did the war end?

The USA declares war
The USA did everything it could to help the Allies except fight along side them. Then Germany began to use submarines to sink any ship that might be helping the Allies. One of these ships was the *Lusitania*. The deaths of American passengers raised an outcry. In April 1917, the USA declared war on Germany.

The Germans were alarmed. With American help, the Allies could win the war. The USA had hundreds of thousands of soldiers, and vast numbers of guns and other supplies. The Germans had to do something quickly, before the large numbers of Americans arrived.

Germany hits back
In March 1918, **General Ludendorff** started a massive attack along the River Somme. Some German troops nearly reached Paris. But they had gone too far, too fast. The rest of the German army was too far behind. Supplies could not reach the men at the front.

Then in August the Allies hit back. American troops arrived and soon the Germans were in retreat. By September, the Allies had taken more than 400,000 German prisoners.

The end of the Great War
Germany was in a desperate state. Thousands of people were starving.

By 4 November 1918, Bulgaria, Austria and Turkey had all surrendered. On 11 November 1918, the German government agreed to a cease-fire. The Great War was over.

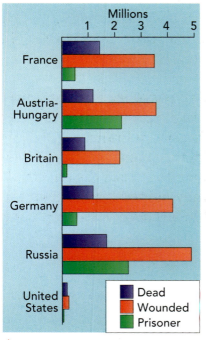

▲ Losses in the war.

SUMMARY

The end of the war

- ▶ Civilian hardship during the war.
- ▶ Mounting death toll at the Front.
- ▶ The importance of the USA's entry into the war.
- ▶ Ludendorff's final gamble.
- ▶ Germany and its allies surrendered.

QUESTIONS

1. Explain: DORA, conscription, conscientious objector.
2. a What work did women do in the war?
   b Why did this make it more likely that Parliament would give them the vote when the war ended?

1.9 Exercise

Source 1

▲ A British poster from 1915.

Source 2

▲ Australians in a front-line trench, May 1916.

Source 3

The trenches on the whole were in very good condition and there were wooden floorboards practically everywhere and with the weather dry too, it was really quite comfortable. We had a very quiet time. The Germans behaved in a very gentlemanly-like manner and did not fire any shells.

▲ Major Walter Vignoles of the Grimsby Chums describing his first taste of trench life in a letter home to his family. The Grimsby Chums was a 'Pals' regiment. These were regiments of friends who joined up together, and came from the same streets or areas of towns or cities.

Life in the trenches

1. Look at Sources 1, 2 and 3. If you only looked at these three sources, what would you think life was like in the trenches?

2. Now look back at pages 12 and 13. Use the information there to explain which of Sources 1, 2 or 3 on this page gives you the most accurate picture of life in the trenches.

CHAPTER 2

INTERNATIONAL RELATIONS 1919–39

After the First World War, the victorious Allies met at Versailles, outside Paris. They had to decide what to put in the peace treaties. Some wanted revenge on Germany. Others wanted to make sure there would never be another war. Because of these different ideas, the treaties they wrote became an important cause of the Second World War, twenty years later.

The peace treaties also set up the **League of Nations**. This was an international organization to keep peace.

Source A

All peoples and nationalities have a right to live on equal terms of liberty and safety with one another, whether they be strong or weak.

▲ Adapted from Woodrow Wilson's 'Fourteen Points' speech, 8 January 1918 (see below).

2.1 How was peace restored after the First World War?

The Fourteen Points

Before the war ended, **President Woodrow Wilson** of the USA set out **Fourteen Points**. He wanted these to be part of the peace treaties. But when the Germans surrendered, they found out that the other Allied leaders had different ideas.

Who went to the Peace Conference?

In January 1919, people from the Allied countries met at Versailles. They did not ask the defeated countries (Germany, Austria-Hungary, Turkey and Bulgaria) to join them. And they did not invite Russia, even though Russia had fought with the Allied powers. This was because the Allies were angry at the way Russia had dropped out of the war. They did not trust the new communist government, either.

Point 1: There should be no secret treaties between countries.

Point 4: There should be a reduction in arms.

Point 10: The people of Austria-Hungary should be able to rule themselves (self-determination).

Point 14: There should be a 'general association of nations' to prevent further warfare.

▲ Some of President Wilson's Fourteen Points.

The Big Three
The really important decisions about the peace treaties were made by the leaders of France, Great Britain and the USA. They were nicknamed the **Big Three**. They were **Georges Clemenceau**, Prime Minister of France, **Woodrow Wilson**, President of the USA, and **David Lloyd George**, Prime Minister of Great Britain. They had other experts to help them.

What did the Big Three want?
Clemenceau wanted Germany to be made so weak that it would never attack France again. He also wanted Germany to pay for the damage the war had caused. But Lloyd George did not want Germany to be treated too badly. He thought Germany might take revenge on the Allies if the peace terms were too harsh. Wilson saw himself as a peacemaker. He believed that the war was not entirely Germany's fault. He thought the Big Three should be looking to avoid wars in the future rather than thinking about revenge.

How did Germany react?
After five months, the Big Three decided on the terms of the peace treaty with Germany. When the Germans saw the treaty, they were horrified. The German Chancellor resigned in protest, but there was nothing else the Germans could do. They could hardly start the war all over again. Reluctantly, two members of the German government signed the **Treaty of Versailles** on 28 June 1919.

The Diktat
Many German people were extremely angry when they heard how the Allies were going to treat them. The German government had not been allowed to take part in the peace talks. Instead the government had been forced to agree to the treaty. Germans called it a 'Diktat' – a dictated peace.

Forest laid waste (sq. kilometres)
2,971

Farmland laid waste (sq. kilometres)
12,800

Houses destroyed
300,000

Factories destroyed
6,000

Livestock lost
1,300,000

▲ French losses in the First World War.

Source B

'Our peace ought to be dictated by men who act in the spirit of judges . . . . . and not in the spirit of vendetta.

▲ David Lloyd George, speaking at the Versailles Peace Conference in 1919.

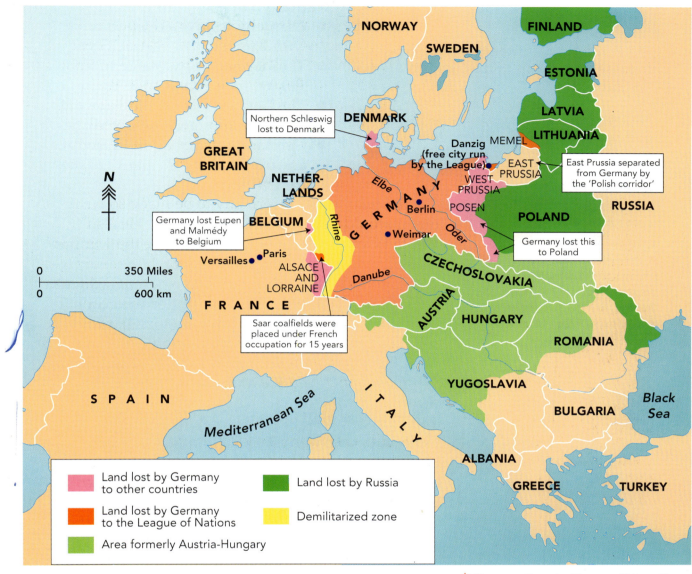

▲ Europe after the Treaty of Versailles and St Germain.

What did the terms of the Treaty of Versailles do to Germany in June 1919?

Territorial losses
- Germany lost all the land it had gained from Russia by the **Treaty of Brest-Litovsk** (1918).
- Poland was remade with land that had been part of Germany, Russia and Austria-Hungary. Poland was given a 'corridor' of land to the sea.
- Alsace and Lorraine went to France.
- Eupen and Malmedy went to Belgium.
- North Schleswig went to Denmark.
- Danzig and Memel were controlled by the League of Nations.
- The Saar coalfields were run by the League of Nations for France.
- Germany lost all its colonies. They were run by other countries under League of Nations control.

2.1 HOW WAS PEACE RESTORED AFTER THE FIRST WORLD WAR?

Source C

The Prime Minister went down to Versailles to present the terms to the German delegates . . .

He says the Germans were very arrogant and insolent and that it has made him more angry than any incident in the war, and if the Germans do not sign he will have no mercy on them.
He says that for the first time he has felt the same hatred for them that the French feel.

▲ An extract from the diary of Frances Stevenson. She was the personal secretary to Lloyd George, in 1919. Lloyd George was Britain's Prime Minister.

Military terms
- Germany was forbidden to unite with Austria.
- The German army was reduced to 100,000 men.
- The German navy could have only six battleships and no submarines.
- Germany was not allowed to place any troops along the banks of the River Rhine.

Economic terms
- Germany had to accept full blame for starting the war.
- Germany had to pay **reparations** to the Allies. Reparations were a bill given to Germany to make amends for starting the war. In 1921, the amount of reparations was fixed at £6,600 million.

Source D

Germany accepts the responsibility of Germany for causing all the loss and damage which the Allies suffered because of the war forced on them by the aggression of Germany.

▲ Adapted from the War Guilt Clause, (Article 231).

The Treaty of Versailles hit Germany hard. The German people were starving and ill. German industry had been damaged because the land taken away included coal mines and iron ore fields. So there was no way in which Germany would be able to meet the reparation payments demanded by the Allies.

What happened to the other defeated countries?

The Allies made the **Treaty of St Germain** with Austria in 1919 and the **Treaty of Trianon** with Hungary in 1920. They also made The **Treaty of Sèvres** with Turkey in 1920. The peacemakers tried to follow the idea of **self-determination**. This meant that they tried to draw new boundaries around countries so that people of the same race governed themselves.

Austria-Hungary
- Austria and Hungary became separate countries.
- Two new countries, Czechoslovakia and Yugoslavia, were formed. Czechoslovakia still contained different races. There were six million Czechs, two million Slovaks and three million Germans.
- Some land in Austria-Hungary was given to Italy, Poland and Romania.

Bulgaria
The Allies made the **Treaty of Neuilly** with Bulgaria in 1919.
- Small areas of land in Bulgaria went to Yugoslavia and Greece.

Turkey
The Allies made the **Treaty of Sèvres** with Turkey in 1920.

- Turkey lost most of its land in Europe.
- The Turkish empire in the Middle East was divided between the British and the French. Britain and France ran the empire for the League of Nations.
- Turkey had to pay reparations to the Allies.
- Turkish armed forces were reduced.

Mandates
The League of Nations took over some countries. It asked Britain and France to run these countries until they were ready for independence. These were called **mandates**.

▲ The Turkish Empire after the Treaty of Sèvres in 1920.

QUESTIONS

Look at page 24

1. a Which statesmen, from which countries, drew up the Treaty of Versailles?
   b What different ideas did they have about how Germany should be treated?
   c Now read the **Treaty of Versailles** on pages 25 and 26. Whose ideas come through strongest in this Treaty?

SUMMARY

▶ **1918** Germans surrendered hoping for peace based on the Fourteen Points.

▶ **1919** Victorious nations met at Versailles.
Treaty of Versailles imposed harsh terms on Germany.

Treaty of St Germain with Austria.

Treaty of Neuilly with Bulgaria.

▶ **1920** Treaty of Trianon with Hungary.

Treaty of Sèvres with Turkey.

▶ **1921** Figure for reparations set.

2.2 What was the League of Nations?

One of Woodrow Wilson's Fourteen Points was that there should be an world peace-keeping organization. The other Allied countries agreed with this. So, as well as dealing with Germany, the Treaty of Versailles set up the **League of Nations**.

What were the aims of the League?

The League wanted all quarrels between countries to be sorted out peacefully. It wanted countries to work together on matters that concerned them all, like fighting disease.

How was the League organized? The Assembly

Every member country could send three people to the Assembly. Each country, no matter how large or small, had one vote. Any decision reached by the Assembly about world peace had to be agreed by all the members.

The Council

The Council was supposed to reflect the balance of power in the world. There were to be five permanent, and four non-permanent, members. The permanent members were to be the victorious Allies. But not all the Allies joined the League. The Council listened to disputes and recommended action to the Assembly.

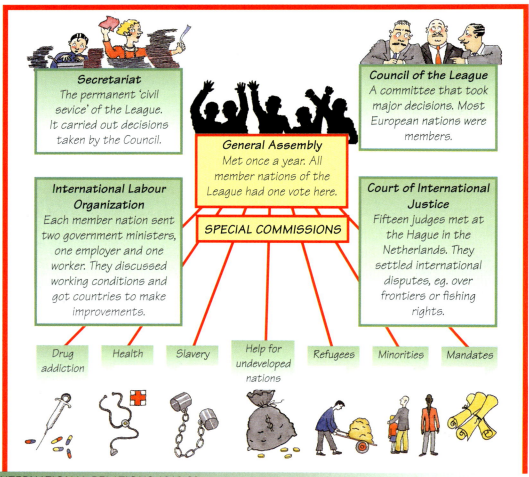

▶ The organization of the League of Nations.

The Secretariat

The Secretariat provided all the back-up information that League members needed. People from all the countries in the League worked for the Secretariat. It was based in Geneva, Switzerland.

The Court of International Justice

This Court was set up in The Hague, Holland, in 1922. The judges who ran the Court were from countries that were members of the League. They made decisions about the law on international problems, such as which countries were allowed to fish in which areas. But the Court could not force countries to bring their disputes before it. And the countries did not have to accept its decisions.

The International Labour Organization (ILO)

The aim of the ILO was to improve people's living and working conditions. Every country in the League sent four people to an ILO conference. Two of these people represented the government of that country, one person represented the employers, and one person represented the workers. The conferences were held every year.

The ILO told governments which belonged to the League how they needed to change their laws to make conditions better for working people. It managed to get members to agree on things like working hours and the right of every worker to join a trade union.

Special commissions

The League set up commissions to deal with special problems. For example, the Drugs Commission tried to deal with the illegal trade in drugs between countries. The Minorities Commission tried to make sure that people were not treated badly because of their religious beliefs, or because of the race they belonged to.

Experts from many countries worked with each other to find solutions to problems they all faced. They were not politicians, and could make their own decisions. So the Commissions got a lot of work done.

Source A

In 1924 the League of Nations established a slavery commission.

It decided to ask members to help stamp out the buying and selling of the slaves.

▲ Adapted from S.R. Gibbons and P. Morican, *The League of Nations*, 1983.

QUESTIONS

1. Whose idea was the League of Nations?
2. What were the aims of the League of Nations?
3. What work was done by:
   a The Assembly?
   b The Council?
   c The Secretariat?

Membership of the League

The major countries of the world were not all members of the League at the same time. Some joined and then left. Some joined later. Others never joined. Some joined and were later thrown out by other members. Great Britain and France were the only Great Powers which were members from beginning to end.

Although President Wilson thought up the idea of the League of Nations, the USA never joined. In the 1920s, the American government tried to keep the USA out of world affairs. This policy was called **isolationism**.

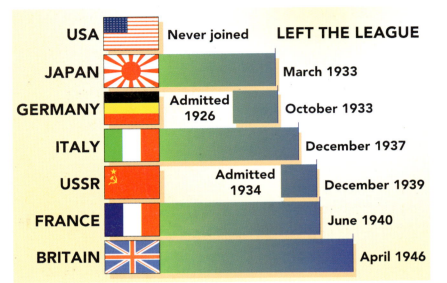

▲ Membership of the League of Nations. The League was disbanded in 1946.

Germany was not allowed to join the League until 1926, and it left in 1933. Japan left in the same year, and Italy left four years later. The USSR (as Russia became) joined the League in 1934 and was thrown out in 1939.

The League's powers

There were three ways in which the League could settle disputes:

- A country not involved in the quarrel could decide what should happen.
- The International Court of Justice could sort things out.
- The Council of the League could inquire into matters.

If a country refused to do what the League wanted, there were three things the League could do:

Source B

If any member goes to war, all member countries will behave as if that member country had declared war on them. All the other members of the League will stop trading with it.

They will advise the Council about any armed action that should be taken.

◄ Adapted from Article 16 of the Covenant of the League of Nations.

Shame
The League could show the country that the rest of the world was against it, and so try to shame the country into accepting the League's decision.

Sanctions
The League could apply **economic sanctions**. This meant that no member of the League would trade with the country until it accepted the League's decision.

Soldiers
The League could ask member countries to supply soldiers to make up a League army. This army could be used to make the country accept the League's decision.

Did it work?
This was all very well in theory. But as it happened, very few countries would take part in economic sanctions. This was because sanctions would harm the countries' own economy.

None of the major powers was willing to supply troops for a League army, either. So the League of Nations had to rely on persuasion. During the 1930s, this simply did not work.

Source C

In the 1920s everything seemed to be going very smoothly. The League's agencies [commissions] were working extremely well and the world's statesmen were actually getting together and talking with each other. They met at the League's headquarters [in Geneva], where they were able to sort out international problems over brandy and a cigar in front of the fire.

▲ S. Lang, *The League of Nations*, 1990.

▼ The successes and failures of the League of Nations in the 1920s.

SUCCESS
- Aaland Islands
- Upper Silesia
- Austrian economy
- Bulgarian invasion of Greece
- Work of commissions

FAILURE
- Vilna
- Memel
- Corfu

How successful was the League in the 1920s?

Successes
- Settled a quarrel between Sweden and Finland over who owned the **Aaland Islands** (1920).
- Divided **Upper Silesia** between Poland and Germany (1920).
- Organized financial help for Austria (1922).
- Stopped a Greek invasion of Bulgaria (1925).

Problems
- Poland seized **Vilna**, the capital of Lithuania. The League took no action.
- Lithuania seized Memel, a port under international control. The League took no action.
- Italy bombarded the Greek island of Corfu. The League of Nations ordered Italy to stop. It did. Then the Great Powers stepped in. They made the Greeks pay compensation to Italy. This made the League look weak.

SUMMARY

The League of Nations
- The League began in 1920.
- Not all countries joined.
- Decisions were to be enforced through sanctions.
- The League had successes but also failures in the 1920s.

QUESTIONS

1. **a** Look at pages 30–31. How was the League of Nations supposed to sort out quarrels between countries?
   b Why did this not always work?

2.3 How did countries try to avoid war after 1919?

International Co-operation
One of the ideas behind the League of Nations was that countries should settle their differences peacefully. It was better, of course, if they did not have any disagreements at all. So the Great Powers tried to arrange matters so that arguments between countries were less likely to happen.

The Dawes Plan 1924 and the Young Plan 1929
These two plans helped the German economy to get better. The **Dawes Plan** showed how Germany could make its money more stable. The **Young Plan** reduced German reparations by 75%. The Great Powers hoped that, because of these plans, Germany would resent the Treaty of Versailles less.

► A cartoon from the *Evening Standard*, published in May 1934, commenting on the failure of the Disarmament Conference of 1932.

The Kellogg–Briand Pact 1928
Sixty-five countries signed this pact. They agreed not to go to war except in self-defence.

The Disarmament Conference 1932
Sixty-one countries met in Geneva to talk about **disarmament**, or getting rid of their weapons. The USSR wanted every country to disarm. But Germany wanted every country to be equal in the arms they held. Other countries emphasized the importance of the League of Nations. Not surprisingly, the conference failed.

The end of world peace
World peace was shattered before the conference met. In 1931 Japan invaded the Chinese province of Manchuria.

SUMMARY

Attempts to strengthen peace
► **1921** Washington Conference.
► **1924** Dawes Plan.
► **1928** Kellogg–Briand Pact.
► **1929** Young Plan.
► **1932** Disarmament Conference.

QUESTIONS

1 How might
   a The Kellog–Briand Pact (1928) and
   b The Young Plan (1929)
   have prevented the Second World War?

2 What point is being made in the cartoon (Source A)?

2.4 The road to war: the League discredited

▲ The Japanese invasion of Manchuria.

The Japanese invasion of Manchuria

Japan was a small country and had developed a great deal since 1900. It needed more space and a better economy.

Japan's economic problems

- Japan's population was increasing at the rate of one million a year. By 1929, the Japanese population was 65 million. There were not enough jobs for everyone.
- Japan had no raw materials like coal and iron ore.
- Japan's only exports were raw silk and manufactured goods. When the world economy collapsed in 1929, Japan found it hard to sell goods abroad. By 1931, half Japan's factories were closed. Millions of people were starving.

The army's solution

Japan needed raw materials, countries in which to sell its goods and living space for its people. The army generals believed they had the answer. They said that the army should be increased in size and then it could capture land abroad. The government in Tokyo did not agree with this idea. But the army leaders had great influence, and they did not always do what the government said.

The railway

Japan had built a railway in Manchuria. Manchuria was part of China, but Japan controlled the land through which the railway ran. Then, in 1931, part of the railway line was destroyed by a bomb. So the Japanese army moved into Manchuria to protect the railway line. But Chinese troops opened fire on the Japanese, and then the Japanese fought back.

Source A

A force of Chinese troops totally destroyed the railway tracks at Mukden and attacked our railway guards.
The Japanese army has had to act swiftly to occupy the surrounding area so as to prevent further outrages.
The Japanese army has no territorial designs on this area of China.

▲ A statement issued by the Japanese government in September 1931.

34 CHAPTER 2 INTERNATIONAL RELATIONS 1919-39

Who planted the bomb?

Many historians believe that Japanese troops planted the bomb themselves, to give Japan an excuse to go to war with China. Manchuria was rich in iron ore and oil, and Japanese people could also settle there.

Who won the war?

By the end of 1931, the Japanese army had captured most of Manchuria. After that the Japanese changed the name of Manchuria to Manchukuo.

'Wait a minute! I am going to tell the League of Nations'

▲ A cartoon published in Germany in 1931.

What did the League of Nations do?

Most countries were horrified at what Japan had done. China asked the League of Nations for help. The League condemned Japan's actions and refused to accept that Manchukuo was a country separate from China.

How did Japan react?

Japan left the League of Nations straight away and began preparing for a general war against China. By 1938, after a year of fighting, Japan controlled most of eastern China.

What was the effect on the League of Nations?

The Japanese invasion of Manchuria showed how weak the League really was. The League did not ask its members to apply any sanctions against Japan. Britain and France, the major powers in the League, would not take any action at all. And Japan simply ignored what the League asked it to do.

QUESTIONS

1. Why did Japan invade Manchuria?
2. What action did the League take?
3. What were the effects of this action on Japan?
4. Why do you think the League did not do more?
5. Do you think that the cartoonist in Source B was praising or criticizing the League? Explain your answer.

The Italian invasion of Abyssinia

Why did Italy want to invade Abyssinia?
- Benito Mussolini became leader of Italy in 1922.
- Mussolini wanted an Italian empire in Africa.
- Italy already owned Eritrea, Libya and Somaliland, in Africa, and Mussolini wanted Abyssinia too.

The invasion
In 1935, some Abyssinians killed 30 Italian soldiers on the border between Abyssinia and Somaliland. So then Mussolini ordered the Italian army to invade Abyssinia. The Abyssinian army was badly equipped and soon retreated. The leader of Abyssinia, Haile Selassie, asked the League of Nations for help.

What did the League do?
The members of the League decided to apply economic sanctions against Italy. But these sanctions did not include steel, coal and oil. This meant that League members could still trade in these goods with Italy. What was more, Germany and Austria refused to apply any sanctions at all.

What did Britain and France do?
Britain and France wanted to support the League. But at the same time, they did not want to upset Mussolini. This was because they believed Mussolini would be a good ally against Nazi Germany. So they did not stop Italian ships carrying supplies through the Suez canal to Italian soldiers in Abyssinia.

Source C

I, Haile Selassie, am here today to claim justice for my people. I claim, too, the help promised eight months ago when the League agreed that aggression had been committed against my country.
The League must uphold its promises that our independence and integrity will be supported. If it does not, the very existence of the League is threatened. God and History will remember your judgements.

▲ A speech made to the League of Nations by the Emperor of Abyssinia, Haile Selassie.

Source D

Four members of the League refused to apply any sanctions at all against Italy. Seven did not stop selling arms and thirteen continued to buy Italian goods.

▲ From a speech made by the Soviet representative at the League of Nations in 1936.

▼ Foreign possessions around Abyssinia, 1935.

The Hoare–Laval Pact
This Pact was signed by Britain and France. In the Pact, Britain and France agreed to let Italy keep two-thirds of Abyssinia if Mussolini agreed to stop fighting. But there were huge protests when news of the Pact leaked out. So the Pact was dropped.

But even though the pact was dropped, it had done enormous harm. Britain and France had shown they were prepared to go against the League if it suited them. Mussolini went ahead and conquered the whole of Abyssinia. Haile Selassie, the leader of Abyssinia, fled abroad.

What was the effect on world peace?
The League had failed as a peace-keeping organization. What is more, Britain and France failed to keep Mussolini as an ally. In 1936, Germany and Italy became allies. They signed the **Rome–Berlin Axis**.

In 1937, Italy left the League of Nations.

Source E

▲ Italian troops advance from the southern front in Somaliland, February 1936.

Source F

If the League had extended economic sanctions to oil, I would have had to withdraw from Abyssinia within a week.

▲ Mussolini, talking about sanctions, after he had conquered Abyssinia.

QUESTIONS

1. **a** Why did Italy invade Abyssinia?
   b What did the League of Nations do?
   c What did Britain and France do?
   d Why did some people think Britain and France were damaging the League of Nations?
2. Read Source F
   a What would Mussolini have done if the League had extended sanctions to oil?
   b Why, then didn't the League extend sanctions to oil?

SUMMARY

▶ **1931** The Japanese army invaded Manchuria.
▶ **1933** Japan left the League of Nations.
▶ **1935** Italian invasion of Abyssinia. The League imposed sanctions on Italy. The Hoare–Laval Pact was signed.
▶ **1936** Mussolini completed the conquest of Abyssinia.
▶ **1937** Italy resigned from the League. Japan invaded China.

2.5 Hitler and the expansion of Germany

Hitler's aims
Adolf Hitler came to power in Germany in 1933 (see Chapter 4). Even before he became Germany's leader, he knew what he wanted German policy to be:

- The Treaty of Versailles should be torn up.
- Germany should begin to build up its armed forces.
- All Germans should be brought together in one large country – a **Greater Germany**.
- Eventually Germany would need extra living space, or **Lebensraum** for all its people. This extra land would come from the Slav lands of Eastern Europe.

Rearmament
Hitler took Germany out of the League of Nations and began rearming. This was against the Treaty of Versailles.

- The **army** was equipped with new tanks. Hitler also wanted the army to be 600,000 men strong. So he introduced **conscription**. This meant that all men had to serve in the army for a certain length of time, whether they wanted to or not.
- The **navy** was equipped with new submarines. And in 1936, the Germans launched a new battleship called the *Admiral Graf Spee*.
- The **airforce** (**Luftwaffe**) began building new, twin-engined bombers.

Naval Agreement
In June 1936, Britain and Germany signed a **Naval Agreement**. They agreed that the German navy could be up to 35% of the size of the British one. Britain seemed to be helping Germany to break the Treaty of Versailles.

The Saar coalfields
The Treaty of Versailles said that the Saar coalfields had to be run by the League of Nations for fifteen years. But when the fifteen years ended in 1935, 90% of the people living in Saar voted to become part of Germany.

Source A
The principal effect of every war is to destroy the flower of the nation. Germany desires peace!

▲ Speech by Hitler to the German parliament (the Reichstag) in 1935.

Source B
Herr Hitler returned here yesterday, a conquering hero

... His triumphant welcome was shared by the army he sent into Austria; flowers were strewn in the path of their armoured cars.

If any Austrians were against him on Friday, they either hid their faces or were completely converted yesterday and today . . .

▲ A report from Germany published in *The Times*, on Monday 14 March, three days after German troops entered Austria.

The Rhineland

In March 1936, Hitler sent troops into the Rhineland. This was forbidden by the Treaty of Versailles. The German troops had instructions to turn back if they were challenged. But neither Britain nor France tried to stop them.

Hitler grew more and more confident that no one would stop him tearing up the Treaty of Versailles.

Guernica

In 1936, a civil war started in Spain. Hitler supported the Fascists, who were led by **General Franco**. Hitler sent 10,000 soldiers and the airforce to help. This gave the soldiers experience of real fighting. It also gave the airforce practice in bombing. They destroyed the Spanish town of Guernica.

Anschluss (union)

One of Hitler's aims was to unite Germany and Austria. This was forbidden by the Treaty of Versailles. In 1938, the new leader of Austria, **Seyss-Inquart**, was a supporter of Hitler. He invited German troops into Austria. Then the Austrian people voted for or against uniting with Germany. Officially, 99% of Austrians said they wanted to unite with Germany. But no one believed the figures.

Britain and France did nothing to stop the German take-over of Austria. This was because they did not want to risk a war. Many politicians believed that there was nothing wrong in Germany and Austria uniting. After all, they were both German-speaking countries. So Hitler was even more convinced that no one would stand in his way.

Source C

Throughout these events His Majesty's Government have remained in the closest contact with the French government...

both governments have entered a strong protest in Berlin...

It seems to us that the methods adopted call for the severest condemnation (disaproval)....

▲ Said by the British Prime Minister, Neville Chamberlain, on 15 March 1938 after the Germans marched into Austria.

▼ Germany gains more land 1933–9.

The policy of appeasement

Between 1933 and 1938, Britain and France did not want to take any action against Germany. There were many reasons for this:

The Great Depression

Britain and France were both trying to deal with economic problems (see page 63). One of their solutions was to lower taxes and cut government spending. This meant that there was less money to spend on the armed forces – and no money for a war.

The First World War

Many people could remember the horrors of the First World War. They would do anything to stop war breaking out again.

The Treaty of Versailles

Many people thought that Germany had been treated too harshly by the Treaty of Versailles. They thought that Germany should be allowed to rearm. They also thought Hitler was bringing stability to Germany. Best of all, Hitler was a bitter enemy of **communism**. So they believed it would do no harm to let him achieve some of his foreign policy aims.

Source D

There can be no doubt that Hitler has a achieved a marvellous transformation in the spirit of the people. The old trust him, the young idolise him.

The Germans no longer have any desire to invade any other land.

▲ A comment made by the ex-Liberal Prime Minister, David Lloyd George, after a visit to Germany in 1936.

Source E

▲ A protest march for peace in London in 1931.

▲ The Sudeten crisis, 1938. From this map it is easy to see why Hitler, once he had control in Austria, wanted to take over Sudetenland. And from there it was an easy step to go further into Czechoslovakia (see over the page).

Neville Chamberlain

In May 1937, Neville Chamberlain became Prime Minister of Great Britain. He wanted to avoid war at all costs, and thought that the best way of avoiding war was by talking to Hitler. As long as the demands Hitler made were not too damaging, Chamberlain was going to give in to them. This was known as the policy of **appeasement**. Appeasement was an important part of Britain's foreign policy between 1936 and 1939. France had the same policy.

From appeasement to war: the Sudeten crisis 1938

Why was Hitler interested in Czechoslovakia?
- The part of Czechoslovakia closest to Germany was the **Sudetenland**. Three million Germans lived there. So Hitler wanted the Sudetenland to become part of Germany.
- The Sudetenland was rich in coal and iron ore.
- There were many armament (weapons) factories in the Sudetenland.

Source F

How horrible it is that we should be digging trenches and trying on gas masks here because of a quarrel far away between people we do not know.

▲ Part of a broadcast by Neville Chamberlain to the people of Britain on 27 September 1938.

Source G

▲ A cartoon of Neville Chamberlain travelling to Munich entitled 'Still hope'.

▼ Hitler at a rally in 1938.

Source H

▼ Neville Chamberlain holding the Anglo-German agreement.

Source I

How did Hitler threaten Czechoslovakia?

In June 1938, Hitler began a **propaganda** campaign with the aim of bringing the Sudetenland into Germany. Members of the Nazi Party in Czechoslovakia began to complain that they were being badly treated by the Czech government. That gave Hitler an excuse to move troops to the Czech border. He was ready to invade.

What did Czechoslovakia, Britain and France do?

President Benes of Czechoslovakia asked France for help. But France would not do anything without Britain. Then **Edouard Daladier**, Prime Minister of France, and Neville Chamberlain, Britain's Prime Minister, flew to Germany to meet Hitler. They all decided that Czechoslovakia should give Germany those parts of the Sudetenland where more than half the people were German. Reluctantly, President Benes agreed. But then Hitler upped his demands. He said he wanted the whole of the Sudetenland.

The Munich agreement

On 29 September 1939, Hitler, Mussolini, Daladier and Chamberlain met at Munich. The Czechs were not invited. The Soviets were not invited either, even though Czechoslovakia was on the border of the USSR. At the Munich Conference, Germany, Italy, France and Britain agreed that the whole of the Sudetenland should be given to Germany. France told the Czechs that they had to accept this Munich agreement. If they did not, they would be left fighting Germany on their own.

Source J

When I think of those four terrible years, and I think of the millions of young men who were killed... and the misery and suffering of the mothers and the fathers of those killed – then I am bound to say, 'In war... there are no winners, but all are losers... It is my duty to strain every nerve to avoid a repetition of the Great War.

▲ Prime Minister Chamberlain talking to his supporters in 1938.

▶ Daily Express, 30 September 1938.

Source K

Daily Express

Fleet Street, London,
Central 8000
September 30, 1938

PEACE

Be glad in your hearts. Give thanks to your God.

The wings of peace settle about us and the peoples of Europe. The prayers of the troubled hearts are answered.

People of Britain, your children are safe. Your husbands and your sons will not march to battle.

A war which would have been the most criminal, the most futile, the most destructive that ever insulted the purposes of the Almighty and the intelligence of men has been averted.

It was the war that nobody wanted. Nobody in Germany. Nobody in France. Nobody, above all, in Britain, which had no concern whatever with the issues at stake.

No war for us

Through the black days, this newspaper clung to the belief that peace would prevail, that common sense would triumph.

Over and over again we said it: "Their will be no European war involving Britain this year, or next year either."

Now, in the moment when our persistent faith is justified, it is no time to estimate who has emerged the victor from the long controversy. Peace is a victory for all mankind.

To him the laurels

If we must have a victor, let us choose Chamberlain. For the Prime Minister's conquests are mighty and enduring – millions of happy homes and hearts relieved of their burden. To him the laurels!

And now let us go back to our own affairs.

We have had enough of those menaces, conjured up from the Continent to confuse us.

Source L

We, the German Führer and Chancellor and the British Prime Minister, have had a further meeting today and are agreed in recognising that the question of Anglo-German relations is of the first importance for the two countries and for Europe.

We regard the agreement signed last night and the Anglo-German Naval Agreement as symbolic of the desire of our two peoples never to go to war with one another again.

We are resolved that the method of consultation shall be the method adopted to deal with any other questions that may concern our two countries, and we are determined to continue our efforts to remove possible sources of difference and thus to contribute to assure the peace of Europe.

A. Hitler
Neville Chamberlain

September 30. 1938.

'Peace for our time'

At Munich, Chamberlain and Hitler also signed another agreement. They said that Britain and Germany would never go to war against each other again. Instead, they would settle their differences through negotiation. People welcomed Chamberlain back to Britain as if he was a hero. He said he had won 'peace for our time'.

◀ The agreement signed by Chamberlain and Hitler at Munich on 30 September 1938.

Hitler takes Czechoslovakia

Chamberlain was an honourable man. He thought Hitler would keep his promises. But Hitler had no intention of doing so. In March 1939, German troops invaded Czechoslovakia and took control of the whole country. Chamberlain was shocked. The British government quickly began increasing the strength of the armed forces. It also introduced conscription for men aged twenty and over.

It was clear that war was very near.

The Nazi-Soviet Pact

In March 1939 the USSR opened talks with France and Britain to discuss ways of preventing Nazi aggression. But France and Britain were afraid to set up a united front against Hitler. The talks broke down in July (see Sources M and Q).

Source M

Why did Chamberlain and Daladier (of France) help Hitler to achieve his aims? They hoped to appease Hitler by giving him some Czech land. They wanted to direct German aggression eastwards towards the USSR . . .

As a result the USSR stood alone in the face of the growing Nazi threat. In this situation the USSR had to make a treaty of non-aggression with Germany . . . this gave the USSR time to strengthen its defences.

▲ A Soviet historian writing in 1981.

Source N

We have sustained a total defeat. All the countries of Middle Europe will be drawn into the vast system of Nazi policies. Is it the end? It is only the beginning.

▲ Adapted from a speech by Winston Churchill, about the Munich Agreement. Churchill was an outspoken critic of the policy of appeasement.

Source O

◀ The people of Prague forced to give the salute, 'welcome' to the German troops.

On 23 August, to everyone's astonishment, the USSR and Germany signed the **Nazi-Soviet Pact**. They agreed not to fight each other, and to divide Poland up between them.

Poland

The Germans were angry that the Treaty of Versailles made them give up the city of Danzig and some other land, so that Poland could reach to the sea. Might Hitler try to overturn this by invading Poland? Now, France had an alliance with Poland. And Chamberlain told the Poles that if there was a war, they could count on Britain's support too.

This marked the end of appeasement.

War!

On 1 September 1939, Hitler invaded Poland. He knew that, because of the Nazi–Soviet Pact, the USSR would not act against him. And Hitler did not believe that Chamberlain and Daladier, the 'men of Munich', would go to war to defend Poland. But Hitler was wrong. On 3 September 1939, Great Britain and France declared war on Germany.

Source P

Chamberlain had feared that history might judge him harshly, and he was correct.
The opening of new records explains his policy.
His was the only policy which offered any hope of avoiding war – and of saving lives and the British Empire.

▲ John Charmley used new evidence based on Chamberlain's private papers when he wrote this in *Chamberlain and the Lost Peace*, 1989.

Source Q

▶ A Soviet cartoon, published shortly after the Munich Agreement. It shows Daladier and Chamberlain pointing Germany towards the East.

Source R

◀ A cartoon by David Low which appeared in the *Evening Standard* on 20 September 1939. Hitler and Stalin are 'greeting' each other over the dead body of Poland.

SUMMARY

▶ **1933** Germany withdrew from the League of Nations.

▶ **1933-6** German rearmament (forbidden by the terms of the Treaty of Versailles):
Conscription.
New aircraft, tanks and submarines built.
Admiral Graf Spee launched.
Anglo-German Naval Agreement.

▶ **1933-8** Policy of appeasement in Britain.

▶ **1936** German invasion of the Rhineland.
Spanish Civil War.

▶ **1937** Neville Chamberlain became Prime Minister of Britain.

▶ **1938** German invasion of Austria.
Sudeten crisis.
29 September – Munich Conference.

▶ **1939** German invasion of Czechoslovakia.
Nazi-Soviet Pact.
1 September – German invasion of Poland.
3 September – Britain and France declared war on Germany.

QUESTIONS

1. Read pages 40–1
   a. What is appeasement?
   b. Why did Great Britain follow this policy in the 1930s?

2. a. Make a timeline of events leading to war in September 1939. Begin with Hitler's invasion of the Rhineland in March 1936 (page 39).
   b. Do you think war could have been avoided?

3. War broke out on 1 September 1939. Does this mean that Chamberlain's policy of appeasement was a total failure?

2.6 Exercise

Source 1

I assert that the problem is a much wider one than the settlement of aggression. It is the very existence of the League of Nations. It is the value of promises made to small states by the league. God and History will remember your judgements.

▲ Emperor Haile Selassie of Abyssinia addressing the League of Nations in 1936.

Source 2

What had failed, for the second time since 1931, was the League of Nations.

The story of the Abyssinian War was the last nail in the coffin of the League, and after 1936 men sought other ways of maintaining peace.

▲ A modern historian commenting on the League's involvement in the Abyssinian affair.

Source 3

▶ A British cartoon called 'Putting the clock back', published in 1935.

Source 4

◀ A cartoon from *Punch*, December 1935. The caption reads: THE SWEETS OF AGGRESSION. Haile Selassie: "Have I got this right? He's taken nearly half of what I had and now you gentlemen want to discuss whether he should take any more!"

1. In Source 3 Mussolini is putting the clock back, from 'Peace' towards '1914'. What point is the cartoonist trying to make?

2. Look at Source 1.
   What do you think Haile Selassie meant when he said:

   the Italian invasion of Abyssinia was a matter of 'the very existence of the League.'

3. Read Source 2 and look back over 2.4. Make a list of the ways in which, after 1936, people looked for 'other ways of maintaining peace' without involving the League of Nations.

4. Which of the four sources in this exercise do you think is the most useful for a historian studying the League of Nations? Explain your answer carefully.

5. Do you think that establishing the League of Nations in 1919 was a waste of time? Use these four sources and your own knowledge to answer the question.

CHAPTER 3

THE UNITED STATES OF AMERICA 1918–41

▲ The United States of America, 1918–41.

After the First World War, the American government decided that it did not want the USA to be involved in world affairs any more. This is called **isolationism**.

In 1929, the Great Depression began. Millions of workers lost their jobs. When Franklin D. Roosevelt became President of the USA in 1933, he promised the American people a 'New Deal'. He wanted to give them back their jobs and make the American economy strong again.

In 1939, war broke out in Europe. American factories began making war goods for the Allies, and thousands of people were back in work. The American economy became strong again. In 1941, the Japanese airforce bombed Pearl Harbor, an American naval base in the Pacific Ocean. Then the USA ended its isolationism and entered the Second World War.

Source A

Faced with the leadership of the world, the US backed out of the room, frightened and stammering.

▲ From *The History of the American Presidential Elections* by A. Schlesinger and H. Israel.

3.1 Why did the USA decide to follow a policy of isolationism?

America and the First World War

In April 1917, the USA joined the First World War on the side of the Allies. This was very important in helping the Allies win the war (see Chapter 1). The American President, Woodrow Wilson, played a major part in putting together the Treaty of Versailles after the war (see Chapter 2).

The League of Nations

President Wilson had persuaded the peacemakers at Versailles to include a section in the treaty setting up a League of Nations. He hoped that the League would watch over world affairs and help to prevent war in the future.

Woodrow Wilson

*Woodrow Wilson was elected President of the USA in 1912. He kept his country out of the First World War until 1917. Towards the end of the war he issued his **Fourteen Points** as a basis for peace talks, and represented the USA at Versailles, where he proposed a League of Nations should be set up. However, he could not persuade the Americans to join. In 1919 he suffered a stroke and died in 1924.*

America and the League

People in the government were worried that, if the USA joined the League of Nations, the USA could be drawn into wars again and again. Over 100,000 American soldiers had been killed in the First World War. They did not want this to happen again. So they refused to agree to the Treaty of Versailles.

Immigration

Some American politicians thought that too many people were coming to live in the USA. Between 1901 and 1911, eleven million men, women and children **emigrated** to the USA from Europe alone. Some politicians began to say that fewer people should be allowed to come and live in the USA. They thought that America should be for the Americans. So the American government passed laws which said how many people could come into the USA each year.

The President

President Wilson believed that the USA should play an important part in world affairs. But he lost the 1920 election and from then on the USA kept out of world affairs.

▲ Front cover of the weekly American magazine *The New Republic*, published in 1919.

▲ A cartoon from the British magazine *Punch*, published in 1919.

QUESTIONS

1. After the First World War the USA followed a policy of isolationism. What does isolationism mean?

2. Why did the USA follow this policy in the years after 1918?

3. Look at Source B. What point was the cartoonist making about the USA's refusal to join the League of Nations?

4. Look at Source C. Why does the writer believe America should not get involved with Europe?

3.2 How did the policy of isolationism work?

After the First World War, the USA tried to avoid getting involved in international disputes.

Treaties
One of the ways in which the USA tried to avoid disputes was by signing treaties to keep the peace. The Washington Naval Agreements (1921–2) limited the size of various countries' navies.

Conferences
The USA believed that talking could sometimes stop fighting later on. The Americans took part in the Geneva Peace Conference (1932) and the World Economic Conference (1933).

Economic help for Germany
The American government believed that the only way to keep peace in Europe was for Germany to be strong. So in 1924, a team of American experts worked out the **Dawes Plan**. This helped sort out a new currency for Germany and loaned the German government $200 million.

Economic help for South America
The American government gave aid to countries in South America like Nicaragua and the Dominican Republic. This was to make sure their governments did not threaten the USA.

Amounts loaned by the USA to different areas of the world, 1924–8

To Asia and Australia $588m
To Canada $936m
To Europe $2,815m
To South America $1,421m
Total of loans made by the USA between 1924 and 1928 $5,785m

Amounts loaned each year by the USA					Total
1924 $969m	1925 $1,076m	1926 $1,125m	1927 $1,337m	1928 $1,251m	1924–8 $5,758m

Economic help for the USSR
The American government hated communism. But the American government still sent aid to the communist USSR because it wanted to help stop starvation and disease there.

The results of isolationism
The USA did not join the League of Nations. It did nothing to stop Japan's invasion of Manchuria in 1931, or Italy's invasion of Abyssinia in 1933.

> **QUESTIONS**
>
> 1 Explain the importance to the USA of:
>   a The Washington Naval Agreements
>   b the Dawes Plan
>   c economic aid to South America.
>
> 2 Read pages 51–2. Have you read anything that might make you think America was *not* really following a policy of isolationism? Give your reasons.

3.3 The USA in the 1920s – was there a 'Golden Age'?

Economic boom
The USA had raw materials like coal, iron ore and oil. It also had skilled inventors and business people. After the First World War, these people helped make the country rich. The amount of goods produced by factories doubled. This brought great wealth to many people.

Automation
The main reason for the USA's economic boom was **automation**. For the first time, goods like radios and cars were produced using lines of machines. This saved a lot of money, and meant that the goods were much cheaper. For example, in 1908, a new car called the 'Model T' Ford cost $850. But by 1925, its price had dropped to just $290. Four years later, there were 26 million cars on American roads.

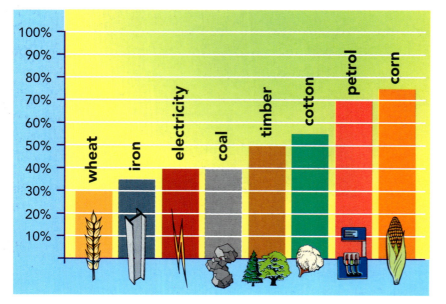

◀ In the 1920s the USA produced a high percentage of the world's basic goods; here are some examples.

Hire-purchase

In the 1920s, Americans could buy goods like vacuum cleaners, radios and cars on **hire-purchase**. This meant that they could pay for the goods gradually over a long time. But thousands of Americans got into debt in this way.

Advertising

People were encouraged to buy consumer goods by the increase in advertising. Colourful billboards, newspapers and the new cinemas all advertised the latest gadgets.

Tariffs

The American government put a tax, called a **tariff**, on all goods that came into the country. These import duties meant that American goods were cheaper than foreign goods.

The government also cut the taxes paid by rich people and companies. It wanted people to have as much money as possible, so that they could invest in American businesses and create even more jobs.

SUMMARY

Reasons for the economic boom in the 1920s

- Raw materials.
- Mass production.
- Hire-purchase.
- Advertising.
- Import duties.
- Low taxation.

Source A

It is often said that 'money can't buy everything', but many Americans in the 1920s thought that it could!
They would scrimp and save to buy the things which seemed to lead to the good life.
Mr A. had to show Mr B. his superiority, not by anything he did, . . . but by the number and size of his cars and the splendour of his house.

▲ Harriet Ward, *World Powers in the Twentieth Century*, 1978.

Source B

▲ The main street of a small town in California in the 1920s. By the early 1920s, the number of motor cars on the road was on the increase.

Spare time
Americans had more money to spend and more goods to spend it on. There was more for them to do in their spare time as well. They listened to records and went to dances. They also went to the cinema and watched great stars like Charlie Chaplin and Greta Garbo. American companies began making films in **Hollywood**.

More and more Americans owned cars, and at weekends they went on trips into the countryside.

Buying and selling shares
Ordinary Americans had more money than ever before. Some of them began investing in American companies. They bought **shares** in whatever company they chose. Every year the **shareholders** were paid a share of that company's profits. This is called a **dividend**. If a company was doing well, the dividends would be high.

Shareholders could make money in another way. If a company's dividends were high, more and more people would want to buy shares in that company. Then shareholders could sell their shares for more than they paid for them. So that way they would make a profit.

Buying on the margin
Some Americans borrowed money from banks so that they could buy shares. These people paid the banks back from the profits they made. This is called buying **on the margin**.

Buying on the margin only worked when profits, and therefore dividends, were high. If profits were low and there was no dividend, shareholders could not pay back their bank loan.

Source C

▲ An advert for a consumer product in the 1920s.

▲ Buying shares 'on the margin'.

QUESTIONS

1. Look at the summary box on page 53. It lists six reasons for the economic boom in the USA in the 1920s. Explain how *each* of the reasons made people richer.

2. How did American peoples' lives change as a result of the economic boom?

3. Why did so many people want to buy shares?

4. Read page 56.
   Were all Americans well off in the 1920s? Explain your answer.

Were all Americans rich?

Many Americans were rich or very rich. But over half of all Americans were very poor indeed. They could not buy shares or cars. In fact, they were so poor that they could not buy proper clothes or decent food for themselves and their families.

Farmers

Many American farmers had done well by selling grain to Europe during the First World War. But after the war, more and more machinery was used on American farms, so crops were cheaper to grow. The price of grain fell, and many farmers were forced to sell their farms.

Black workers

Most people working on farms in the southern American states were Blacks. When the farmers sold their farms, the Blacks lost their jobs. Many Blacks moved to the industrial cities of the north. But they could not earn much money there because they did not have the skills that factory owners in the north wanted. As the Blacks had such little money, they lived in terrible conditions.

American Indians

Indians lived in the USA long before white people went there. By the beginning of the 20th century, most American Indians lived on **reservations**. These were special areas set aside for the Indians by the American government. Reservations mostly had poor soil, so Indians found it difficult to grow crops. The American government had forced the Indians into reservations, but it gave the Indians very little help to survive.

▼ A poor farming community in Virginia in the 1920s.

Source D

3.4 Why did government policy towards immigration change in the 1920s?

Before 1921, nearly everyone who wanted to go and live in the USA could do so. This is often called the **open door** policy. After 1921, this policy changed for two main reasons:

- Some politicians thought that many of the **immigrants** going to live in the USA brought with them 'un-American' ideas like communism.
- Many people believed that these new immigrants took jobs away from the 'real' Americans.

The quota system 1921

Before 1921, nearly one million people had gone to live in the USA every year. But in 1921, the American government said that only 357,000 immigrants would be allowed in each year. They would be allowed into the USA in proportion to the numbers of their fellow countrymen already there.

The Immigration Act 1924

This cut the number of immigrants allowed in each year from 357,000 to 164,000.

The 'open door' had closed.

Source B

Whenever I begged for food my mother would pour me a cup of tea. This settled my stomach for a moment or two, but a little later I would feel hunger nudging my ribs, twisting my empty guts until they ached.
I would grow dizzy and my vision would dim.

▲ A poor Black remembers what it was like in the south of the USA in the 1920s. From R. Wright, *Black Boy*, 1947.

Andrew Carnegie

Andrew Carnegie was born in Scotland and went to the USA when he was a small boy. He started work in a Pittsburgh mill at the age of 13, working for just over one dollar a week. By the time he was 30 he had investments in iron and oil companies which earned him over $40,000 dollars a year. By 1900 his income was estimated at $23 million dollars a year – 20,000 times the average wage. In 1901 he sold out and devoted his life to founding libraries and universities.

▼ A poor area of New York, 1922.

Source A

3.5 How were the immigrants treated?

White people
There were more white Europeans living in America than any other group. Many Americans began to believe that the only 'true' Americans were Whites.

Black people
Most people in America in the 1920s were **prejudiced** against Blacks. In some states, Blacks were not allowed to vote and their children were not allowed to go to school with white children.

The Ku Klux Klan
The Ku Klux Klan was based in the southern states of America. Members of the Klan believed that Whites were better than Blacks.

Klan members met at night by the light of flaming torches. They dressed in long white robes with pointed hoods over their heads. They burned houses and businesses to the ground. They flogged, tarred and feathered Blacks, as well as Jews and Catholics. Sometimes they put people to death without a trial. These murders are called **lynchings**.

Why were the Klan not caught?
In many towns, Klan members held important jobs in the police or the law courts. So it took a lot of bravery, too, for someone to give evidence against a Klan member, or to sit on a jury which sent a Klan member to prison.

Source A
The Negro was chained to a tree stump by over 500 Klan members and asked if he had anything to say.
Castrated and in indescribable torture, the Negro asked for a cigarette, lit it, and blew smoke in the face of his tormentors.
The fire was lit and everyone danced around.

▲ Account of the lynching of a man convicted of killing a white woman in Georgia in 1921, published in the *Washington Eagle*.

▼ Victims of a Ku Klux Klan lynching in 1930.

Source B

QUESTIONS
1. What was the Ku Klux Klan?
2. Why were Klan members not always punished when they broke the law?
3. What does Source A above tell you about attitudes of Whites to Blacks and Blacks to Whites?

3.6 What was prohibition?

In 1919, the American government said that no one was allowed to make or sell alcoholic drink anywhere in the USA. This was called **prohibition**.

Why did the American government introduce prohibition?

Different groups of people wanted the American government to ban alcohol.

- Women's organizations wanted alcoholic drink banned so that husbands would stop wasting money in saloons.
- The Church wanted alcohol banned so that family life would get better.

Speakeasies

Most Americans could not see what was wrong with having a drink. They wanted to carry on buying alcohol. Hundreds of illegal bars sprang up all over the USA. These bars were called **speakeasies**. Because they were illegal, they had to be kept secret. At speakeasies, people could buy **bootleg** (alcohol from abroad) or **moonshine** (alcohol made illegally in the USA). Millions of Americans turned themselves into criminals by going to speakeasies and buying illegal alcohol.

Source A

"THE POOR MAN'S CLUB."
THE MOST EXPENSIVE IN THE WORLD TO BELONG TO

A CLUB MEMBER IN GOOD STANDING
"PAYING HIS DUES"

SLAVES OF THE SALOON

A woman entered a barroom, and advanced quietly to her husband, who sat drinking with three other men. "Thinkin' ye'd be too busy to come home to supper, Jack, I've fetched it to you here."

And she departed. The man laughed awkwardly. He invited his friends to share the meal with him. Then he removed the cover from the dish. The dish was empty. It contained a slip of paper that said: "I hope you will enjoy your supper. It is the same your wife and children have at home." – Chicago Chronicle.

▲ A poster issued by the Anti-Saloon League in 1920.

Source B

The result of introducing prohibition was that many Americans began to lose their respect for law and order. In Chicago, for example, the gangster, 'Scarface' Al Capone, with his private army of gunslingers, had more real power than the mayor.

▲ Adapted from D. B. O'Callaghan, *Roosevelt and the United States*, 1966.

Protection rackets

Gangsters ran the speakeasies. They also ran gambling dens and brothels. They made a lot of money from **protection rackets**. In these, business owners were forced to pay the gangsters money each week to have their premises looked after. If the owners refused to pay, the gangsters would break up their premises.

Al 'Scarface' Capone

Al Capone was one of the most famous of all American gangsters. He made a fortune – $105 million in 1927 alone – from selling illegal alcohol. He bribed police and politicians, and in 1927 managed to get one of his henchmen elected mayor of Chicago. Al Capone stopped other gangsters operating in 'his' area. On 14 February 1927, his gangsters shot down a rival gang in the streets of Chicago. This was called the **St Valentine's Day Massacre**. But the police were never able to prove Capone's part in the murders.

Why did prohibition end?

Ordinary men and women began to lose faith in the law. Gangsters fought on the streets as they struggled to control the trade in illegal alcohol. The police seemed powerless.

In February 1933, the American government **repealed** the law against the sale of alcohol. Prohibition had failed. Americans were free to drink alcohol legally once more.

> **QUESTIONS**
>
> 1. Explain the following:
>   a. Prohibition
>   b. Speakeasies
>   c. Moonshine
>   d. Bootleg
>   e. Protection.
> 2. Why did the government find it so hard to enforce prohibition in the United States in the 1920s?

▼ Profits made by Al Capone in 1927.

3.7 What were the effects of the Wall Street Crash?

What was the Wall Street crash?

In the 1920s, Americans who invested in shares (see page 54) made good profits. Business boomed as more and more people bought cars and washing machines, radios and telephones. But in the end there is a limit to the number of goods like these that people can buy. Sales began to drop. By 1929, some companies' profits were beginning to fall. This meant that the dividends that companies could pay to their shareholders began to fall, too. Many shareholders had borrowed money from stockbrokers or banks to buy their shares. They thought they could sell them again for more than they had paid for them.

As profits started to fall, some cautious investors began selling their shares. Once this happened, the prices of shares began to fall. More and more people sold their shares. Panic set in. On 23 October 1929, 13 million shares were sold. Five days later over 16 million shares were sold, and prices tumbled hour by hour.

The **Wall Street Crash** is named after the street in New York where the shares were bought and sold.

▼ A victim of the Wall Street Crash tries to sell his car for a bargain price, October 1929.

Source A

What happened to the shareholders?

Many shareholders sold their shares for much less than they had paid for them. Others could not sell their shares at all. Many thousands of people were ruined. Some even killed themselves.

What happened to industry and to business?

Industries had to cut down on the amount of goods they produced. This meant that fewer workers were needed, so thousands lost their jobs. Banks which had lent money to businesses wanted their money back. Many companies could not repay the loans, so they had to close down. Even more jobs were lost.

Source B

They used to tell me I was building a dream
And so I followed the mob
When there was earth to plough or guns to bear
I was always there – right on the job.

They used to tell me I was building a dream
With peace and glory ahead
Why should I be standing in line
Just waiting for bread?

Say don't you remember, they called me Al
It was Al all the time
Say don't you remember, I'm your Pal –
Buddy can you spare a dime?

▲ Extracts from 'Buddy can you spare a dime?'. This song was written in 1932 and was very popular during the 1930s.

▼ Rising unemployment in the USA, 1929–33.

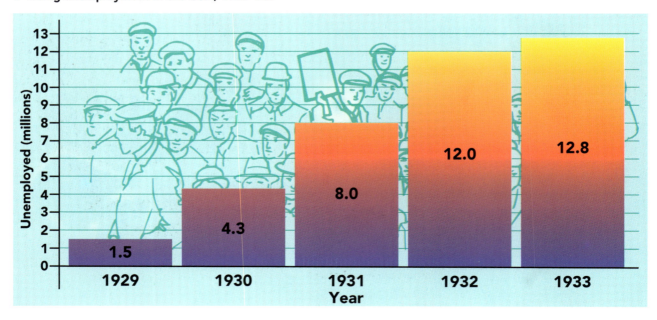

What happened to ordinary people?

- **Unemployment**. Throughout the USA, four people in every ten were unemployed. In some states, unemployment was as high as 70%. The **Great Depression** had begun.

- **Housing**. Thousands of people could not pay their rent or their mortgage. They moved into makeshift **shanty towns** on the outskirts of big cities. People called these towns **Hoovervilles** after the President, Herbert Hoover, who seemed to do nothing to help.

- **Money**. There was no social security or unemployment benefit. Some unemployed people stole in order to eat. Charities set up soup kitchens to stop men, women and children starving.

- **Farmers**. People had less and less money to spend on food. Shops and canning factories had less money to pay the farmers. Farmers' incomes fell, and they had less money to spend on rents and mortgages. Many farmers could not pay their rent at all, and drifted into towns looking for work.

To make matters even worse, a drought in the Midwest meant that the soil simply blew away in dust storms. Millions of acres were turned into a Dust Bowl. The land could not be farmed. Even more farmers were out of work.

> **QUESTIONS**
>
> 1 Why did share prices fall in 1929?
>
> 2 How were the following affected by the Wall Street Crash:
>
>   a Ordinary investors
>   b Banks
>   c American industry
>   d Factory workers
>   e Farmers
>   f Foreign countries?
>
> Who was worst hit?

▶ The downward spiral.

3.7 EFFECTS OF THE WALL STREET CRASH

Source C

▶ Unemployed workers in Times Square, New York. They are queuing for free bread provided by one of the big newspapers.

How did the Great Depression affect foreign countries?

During the 1920s, the USA loaned $5,758 million to other countries. In 1929, the USA needed the money and asked for these loans back. This had a terrible effect upon the other countries. Factories and businesses closed and thousands of people became unemployed.

SUMMARY

USA in the 1920s – a time of turmoil?

- Half the population below the poverty line.
- Prices of farm produce dropped.
- Farm labourers lost jobs.
- Low wages and poor conditions in factories.
- Opposition to immigration.
- The Ku Klux Klan.
- Prohibition – widespread breaking of law.
- Gangsters.
- The Wall Street Crash – 1929.
- The Great Depression.

Source D

◀ A farmer and his sons run for shelter during a dust storm in Oklahoma.

3.8 How successful was President Hoover in dealing with the Depression?

What did Hoover think should happen?

President Hoover was a member of the Republican Party. Republicans thought that the government should not interfere in the ways in which business and industry worked. President Hoover believed that the USA had become prosperous in the 1920s without any help from government. The USA would become prosperous again, he thought, if business and industry were left to sort things out themselves.

Money for the poor

President Hoover believed that money given to unemployed people should not come from the taxes paid by people still in work. He made arrangements for town councils and state governments to borrow money from the federal (national) government. But this money had to be paid back when times were better.

Source A

One of the oldest hopes has been the abolition of poverty.
We Americans are nearer the final triumph over poverty than ever before . . .

▲ President Hoover speaking to the American people in 1928.

▼ A 'Hooverville', in Central Park, New York, 1932.

Source B

Source C

▶ Police and the Bonus Army clashing in Washington in March 1932.

Was President Hoover hard-hearted?

Many people thought that President Hoover should use government money to start the economy up again. They believed he should use government money to help people who had fallen on bad times. They did not understand how he could let decent, ordinary men, women and children end up living in Hoovervilles.

The Bonus Army

Many people were shocked by Hoover's treatment of the 'Bonus Army'. At the end of the war in 1919, the soldiers who survived were promised a bonus. This bonus was to be paid in 1945. In 1932, 25,000 of these ex-soldiers marched to Washington to ask for their bonus then and there, so that they would be helped through the bad times. President Hoover refused. He sent soldiers with tanks and tear gas to drive the ex-soldiers out of Washington.

The end of President Hoover

The people had had enough. In the election for President in 1932, the leader of the Democrats, Franklin Delano Roosevelt beat Herbert Hoover easily.

Source D

The Depression brought tragedy to thousands of families; the old man who sees his life's savings vanish, the ragged child surviving on the one 'meal' a day of dough fried in last week's bacon dripping, the young wife who watches her energetic and handsome husband become by degrees, idle, then irritable, then scared, then just listless.

▲ D. Snowman, *The Effects of the Depression: America Since 1920*, 1968.

QUESTIONS

1 What part did President Hoover think the government should play in the American Depression?

2 Why was President Hoover so unpopular with the American voters after 1932?

3.9 What steps did President Roosevelt take to end the Great Depression?

Roosevelt's policies were completely different from those of Hoover. He promised a **New Deal** for the American people.

The Emergency Banking Act

During the Great Depression, some banks found it hard to pay out money to the men and women who had put their savings into the banks. This was because the banks had loaned the money to companies and businesses. So hundreds of banks were forced to close, and thousands of people lost all their savings. Millions of American people lost their faith in banks, and kept what money they had in their own homes.

Roosevelt knew that, if American industry was to grow, the banks had to have money to lend out to businesses. So people had to be persuaded to put their money back into the banks.

Roosevelt closed all the banks. Then he had them inspected, and only those that were found to be all right were allowed to re-open. People began to believe once more that banks would not close overnight. They began trusting banks with their money again.

Roosevelt also stopped banks from investing on the Wall Street stock market. He did not want a repeat of the problems of 1929 when the banks lost their customers' money through buying and selling shares.

Source A

The only thing we have to fear is fear itself. This nation asks for action, and action now. Our greatest task is to put people to work. This problem can be solved in part by the government creating jobs and treating the task as we would treat the emergency of war.

▲ An extract from Roosevelt's first speech as President, made to the American nation in March 1933.

Source B

▶ An American newspaper cartoon published in 1933.

3.9 ROOSEVELT AND THE GREAT DEPRESSION

Fireside chats

Roosevelt was determined to explain his policies to the American people. He was the first President to use radio to do this. He made a series of broadcasts in which he told people about government policies and chatted about his own family and his dog, Fala. For millions of people, President Roosevelt was almost like an old friend who sat and chatted in their sitting room. His broadcasts became known as 'fireside chats' and were very popular. Most people trusted him to do what was best for them.

Relief for the unemployed

In 1933 millions of Americans were out of work and hungry. Roosevelt set up an organization to provide emergency relief (**FERA**) for the hungry and homeless. To help pay for this relief, the salaries of government employees were cut.

Getting the USA back to work

Roosevelt believed that in an emergency like the Great Depression, it was up to the government to create jobs for people. This would put money into their pockets. They would then begin to spend this money, and so more goods would be sold. Factories would get going again, and more and more people would be employed. Those people, in turn, would have money to spend. Gradually the economy would get better, and government help would not be needed any more. Roosevelt called this way of getting the USA back to work 'priming the pump'.

▲ The symbol of the National Recovery Administration was displayed in shop windows and advertisements.

QUESTIONS

1. Read page 67.
   Why did President Roosevelt act quickly to deal with problems facing American banks?

2. Roosevelt had many serious problems to deal with in the USA. Why, then, did he bother to tell the American people about his dog?

3. Read the section 'Getting the USA back to work'.
   Why did Roosevelt believes it was important to create jobs for people?

The Alphabet Agencies

The American Congress agreed with Roosevelt. This was important because without the support of Congress, Roosevelt could not possibly expect his ideas to become law.

Between 1933 and 1935, Congress set up a large number of organizations, called agencies, which were aimed at getting people back to work. The agencies were known by their initials. For example, there was the Civilian Conservation Corps (the CCC), which employed young people to plant trees to stop soil erosion. Because the agencies were known by their initials, they were called the **Alphabet Agencies**. (see page 70)

Security at work

Roosevelt also wanted to improve working conditions for the workers. He wanted to bring in laws allowing them to join a trade union. He persuaded Congress to pass an Act giving them the right to belong to a trade union as well as better wages.

In 1935 the **Social Security Act** was passed. This was the beginning of pensions for workers aged 65, and also unemployment benefit.

Help for Farmers

A major problem for farmers was that they were producing too much. This kept prices low. The **Agricultural Adjustment Act (AAA)** gave special payments to farmers who agreed to produce less.

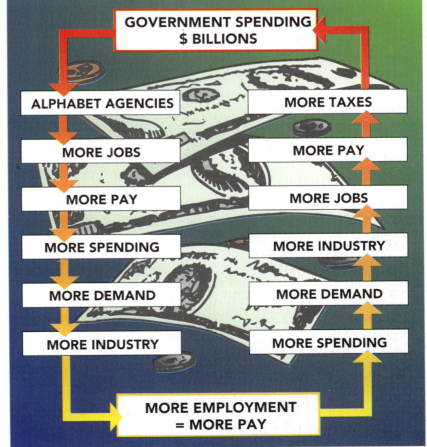

▶ Roosevelt believed that the government should create jobs to help unemployment. This policy was called 'priming the pump'.

The main Alphabet Agencies

Civilian Conservation Corps (CCC) 1933
This provided work for 18 – 25-year-olds. Camps were set up in the countryside for conservation work, such as planting trees, digging canals, strengthening river banks against flooding and stocking rivers with fish.

Tennessee Valley Authority (TVA) 1933
The TVA was not set up as a means of creating work for the unemployed, but aimed to help one of the poorest areas of the USA. The Tennessee Valley suffered from poor soil and high unemployment. The TVA built 20 dams and a large system of inland waterways. It also planted trees. Its work stopped nearly all the flooding in the region. Farming improved, and the growth of tourism began.

Public Works Administration (PWA) 1933
This scheme was given a lot of money to spend on public works such as building hospitals, bridges, sewage plants, and schools. It was also responsible for clearing large slums in the cities and replacing them with new housing.

Civil Works Administration (CWA) 1933
This provided temporary work for unemployed adults in building roads, schools, airfields and playgrounds. In 1934 there were more than 4 million workers on the scheme. It was replaced by the **WPA** in 1935.

Works Progress Administration (WPA) 1935
This organization carried out the same sort of work as the PWA. It built 2,500 hospitals and nearly 6,000 schools and playgrounds. It also found work for artists and writers (for example, producing murals and guide books) and set up schemes for unemployed actors.

Source C

▲ Farmland in the Tennessee Valley in the early 1930s.

Source D

During the last three months I have visited some twenty states of this wonderfully rich and beautiful country.

At Montana citizens told me of thousands of bushels of wheat left uncut in the fields on account of its low price that hardly paid for its harvesting.

In Oregon I saw thousands of bushels of apples rotting in the orchards. Yet there are millions of children who, on account of the poverty of their parents will not eat one apple this year.

In this country we have reached the stage where we are producing too much and using too little at the same time

◀ From the *Report of the Government Committee on Unemployment in the United States, 1932.*

QUESTIONS

1 a What were the 'Alphabet Agencies'?

  b Choose TWO agencies and explain how they helped America to recover from the Great Depression.

2 a What was the work of the Tennessee Valley Authority?

  b Why was this work important in helping America recover from the Great Depression?

3 a What was the problem described in Source D?

  b How did the problem come about?

  c How did the Agricultural Adjustment Act help (see page 69)?

3.10 What opposition was there to the New Deal?

Source A

Population of United States	124,000,000
Eligible for Old age pension	30,000,000
That leaves to do work	94,000,000
Working for government	20,000,000
That leaves to do work	74,000,000
Forbidden to work by the Child Labour Law	60,000,000
That leaves to do work	14,000,000
Number unemployed	13,999,998
That leaves to do work	2

ME AND THE PRESIDENT

HE HAS GONE FISHING

AND I'M GETTING DAMN TIRED

▲ This was sent out by an American company in 1936. It was supposed to be a joke.

Source B

The President didn't understand that when you give to people you hurt them.
In the Depression people lost confidence in themselves.
Welfare kills a man's spirit because it makes him lose the will to fend for himself.
If you want a man to be successful, he needs to face the setbacks of life.

▲ An American businessman remembers the New Deal.

Roosevelt's policies were intended to end the Great Depression and make the USA rich again. But there were some people who did not like what Roosevelt did.

Why were some people against the New Deal?

People who did not like the New Deal said that:

- Rich people were taxed heavily to pay for it, and this was not fair.
- Huge sums of money were paid to unemployed people for planting trees and painting murals, and this was silly.
- Roosevelt had no right to interfere in the ways in which Americans ran their own businesses – for example, by limiting the hours people could work. This was making the USA more like the communist USSR.
- The new sickness benefits and pensions were state handouts. People should save in good times and so be able to look after themselves in bad times.
- Roosevelt's scheme to pay farmers for producing less food was stupid when so many people were starving.
- Pouring huge sums of government money into schemes like the Tennessee Valley Authority was not the American way of doing things.
- Some people like Governor Huey Long of Louisiana, thought the New Deal did not go far enough. He wanted the government to take from the rich and give to the poor in a far more direct way.

The Supreme Court

In 1933, Roosevelt set up the **National Recovery Administration** (NRA). He wanted to improve the conditions of people at work, and to make their jobs more secure.

But in 1935, the Supreme Court said that the NRA was against the American Constitution. The judges said that the President did not have the power to tell employers how they should treat their workers.

So then Roosevelt threatened to create new judges. He said he was going to do this to make the Court more efficient. But most people believed it was to make sure that most of the judges supported him.

There was so much opposition that Roosevelt dropped this idea. But he had frightened many Americans. They believed he was getting too powerful.

Was Roosevelt popular with ordinary voters?

Some people were very critical of Roosevelt and what he was doing. Others thought that his policies were just plain wrong. But Roosevelt was very popular with most people, and he was re-elected President in 1936, 1940 and 1944.

Source C

THE ILLEGAL ACT.

PRESIDENT ROOSEVELT. "I'M SORRY, BUT THE SUPREME COURT SAYS I MUST CHUCK YOU BACK AGAIN."

▲ A cartoon published in the British magazine Punch in June 1935. The man in the rowing boat is Roosevelt.

SUMMARY

- Hoover did not believe in government interference.
- Roosevelt promised a 'New Deal'.
- Alphabet Agencies.
- 'Priming the pump' – to help the workers.
- Agricultural Adjustment Act.
- Opposition to Roosevelt's measures.
- President's powers challenged by the Supreme Court.

3.11 War – the end of isolationism and the end of the Depression

Roosevelt's policy had been to spend government money to create jobs. But in 1939, there were nine million people in the USA without a job. This was six times as many as in 1929.

During the 1920s and 1930s, the American government did everything it could to avoid being dragged into a European war (see page 49). But when the Second World War broke out in Europe in 1939, Roosevelt wanted the USA to do what it could to oppose Hitler.

American industries provided goods that the Allies needed. In order to do this they had to produce more in their factories. This created thousands of new jobs.

Lend-Lease
In March 1941, Roosevelt agreed to lend Britain up to $7,000 million worth of arms and other vital supplies. Officially, the USA was not on either side at the time, but the American government was happy to provide this sort of help to Britain.

Pearl Harbor
Japan was an ally of Germany in the Second World War. But the Japanese were afraid that the USA would enter the war against Japan and Germany. So the Japanese decided to try to destroy the American Pacific fleet before the USA declared war, and before the Pacific fleet was used against Japan.

In December 1941, the Japanese airforce bombed the American naval base at Pearl Harbor in the Pacific Ocean. As a result of the attack, the USA entered the Second World War on the side of Britain, France, Russia and China against Germany and its allies.

Isolationism was over.

QUESTIONS

1. Read pages 72–3. Roosevelt was working hard to improve life for millions of Americans. Why did some people oppose what he was doing?
2. What was lend-lease?
3. a Why did the USA enter the Second World War?
   b When did the USA's policy of isolationism end?

   Explain your answer.

3.12 Exercise: How successful was the New Deal?

President Franklin Delano Roosevelt took office in March 1933. He had promised the American people a New Deal and immediately set to work to create jobs for the unemployed. As we saw in Section 3.10, there were many who opposed his policies. They did not believe that the government should be spending taxpayers' money to find jobs for the unemployed. Roosevelt felt quite differently. He was perfectly prepared to use government money to 'prime the pump' of the American economy. Between 1932 and 1936 Federal Government spending increased by nearly 80% – most of it on Roosevelt's job creation schemes.

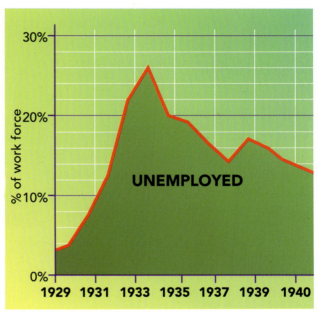

▲ Percentage of the workforce unemployed in the USA, 1929–40.

Source 1

Dear Mr President,

This is just to tell you that everything is all right now. The man you sent went down to the bank with us and the mortgage can go on. I wrote about losing the furniture too. Well your man got that back for us. I never heard of a President like you.

▲ One of several thousand letters received by Roosevelt every day during the New Deal.

Source 2

▲ A cartoon of Roosevelt from a newspaper printed in June 1934.

The voters supported what Roosevelt was trying to do and re-elected him in 1936, 1940 and 1944. The real question, however, is did the New Deal work, or is Roosevelt's image as the saviour of the American economy a false one?

Source 3

Happy days are here again
The skies above are clear again
Let us drink a cup of cheer again
Happy days are here again

▲ Part of a song sung by Roosevelt's supporters in the 1930s.

Source 4

They planted trees, made reservoirs and fish ponds . . . cleared beaches and camping grounds and in a multitude of ways protected and improved parks forests and recreational areas.

Their muscles hardened, their bodies filled out, their self-respect returned.

They learned trades; more important they learned about America, and they learned about other Americans.

▲ Description of men at work on a Civilian Conservation Corps project. From Arthur Schlesinger, *The Coming of the New Deal*, 1959.

Source 5

▲ The Norris dam, the first dam to be completed by the TVA in 1936. The dams built by the TVA allowed 630 miles of river to be navigated for the first time, produced hydro-electricity for local farms, encouraged businesses into the area and helped tourism to flourish. Some historians believe that the Tennessee Valley was the only real success of the New Deal programme.

Source 6

▲ A cartoon published by Roosevelt's opponents during the New Deal. It shows Roosevelt using more and more money to 'prime' the New Deal 'pump'. Lots of the money is shown leaking away.

Source 7

The New Deal left many problems unsolved and even created some new ones.

As late as 1941 the unemployed still numbered six million and not until the war years of 1943 did the army of jobless finally disappear.

▲ William Leuchtenburg, *Franklin Roosevelt and the New Deal*, 1963.

Source 8

The most damning criticism of Roosevelt's policy was that it failed to cure the depression. Despite some $20 poured out in spending and lending, there were still millions of dispirited men unemployed.

▲ The views of a modern historian on the New Deal.

---

1 Look carefully at sources 1–8.

  a Choose the source which you think tells you most about the success of the New Deal.

  b Explain what your chosen source tells you about the success of the New Deal.

2 Do Sources 1–5 give a complete account of the New Deal? If not, what is missing?

3 Look at the two views below:

  View 1
  - The New Deal was a waste of taxpayers' money and achieved very little.

  View 2
  - Roosevelt was a hero. His New Deal solved the USA's economic problems and brought back better living conditions.

Explain which of these two views gives the more accurate picture of the New Deal.

CHAPTER 4

GERMANY 1919–39

In 1919, the victorious Allies forced Germany to accept the **Treaty of Versailles** (see pages 25–6). Many German people just could not accept the treaty which they believed to be unfair. To make matters worse, Germany was hit by an economic crisis in which thousands of people lost their jobs and their savings. This added to their anger and resentment.

The National Socialist German Workers' Party (Nazis) seemed to offer the German people hope for the future. In 1933, the Nazis came to power. They set up a dictatorship under their leader, Adolf Hitler. He increased the size of the army and the navy and reduced unemployment. Then he set about overthrowing the Treaty of Versailles.

▲ Cartoon published in 1919. Children in 1919 would be the soldiers of 1940. The four Allied leaders are, from left to right: Lloyd George (Great Britain), Orlando (Italy), Clemenceau (France) and Wilson (USA). They wrote the Treaty of Versailles.

4.1 How did Germany react to the Treaty of Versailles?

Signing the treaty

The German government was shocked by the terms of the Treaty of Versailles. It had been hoping that the treaty would be based on the **Fourteen Points** put forward by President Wilson of the USA (see page 23). Instead the treaty seemed to be based on revenge. The German government complained bitterly about this to the Allies, but the Allies told the German government that if it did not sign the treaty, Allied soldiers would invade Germany. So the German government signed.

The 'war guilt' clause
One of the items or **clauses** in the Versailles Treaty was Article 231. Article 231 forced Germany to accept responsibility for all the loss and damage caused by the war. The German people thought this was really unfair. They did not believe that they had started the war and, besides, more German soldiers had been killed than French, British or American ones.

A new republic
The German Kaiser (Emperor) had taken the German people into the war. But because Germany had been defeated, he could no longer stay as Emperor. So he gave up his throne.

After this, the German people set up a new system without an emperor, and where everyone could vote to choose the government. This system was called the **Weimar Republic**, because Weimar was the city in Germany where it was agreed.

'Diktat'
The Germans had not taken part in drawing up the Treaty of Versailles. So they began calling it a 'Diktat' – a dictated treaty. Many German people believed that they did not have to obey the terms of the treaty because it had been forced on them.

Who was to blame?
Most Germans blamed the Allies for what happened at Versailles. But some blamed their own politicians. These people said that the German army had not surrendered. And enemy troops had not invaded Germany either. Instead, it was their own politicians who had 'stabbed them in the back' by agreeing to the Treaty of Versailles.

Was there a solution?
A young ex-soldier, Adolf Hitler, began telling people that, if he gained power, he would scrap the Treaty of Versailles. Because so many people hated the treaty, there were plenty of people willing to listen to him.

Source B
The government of the German Republic says it is ready to accept and sign the peace treaty. But the government also believes that the conditions of the peace are unjust.

▲ Said by representatives of the German government before signing the Treaty of Versailles.

Source C
Vengeance!
German nation!
Today in the Hall of Mirrors (at Versailles) the disgraceful treaty is being signed.
Do not forget it.
The German people will regain their rightful place amongst the nations.

▲ Adapted from a German newspaper, *Deutsche Zeitung*, 28 June 1919.

QUESTIONS
1. Read section 4.1. Why did the German people resent the Treaty of Versailles?
2. Look at Source A.
   a. What point in the cartoonist making?
   b. Do you find it odd that, at the end of a terrible war, some people were expecting another one?

4.2 What problems faced the Weimar Republic 1919-24?

Source A

Article 1 The German Reich [state] is a Republic. Political authority comes from the people.

Article 22 Everyone in the country over the age of twenty could vote for delegates to the Reichstag, according to proportional representation.

Article 48 If public order is seriously disturbed, the President can take full control. He may use the army to restore peace if necessary.

▲ Adapted from the Weimar Constitution.

The Weimar Constitution

The German people elected a new Parliament, the **Reichstag**, in January 1919. It was the members of this Parliament who were forced to accept the Treaty of Versailles. In August they drew up a new constitution (rules for government) for Germany, known as the **Weimar Republic**. It was one of the most democratic constitutions in the world.

The Reichstag

All men and women over the age of twenty were allowed to vote, and the vote was a secret one. This was quite new to the German people. They had been used to a strong dictatorship under an emperor and his ministers. Member of the Reichstag were elected by **proportional representation**. This meant that the more people who voted for a political party, the more seats in the Reichstag that party had.

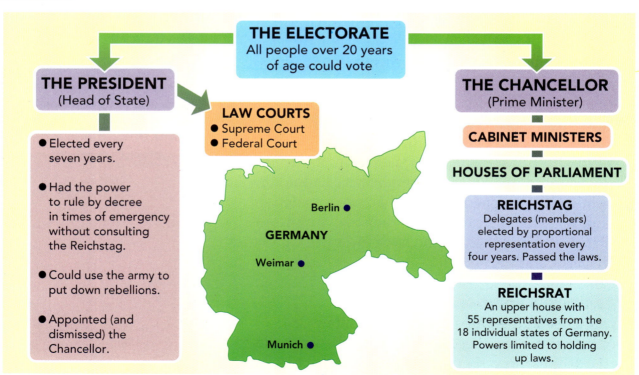

▲ The structure of the Weimar Constitution. It took its name from the small town of Weimar where the government went to escape from the violence in Berlin in early 1919.

80 CHAPTER 4 GERMANY 1919-39

Constitutional problems

There were many problems with the Weimar Constitution:

- The German people thought it was connected with the hated Treaty of Versailles.
- German people were not used to being able to vote for the government they wanted.
- **Proportional representation** meant that German governments were made up of several different parties. In times of crisis, these parties disagreed and governments often fell apart.

Economic problems

By the end of the war in 1918, Germany's economy was in a bad way. But the German government found it difficult to put things right for many reasons:

- The Allies forced Germany to pay for all the losses of the war. These payments were called **reparations**. The Allies said that Germany owed them £6,600,000 million. But they agreed that Germany could pay this in smaller amounts over a period of time.
- In 1923, the German government stopped making reparation payments.
- Then the French government sent troops into the Ruhr, Germany's main industrial region. These troops took over coal and industrial production, and sent the profits to the French government to make up for the missing payments.
- After this, German workers in the Ruhr went on strike. Industrial production there collapsed.
- Because it was short of money, the German government printed more and more of it.
- This made prices rise dramatically. This is called **hyper-inflation.**
- As a result, the value of people's savings fell dramatically. So these people stopped supporting the Weimar Republic.

▼ The rising cost of bread and eggs.

BREAD

1918
0.63 marks

1922
163.15 marks

January **1923**
250 marks

July **1923**
3,456 marks

September **1923**
1,512,000 marks

November **1923**
201,000,000,000 marks

EGGS (1 egg)

1914
0.90 marks

1921
1.60 marks

1922
7 marks

July **1923**
5,000 marks

September **1923**
4,000,000 marks

November **1923**
320,000,000,000 marks

Political problems

Assassinations
- Matthias Erzberger, who signed the Treaty of Versailles on behalf of Germany, was shot and killed in 1921.
- Walther Rathenau, the Weimar Republic's Foreign Minister, was murdered in Berlin by a gang of nationalist youths.

The Social Democrats
At first the Weimar Republic was ruled by moderates: the Social Democrats. They faced threats from groups on the far left and far right of politics. One of the most important challenges from the left came from the Spartacus League. The Kapp Putsch was a challenge from a right wing group.

The Spartacus League
One group of Germans wanted Germany to become a communist state. They called themselves the **Spartacus League**, and were led by **Rosa Luxemburg** and **Karl Liebknecht**. In January 1919, they organized an uprising in Berlin. But the army crushed the rebels and killed the two leaders.

The Kapp Putsch (rising)
On 13 March 1920, Dr Wolfgang Kapp and 5,000 supporters marched on Berlin. They wanted to overthrow the Weimar Republic. But all the workers in Berlin went on strike, because no one wanted to work with Kapp and his followers. So, after four days, Kapp gave up.

Source B
▲ These schoolboys have been allowed to make a kite from German banknotes.

Source C

The main cause of the Kapp Putsch was discontent in the army.
The Versailles Treaty said that the army had to be reduced in size.
A lot of soldiers would lose their jobs.

Most of the army officers were against the Weimar Republic. One of these officers was General von Luttwitz who controlled Berlin. He plotted with Wolfgang Kapp.

▲ Adapted from A. J. Nicholls, *Weimar and the Rise of Hitler*, 1968.

The Munich 'Beer Hall' Putsch

On 8 November 1923, Adolf Hitler's private army, the **Stürm Abteilung** (storm troopers), surrounded a beer hall in Munich. Then Hitler took over the beer hall and told people about his plans for Germany.

The following day, Hitler led about 3,000 supporters in a march to the centre of Munich. They were going to take over the government of Bavaria and then march on Berlin. They were met by armed police. Hitler was arrested, tried and sentenced to five years' imprisonment in Landsberg Castle.

Source D

▲ A painting made in 1933 by a Nazi artist. It shows Hitler in the Munich beer hall in 1923. It is called *In the Beginning was the World*.

Source E

I am not a criminal. There is no such thing as treason against the traitors of 1918. History will judge us as Germans who only wanted to fight and die for the Fatherland.

▲ Hitler speaking to the judges at his trial after the Munich putsch, 1923.

QUESTIONS

1. Read the section headed **Constitutional problems** on Page 81.
   Which constitutional problem do you think was the most serious? Why?

2. Read the section headed **Economic problems** on page 81.
   Which economic problem do you think was the most serious? Why?

3. Read the section headed **Political problems** on page 82.
   a. Was the Weimar Republic put in danger by people on the far left of politics?
   b. Was the Weimar Republic put in danger from people on the far right of politics?

4. Read Source E.
   Why did Hitler believe that he was not a criminal?

SUMMARY

- **June 1919** Germany signed the Treaty of Versailles.
- **January 1919** Spartacist rising in Berlin.
- **January 1919** Elections for Reichstag.
- **March 1920** Kapp putsch.
- **January 1923** German government stopped payment of reparations; French troops invaded the Ruhr.
- **Summer 1923** Hyper-inflation in Germany.
- **November 1923** Munich putsch.

4.3 The Stresemann era 1924-9

There was peace and prosperity in Germany between 1924 and 1929. This was largely due to the hard work of **Gustav Stresemann**.

Source A

▲ Gustav Stresemann, Chancellor of Germany, 1923; Foreign Minister, 1923–9.

The Rentenmark
As soon as Stresemann became Chancellor in 1923, he set about solving one of Germany's most urgent problems: **hyper-inflation**. He brought in a new currency, called the **Rentenmark**, and destroyed all the old bank notes. This worked, and the value of Germany's currency stopped falling.

Reparations
In 1924, Stresemann was made Foreign Minister. He wanted Germany to restart reparation payments. So did the Allies, because they needed the money from Germany to pay their debts to the USA.

The Dawes Plan 1924
Charles Dawes, an American, worked out a plan to help Germany. Under the plan, Germany agreed to give the Allies some of its industrial output each year. In return, France agreed to take French troops out of the Ruhr.

The Young Plan 1929
This plan helped Germany even more. Reparations were cut to 25% of their original amount, and the period over which they were to be paid was extended by 59 years.

But in 1931, the Great Depression forced Germany to stop reparation payments. And in 1933, the new Chancellor, Adolf Hitler, refused to make any more payments to the Allies.

Source B

The policy of making Germany pay is dreadful. It brings misery to thousands of people.

Some preach it in the name of justice. Justice is not so simple.

▲ Adapted from comments made by John Maynard Keynes, a British economist, about reparations.

The Locarno Pact 1925
Under this pact, Britain, France, Germany, Italy and Belgium agreed that the existing borders of Germany, France and Belgium should be kept the same for ever. But there was no pact about Germany's borders with Czechoslovakia, Poland and Austria. Stresemann hoped that Austria and Germany would eventually come together to form one country. So he deliberately kept Germany's eastern borders out of any international agreement.

The League of Nations
The Treaty of Versailles did not allow Germany to join the League of Nations. But Stresemann still thought that Germany should join as soon as possible. In that way, Germany would be seen as equal with the other League powers. Germany finally joined in 1926.

Was Germany breaking the Treaty of Versailles?
All this time, Germany was quietly building up its armed forces. So the German government was already breaking the Treaty of Versailles. The Allied governments knew what Germany was doing. But they were not worried because, throughout the Stresemann era, the German army was never strong enough to threaten international peace.

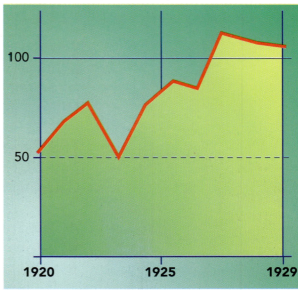

▲ Production of manufactured goods in Germany, 1920–9 (100 = average level of production, 1925–9).

Source C

Germany has made no effort to carry out the peace treaty. This is because she does not believe she has been defeated.

▲ Raymond Poincaré, Prime Minister of France, 1911–13, 1922–4, and 1926–9.

Source D

Because of the peace treaties of 1919, there have been many disagreements between the League and Germany. I hope that, now Germany is a member of the League, we can discuss these disagreements together.

▲ Adapted from Stresemann's speech when Germany joined the League of Nations in 1926.

QUESTIONS

1. Look again at page 81. Now read Source B. Would you agree with what John Maynard Keynes says about reparations? Use the information in this chapter to support what you say.
2. Make a list of the things Stresemann did to help Germany recover from the post war problems of the Weimar Republic.
3. Read Source C. Use the information and the Sources in this section to say if you agree.

4.4 The beginnings of the Nazi Party 1919-29

The Nazi Party began as just one of the many small political parties which sprung up in Germany after 1918. At first, it was called the **German Workers' Party**. Adolf Hitler was in charge of developing the party's ideas.

The Twenty-Five Point Programme

In 1920, Hitler produced a statement of the aims of the German Workers' Party. The most important ones were:

- The Treaty of Versailles should be overthrown.
- Germany should gain more land in Europe.
- Only pure-blooded Germans should be citizens of the new Germany.
- No Jew should be a German.
- There should be very strong state control.

The Nazi Party

The German Workers' Party changed its name to the **National Socialist German Workers' Party** (**Nazis** for short). The Nazi symbol was a black swastika in a white circle on a red background. These were Hitler's ideas.

In 1921, Hitler took over as leader of the Nazi Party.

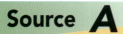

Source A

The new movement is a nationalist party.... filled with blind obedience and inspired by a brutal will.

The new Nazi Party is a party of struggle and actions. Its aims should be pushed with fanatical will and spirit.

▲ From an internal Nazi Party memorandum, 1922.

▶ Hitler at an SA parade in Nuremberg in 1927. Hitler set up the Stürm Abteilung (Storm troopers) in 1921. Brown shirts were part of the SA uniform, and the troopers were often called simply 'Brownshirts'.

How did the Nazis gain support?
Hitler believed that people would vote for the Nazis if they showed that they were a strong and determined party. He was convinced that rallies, parades and marching songs were the way to do this.

The Stürm Abteilung (storm troopers)
Hitler set up his own private army – the **Stürm Abteilung** (SA). He used these storm troopers to break up meetings of his opponents. The troopers frightened people so that they went to Nazi Party meetings, and they kept order at those meetings too.

Mein Kampf (My Struggle)
Hitler was sent to prison after the Munich Putsch (see page 83). Hitler used his time in prison to think. He wrote a book called *Mein Kampf*, in which he set out his ideas about the future of the Nazi Party and the future of Germany. He realized, too, that if the Nazi Party was to gain power in Germany, it had to do so legally. In other words, it had to stand in elections and win more seats than any other party. Once the Nazi Party was in power, then it would change Germany. To start with the Nazis were not very successful at winning seats. Streseman was popular and had brought about economic recovery.

Source C

Instead of an armed rising, we will have to hold our noses and enter the Reichstag against Catholic and Marxist members.

If out voting them takes longer than out shooting them, at least it is by their rules.

Soon we shall have a majority, and after that - Germany!

▲ From a letter written by Hitler while in prison after the failed Munich putsch.

Reorganization
When he was out of prison, Hitler reorganized the Nazi Party.

- He set up branches (called **Gaue**) all over Germany. Each **Gaue** was run by a Nazi official called a **Gauliter**.
- He put Joseph Goebbels in charge of propaganda and made him **Gauliter** of Berlin.
- Propaganda was an important part of Nazi activities. It means the deliberate spreading of ideas and doctrines so as to influence people in your favour.

REICHSTAG ELECTIONS

Date	Nazi seats	Ranking in party size
May 1924	32	6th biggest
Dec 1924	14	8th biggest
1928	12	8th biggest

▲ The Nazi Party's performance in the Reichstag elections, 1924–8.

4.5 How did the Nazis achieve power?

At the beginning of 1929, the Nazis were the eighth largest party in the Reichstag – the German parliament. By the end of 1933, the Nazis were in power and Hitler was Chancellor of Germany. How had this happened?

The Depression
The Wall Street Crash happened in October 1929 (see page 61). It had an enormous effect on Germany:

- The USA loaned German businesses and industry a lot of money. Once the Depression came, the USA wanted its money back.
- Many German businesses collapsed, and thousands more businesses laid people off.
- German people had less money with which to buy goods.
- Factories sold fewer goods and there was no work for thousands of factory workers.
- Farmers could not sell their produce for enough money. So farmers and farm workers were forced out of work.
- Middle-class people lost their savings and their homes.

By 1933, there were six million unemployed people in Germany. Hitler and the Nazi Party offered these people hope.

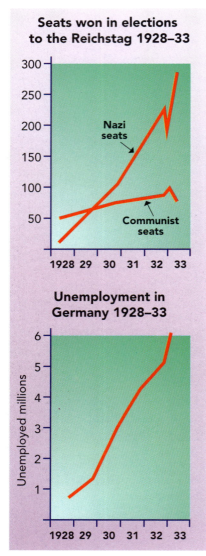

▲ Unemployment and election results in Germany, 1928–33.

Source A

The elections will certainly be the last for the next ten years.

▲ Hermann Goering, a leading Nazi, speaking to a meeting of bankers and businessmen in March 1933.

How did the Nazis gain support?
The Nazis used:
- Posters, books and newspaper articles
- Carefully organized mass rallies
- The effect of Hitler himself. He was a powerful speaker at Nazi rallies
- The SA (storm troopers), who broke up opponents' meetings.
- The efficient organization of the party to win new members
- Fear

Who supported the Nazis?
- Farmers
- Factory workers
- Middle-class families
- Businessmen and industrialists
- People who were afraid of a communist take-over
- People who wanted the Treaty of Versailles overturned.

The 1930 election
The Weimar Republic found it almost impossible to deal with the problems of the Depression. Because of this, the government could not gain the support of enough members of the Reichstag. So President von Hindenburg began ruling without the Reichstag.

To try to improve matters, Hindenburg called elections for September 1930. He hoped for a strong government as a result. What happened was that the Nazis and the Communists both had an enormous increase in their votes. After the election, the three strongest parties in the Reichstag were the Social Democrats, the Nazis and the Communists. But no single party had enough members in the Reichstag to form a government on its own.

Hitler becomes Chancellor
More elections were held in July. This time, the Nazis ended up as the largest party in the Reichstag. The Nazis were not large enough to run Germany on their own, but no other party could form a government either without the support of the Nazis. After months of plotting to keep the Nazis out of office, President Hindenburg finally gave up. In January 1933, he asked Hitler, as leader of the largest party in the Reichstag, to become Chancellor of Germany.

Source B

▲ A 1932 Nazi election poster: 'We want work and bread. Elect Hitler.'

QUESTIONS

1 How did the following groups suffer during the Depression:

　a farmers
　b factory workers
　c industrialists?

Do you think that this was why they supported the Nazi party?

2 Is the poster (Source B) designed to encourage people to vote for Hitler, or to frighten them into doing so?

4.6 How did Hitler become dictator of Germany?

When Hitler became Chancellor of Germany in January 1933, he was one of just three Nazis in the government. By the end of the year, Hitler had complete control of the government of Germany. How had this happened?

The Reichstag Fire

On 27 February 1933, the Reichstag building in Berlin burned down. A young Dutch communist, Marinus van de Lubbe, was caught inside the building. He was carrying matches and firelighters. At his trial later in the year, he confessed to burning down the building. However, the court could not find any connection between him and the German communists who had been rounded up after the fire. They were released and van de Lubbe was executed.

▼ The Reichstag on fire. Many people believed that a fire as big and fierce as this could not have been started by one man.

Source A

Many people, at the time and later, believed that it was actually the Nazis who had planned the fire. No one knows for sure. But what is certain is that the Nazis made good use of the fire:

- All German communist leaders were arrested
- President Hindenburg declared a **state of emergency**.
- Hindenburg gave Hitler special powers to deal with what seemed like a communist threat to Germany.
- The Nazis were able to claim that their enemies the communists were a danger to the peace of Germany.

The March election

In the elections of March 1933, the Nazis did not win as many seats in the Reichstag as they wanted. They needed two-thirds of the members of the Reichstag to be Nazi supporters, so that they would be able to introduce the laws they wanted to run Germany their way.

But Hitler quickly solved the problem. He did a deal with the Centre Party, and he used his emergency powers to stop the Communists taking their seats in the Reichstag. In this way, he had the two-thirds majority he needed.

The Enabling Act 1933

When the new Reichstag met, it passed the **Enabling Act**. This gave the Nazis full control over Germany:

- The German Cabinet could make laws, treaties and changes to the constitution without getting the agreement of the Reichstag.
- Hitler, as Chancellor and leader of the Cabinet, could draw up laws for them to approve.

Only the Social Democrats were brave enough to risk the violence of the SA, and voted against the Act.

Hitler becomes Führer

Hitler was determined to take over from President Hindenburg when the old man died. To do this, Hitler needed the support of the army. But German army leaders were suspicious of the SA, because it acted as if it was Hitler's own private army. In order to gain the trust of the German army, Hitler turned against the SA. On 30 June 1934, he had its leaders killed in the **Night of the Long Knives**. This worked. When President Hindenburg died in August 1934, Hitler took over all his powers. Then he changed his own title to **Führer**, which means 'leader'. The army accepted this, and all German officers took an oath of loyalty to Hitler.

▶ The army's oath of allegiance to Hitler.

Source B

I did not wish to harm private people.
I acted alone.
No one helped me, nor did I meet a single person in the Reichstag.

▲ From a statement made to the police by van der Lubbe on 3 March 1933.

Source C

I hereby declare that I and two SA men set fire to the German Reichstag. We believed we would be serving the Führer and our movement.

▲ From a statement written by Karl Ernst, a member of the SA. It was discovered after his death by Arthur Koestler, a communist.

Source D

I swear before God to give my total obedience to Adolf Hitler, Führer of the Reich and of the German people, and I will observe this oath always, even at the peril of my life.

4.6 HOW DID HITLER BECOME DICTATOR OF GERMANY?

QUESTIONS

1. Read the section headed **The Reichstag Fire** on page 90, and Sources A, B and C.
   Why is it difficult to find out who started the Reichstag fire?

2. Read the section **The Enabling Act 1933**. How did this Act give the Nazis full control over Germany?

3. Read Source D on page 91. What was the importance of this oath?

SUMMARY

▶ **1920** Hitler announced new programme of National Socialist German Workers' Party (formerly the German Workers' Party).

▶ **1921** Hitler became undisputed leader of Nazi party.

▶ **1923** Munich Putsch: Hitler was imprisoned and wrote *Mein Kampf*.

▶ **1928** Nazis had 12 seats in Reichstag.

▶ **1930** Nazis had 107 seats in Reichstag.

▶ **November 1932** Nazis had 196 seats in Reichstag.

▶ **January 1933** Hitler was appointed Chancellor.

▶ **February 1933** Reichstag fire; President Hindenburg ruled by emergency decree.

▶ **March 1933** Nazis had 288 seats in Reichstag; Enabling Act.

▶ **August 1934** Hindenburg died; Hitler became Chancellor and President and called himself Führer of Germany.

4.7 What did Hitler believe in?

Hitler's ideas and beliefs can be worked out from many different sources:

- The two books he wrote: *Mein Kampf* and the *Second Book*
- Thousands of his speeches
- Notes, diaries and letters written by people who met and worked with him

Source A

Germany will follow a policy of expansion.

Germany will concentrate all its forces on providing our nation with sufficient living space.

Such space can only be in the East.

▲ From the *Second Book* by Adolf Hitler, written in 1928 but published after his death.

Nationalism

Hitler believed that Germany was too small to meet the needs of its people. The need for **Lebensraum** (living space) meant that Germany would have to ignore the boundaries set by the Treaty of Versailles. Because of the Locarno Pact (see page 85), Germany would have to expand into Poland and Russia.

Race

Hitler said that the world was divided into different races. He thought the best race was the **Aryan** race, made up of most Germans and some other north Europeans. He thought the worst race was the Jewish race. Hitler blamed them for most of Germany's problems. He said the German people should be 'purified' until all Germans were Aryans.

Struggle

Hitler believed that all life was a struggle. In this struggle, only the toughest would survive and prosper. So Germany had to be tough and ready to fight. Hitler believed that the Aryan people would put right the wrongs of the past and could look forward to a bright future. According to Hitler, Aryan people had the right to take anything they could get.

Leadership

Hitler did not believe in democracy. Because he was Führer of Germany, Hitler believed that the Nazis had to obey him without question. He thought that decisions reached by discussion and compromise were bound to be wrong.

Individual rights and freedom

Hitler believed that individual people did not have any rights. The German state had rights, and so did the German people as a whole, but that was all. This meant that, according to Hitler, it was quite all right for Nazis to imprison individual people without trial, beat them up to stop them voting, and even kill them if they opposed his views.

Source B

▲ 'Purifying' the German people, until all Germans were Aryans, meant that girls were expected to become mothers of at least four babies (see also page 99).

Source C

All art, science and technology have been made by the Aryan.

The Jew makes art, literature and the theatre dirty.

He destroys national feeling.

He overthrows all ideas of beauty.

▲ Adapted from *Mein Kampf* by Adolf Hitler, written in 1924.

4.8 How did Hitler and the Nazi Party control Germany?

Germany becomes a totalitarian state

Hitler and the Nazis turned Germany into a **totalitarian state**. This means that the Nazis used their power to control what people did and even what they thought. They controlled newspapers and the radio, and used **propaganda** (see page 87) to persuade people that their way was the right way. Secret police spied on ordinary people to make sure that no one was disagreeing with the government.

Hitler's powers

The Enabling Act (see page 91) gave Hitler all the powers he needed. He could rule without the Reichstag, and he used this power to ban all the opposition parties. Then he combined the jobs of President and Chancellor and made himself Führer (leader) of all Germany. Finally, he made the army swear an oath of loyalty to him, not to the German state.

The SA and the Night of the Long Knives

Hitler's treatment of the SA shows just how ruthless he could be. The SA had been a great help to Hitler in his rise to power. But then, once he was in power, he set about destroying them. This was partly because he did not want the Nazis to be associated with criminal thugs like the SA, and partly because he needed the support of the army (see page 91).

On the night of 30 June 1934, Hitler's Nazis arrested **Ernst Rohm**, the leader of the SA, along with other important SA members. They were executed on direct orders from Hitler.

The SA itself was not abolished, but it was never a powerful force again.

Source A

I have been leader of the SS for eleven years.
During this time I have had one aim: to make the SS into an Order of Pure Blood for the service of Germany.

▲ Adapted from Heinrich Himmler, speaking in 1940.

▼ Ernst Röhm, head of the SA, pictured with Hitler three weeks before he was arrested and shot by SS Troops acting on Hitler's orders.

Source B

94 CHAPTER 4 GERMANY 1919–39

The SS (protection squad)

The **Schutzstaffel** (SS) was set up in 1925. It was a special, highly disciplined force whose members were totally loyal to Hitler. Hitler used the SS to arrest and execute SA members in the Night of the Long Knives.

From the early days, SS members wore black shirts, and this meant that they were not confused with the SA, whose members wore brown shirts.

From 1929, the SS was controlled by Heinrich Himmler, who used it to enforce Hitler's policies against the Jews. Some members of the SS controlled the concentration camps, while other SS members worked as tip top units within the regular army.

The Gestapo (secret state police)

The **Geheime Staatspolizei** (Gestapo for short) was set up in 1933 by Hermann Goering. The Nazis used the Gestapo to spy on ordinary people. In 1936, it came under the control of the SS. The Gestapo was led by **Reynhard Heydrich**, one of the most ruthless Nazi leaders.

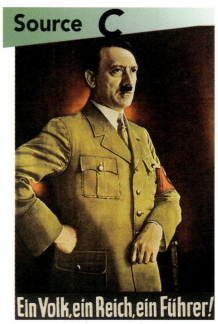

▲ A Nazi Party poster from 1938. The slogan says, 'One People, one Empire, one Leader'.

Concentration camps

In 1932, the Nazis set up the first two concentration camps, at Dachau and Oranienburg. The Nazis used these camps to imprison their opponents. People were very afraid of being informed on by the SS or the Gestapo, and being sent to a concentration camp. This was enough to keep silent those who opposed the Nazis, but who were afraid to speak out.

▶ A Nazi rally in 1935.

Propaganda and censorship

Propaganda and censorship were vital if the Nazi state was going to be successful. Propaganda made people accept Nazi ideas. Censorship stopped them knowing anything different. Joseph Goebbels was the head of the **Ministry of People's Enlightenment and Propaganda**. He used propaganda to persuade people that Hitler and the Nazis were right.

Posters and rallies

Posters were a very early form of Nazi propaganda. They always showed Hitler as a wise and thoughtful leader. Poster campaigns were often linked to rallies. These rallies were huge, stage-managed affairs. They aimed to show Germans just how popular Hitler was, and just how powerful the Nazi state could be.

Radio

More Germans had radios than any other people in Europe. Goebbels made good use of this. The Nazis controlled all radio programmes, and only programmes that supported the Nazis could be broadcast. Hitler's speeches were also broadcast.

Books

The Nazis banned over 2,500 writers – they did not allow German bookshops to sell the books that these people had written. Their books were burned on huge bonfires in the streets.

QUESTIONS

1 Look at Source B on page 94 and Source D on page 95. What can you learn about the Nazi state just by looking at them?

2 Look at Source C on page 95. What were people meant to think about Hitler?

3 'Hitler controlled Germany by terror.'
'Hitler controlled Germany by persuasion.'

Use the information and sources in this section to explain which view you agree with, and why.

4.9 How did the Nazi Party use the German economy?

Source A

▲ Celebrations to welcome the opening of a new autobahn, May 1935.

Hitler's main aim was to make Germany and Germans great again. He wanted to do this by turning Germany into a strong military power. He had first to overthrow the Treaty of Versailles. Then, to make Germany a strong military power, Hitler believed that the Nazis had to control what industry produced and how people were employed.

Hjalmar Schacht

Hitler appointed Hjalmar Schacht to plan the economy. Schacht signed trade treaties with underdeveloped countries. They sent raw materials to Germany and bought manufactured goods in exchange. Gradually the German economy recovered. But this was far too slow for Hitler.

Hitler's Four-Year Plan

In 1936 Hitler replaced Schacht's scheme with his own Four-Year plan. Hitler's Four-Year Plan was directed by **Hermann Goering**. Together, Hitler and Goering made **rearmament** their main aim. This meant that German industry was geared up to produce tanks, guns and planes. This, in turn, meant that the German iron and steel industries had to increase their output enormously.

Autarky

Hitler introduced the idea of **autarky**. By this, he meant that he wanted Germany to produce all its own raw materials. Germany was to become self-sufficient. In this way, it would not be dependent upon any other country.

The Reicharbeitsdienst (National Labour Service)

In 1933, there were 6 million people unemployed in Germany. By 1939, there were only 300,000 people out of work. How had Hitler done this?

He set up the National Labour Service, which told people where they had to work. At the same time, he made government money available for public works programmes. These involved building autobahns (motorways), hospitals and schools. Thousands of young men were sent into the armed forces, too.

The German Labour Front (DAF)

When the Nazis came to power, they banned all trade unions. Instead, the Nazi German Labour Front controlled workers everywhere. It set their rates of pay and the hours they could work.

Source B

If we do not succeed in making the German army the best in the world, then Germany will be lost!

I set the following tasks: the German armed forces must be operational within four years; and the German economy must be fit for war within four years.

▲ From Hitler's notes on the Four-Year Plan, 1936.

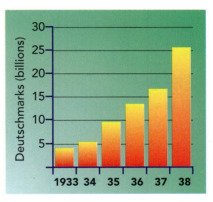

▲ Total military expenditure of the German government, 1933–8.

▼ German unemployment, 1933–9.

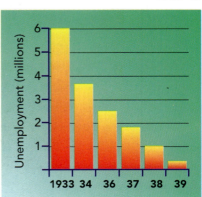

4.9 HOW DID THE NAZI PARTY USE THE GERMAN ECONOMY?

The 'Beauty of Labour' and the 'Strength through Joy' movements

The German Labour Front set up two organizations. **Beauty of Labour** aimed to improve people's working conditions by, for example, providing hot meals at midday in factories. **Strength through Joy** provided activities, such as film shows and coach trips, for workers to do in their spare time.

QUESTIONS

1. Look at Source A on page 96. What is there that looks military? Why would the Nazis want to make the opening of an autobahn look like a military occasion?
2. What is the connection between Source B and the two diagrams on page 97? Use the information in this section in your answer.

4.10 What was everyday life like for young people?

Hitler believed that it was very important to teach Nazi ideas to children and young people. In this way, they would grow up to be good Nazis and would not question the Nazi regime.

Schools

All teachers had to belong to the Nazi Teachers' Association and had to teach Nazi ideas in their lessons. There were lessons about race, in which pupils were taught that the Aryan race was the best. They were also told that Hitler was a great leader, who must never be questioned.

History books were rewritten to make the Jews look dreadful, and to show how unfair the Treaty of Versailles was. In biology lessons, pupils were taught about race and heredity, and were encouraged to measure each other's skulls to see how Aryan they were.

Source A

Periods	Monday	Tuesday	Wednesday	Thursday	Friday	Saturday
8:00 – 8:45	German	German	German	German	German	German
8:50 – 9:35	Geography	History	Singing	Geography	History	Singing
9:40 – 10:25	Race study	Race study	Race study	Ideology	Ideology	Ideology
10:25 – 11:00	Recess, with sports and special announcements					
11:00 – 12:05	Domestic science with mathematics, every day					
12:10 – 12:55	Eugenics – Health Biology, alternating					

▲ A girls' school timetable.

Youth movements

In their spare time, children and young people were expected to join youth movements.

Boys
- **Pimpf** (Little Fellows) was for boys when they were 6 years old. They went hiking and camping, and had lessons based on Hitler's ideas.
- **Deutsche Jungvolk** (German Young People) was for boys aged between 10 and 14. They took an oath of loyalty to Hitler and learned about military discipline.
- **Hitler Jugend** (Hitler Youth) was for boys over 14 years old. They learned how to use guns and read maps; they also went on camps and long marches.

Girls
- **Jungmädel** (Young Maidens) was for girls up to the age of 14. They learned how to keep themselves healthy and look after babies.
- **Bund Deutscher Mädel** (League of German Maidens) was for older girls. They learned how to become good wives and mothers.
- When they married, girls were expected to have at least four Aryan babies.

Source B

▲ A crowd of Jungmädel wait outside the Reich Chancellery in Berlin for Hitler to arrive, May 1939.

Source C

All subjects must concentrate on military matters and the glorification of military service and of German heroes and leaders.

Chemistry will teach a knowledge of chemical warfare, and mathematics will explain artillery, ballistics etc.

▲ From a Nazi publication about education for boys, October 1939.

Source D

▲ Young men of the Hitler Youth parading with spades held as rifles.

QUESTIONS

1. Look at Source A. Which subjects would you be surprised to find on your own timetable? Why did they appear on a timetable of lessons in a school in Nazi Germany?
2. Now read Source C and compare it with Source A. How did the education of girls differ from that of boys?
3. Why were the Hitler Youth movements important?

4.11 The persecution of the Jews

From its earliest days, the Nazi Party blamed the Jews for everything that was not right with Germany. Once Hitler became Führer, he put Nazi words into action.

Source A

▲ Even children's books showed the Jews in a bad light. This illustration is from a book published in 1938.

Source B

▲ A burnt-out synagogue in Munich after Krystallnacht.

Shops and jobs: 1933
On 1 April 1933, SA troops stood outside shops owned by Jews and told people not to shop in them. Only the very bravest dared go in and buy goods.

Six days later, the Reichstag passed a law which said that no Jew could have a government job. This meant that all Jews who worked in the civil service had to give up their jobs. Only those Jews who had fought in the First World War could stay on.

The Nuremberg Laws 1935
These were a series of laws which made life very difficult for the Jews. After the laws were passed, Jews could not go to restaurants, public parks, swimming pools, cinemas or theatres. They were not allowed to be citizens of Germany, and could not marry people who were. Jews could not vote in elections either.

Krystallnacht 1938
In November 1938, a German official in Paris was shot dead by a Jew. Immediately, the Nazis organized a massive attack on Jewish shops, offices, homes and synagogues in Germany. During the night of 9 November, about 100 Jews died in SA attacks. Thousands of Jewish properties were destroyed or damaged. That night was called **Krystallnacht** (Crystal Night) because of all the glass that was broken. Over 30,000 Jews were arrested and sent to concentration camps. Most were released, but only when they promised to leave Germany.

The Jews leave

Between 1933 and 1939, roughly half of all the Jews in Germany fled abroad. Most went to Palestine, but some went to Britain and the USA. One and a quarter million stayed to suffer and die under the Third Reich.

4.12 Exercise

1 Read sections 4.2 and 4.5.
Now draw a chart with these headings:

Failure of the Weimar Republic	
Long-term reasons	Short-term reasons

List the reasons why the Weimar Republic failed under these headings.

  b Write a paragraph explaining why the Weimar Republic failed.

2 Look at Source C on page 87 and read section 4.6 again. Did the Nazis come to power legally or did they seize power? Give reasons for your choice.

3 Read the following two accounts of Nazi Germany:

The only aim of the Nazi state is to prepare the German people for war. The Nazis do this by wiping out any opposition to the idea of a war, and by making the German people completely obedient to the Nazi state. If the idea of war was taken away, the Nazi state would mean nothing at all.

Adapted from Thomas Mann, one of Germany's most distinguished authors, writing to the Dean of Bonn University.

I have just returned from Germany. I have now seen the famous German leader [Hitler] and also something of the great change he has made. Whatever one may think of the way in which he does things, he has changed the German people. They are working together for their own good and to make Germany a prosperous country. Hitler is making sure the German people will never again starve as they did during the last war.

Adapted from David Lloyd George, who was the British Prime Minister during the First World War. He was writing in a British newspaper in 1936 after a visit to Germany.

Work back through this chapter and find the evidence which supports what David Lloyd George wrote and what Thomas Mann wrote.

Why did the authors come to such different conclusions?

CHAPTER 5

RUSSIA 1905–39

Russia in 1905 was a huge country with forests, rivers and mountains; coal, iron ore and oil. There was hardly any industry. Travel was difficult. Many people were very poor, although a few were very rich indeed.

Russia was ruled by a Tsar, who was almost a God to his people. But Russia was so vast that it was a difficult country to govern. Landowners often made their own laws, which peasants had to obey.

By 1939, Russia had completely changed. The Tsar had gone. The communists were in power and the USSR (as the old Russia was now called) was economically and politically strong. The history of Russia from 1905 is the dramatic and often terrible story of how this was done.

5.1 What was Russia like in 1905?

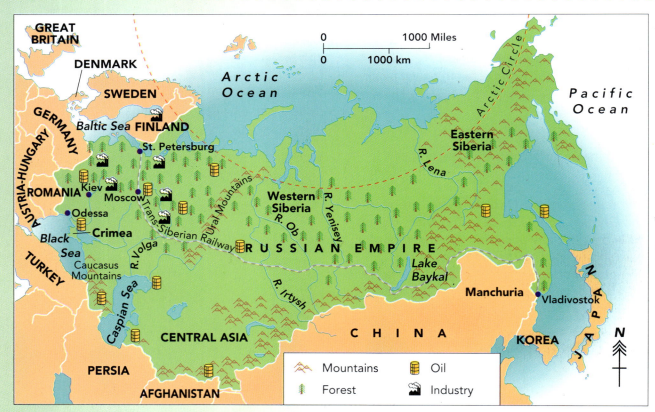

▲ The resources, rivers and main towns of Russia in 1905.

Farming and factories

Most of Russia's wealth came from farming. But farmers used out-of-date methods, so the land did not produce as much as it should have. Terrible winters ruined crops, and farmers often could not get their goods to market because the roads were bad. People in the countryside often starved.

But then people from abroad began investing in Russian industry. Railways and factories were built and businesses set up. Men and women drifted from the countryside to the towns. There they worked long hours and lived in terrible conditions.

The government

Russia was ruled by emperors called **Tsars**. The Tsar had complete control of his government. He did not have to take advice from anyone.

Newspapers were censored. They could only print what the government wanted them to say. The Tsar's secret police, the **Okhrana**, had agents in every town and village. They reported back on anyone who criticized the government.

The people

In 1905, there were over 125 million people living in Russia. They belonged to many different nationalities and spoke many different languages. Almost 80% were peasants, while 10% worked in factories, mills and mines. The Tsar and nobility (about 1%) owned almost all the land.

Source A

▲ In 1894 Nicholas II became Tsar. His wife, Alexandra, became the Tsarina. Alexandra was the granddaughter of the British Queen Victoria. This official photograph of Nicholas and Alexandra was taken in 1890.

Nationality	Population
Russians	55,650,000
Ukrainians	22,400,000
Poles	7,900,000
Byelorussians	5,900,000
Jews	5,000,000
Kirghiz	4,000,000
Tartars	3,700,000
Finns	2,500,000
Germans	1,800,000
Lithuanians	1,650,000
Letts	1,400,000
Georgians	1,350,000
Armenians	1,150,000
Romanians	1,110,000
Caucasians	1,000,000
Estonians	1,000,000
Iranians	1,000,000
Other Asiatic peoples	5,750,000
Mongols	500,000
Others	200,000

▶ The first Russian census was taken in 1897. This shows the numbers of people of different nationalities living in Russia at that time.

QUESTIONS

1. Read the section headed '**Farming and factories**' on this page.
    a. Why was farming backward in Russia?
    b. Why was industry slow to develop?
2. Read these two pages and look at the map. Why was Russia a difficult country to govern?

5.2 Who opposed the Tsar's government?

Many Russian people were unhappy with the way in which their country was run. They talked and plotted in secret about how they could change things. The problem was that the different groups all had different ideas about what should be done.

Liberals
The Liberals were the largest group. They wanted the government of the Tsar to go. In its place they wanted an elected parliament (a **Duma**). They also wanted a written constitution, which all people would have to follow.

Social Revolutionaries
Many teachers and university students became Social Revolutionaries. These people believed that revolution would start with the peasants, who would rise up and take possession of the land on which they worked. The problem was that many peasants were very loyal to the Tsar, and were suspicious of people trying to make them rebel.

In 1874 hundreds of students left their universities and colleges. They went out into the countryside to work amongst the peasants and try to get them to revolt. They were called **Narodniks**. The peasants didn't revolt. A small group of Narodniks called '**The People's Will**' assassinated the Tsar in 1881. The secret police hunted them down and the government put the universities under state control and made all student organizations illegal.

> **Source A**
>
> I am sure that the only way to change this society is by force.
> If anyone could show me a peaceful way, I would follow it.
> But we don't have a free press in this country, and so it is hard to spread ideas. Violence is the only solution.
> I could not follow the peaceful path.

▲ Vera Figner, a medical student, explains why she joined 'The People's Will'. This was a small group of revolutionaries which blew up Tsar Alexander II in 1881.

▼ This is a painting of a religious procession in Kursk (1882). It was painted by Ilya Repin. Find the priest in this painting. Many priests informed on people with 'dangerous' ideas. Some artists tried to present social problems in their paintings.

Source B

Marxists

Many Russians joined the **Social Democratic Party**. They followed the teachings of **Karl Marx**.

- Marx said that in industrialized countries like Britain and the USA the *owners* of mills and mines, factories and workshops had the power. Yet it was the *workers* (the **proletariat**) who actually produced the wealth. For this reason Marx believed that the first revolutions would take place in industrialized countries.
- The workers would rise up and take over the government. All land and all business would be owned by the state. All the wealth in the country would be owned by all the people.
- This form of government is known as **communism**. Communists should work for the good of the people, not just themselves.

Bolsheviks

In 1903, the Social Democratic Party split in two. The **Bolsheviks** were led by **Vladimir Lenin**. They wanted the party to take over power for the peasants and industrial workers. The **Mensheviks**, on the other hand, wanted the middle classes to get power first, and then to help the peasants and industrial workers to take over.

But in 1903 these were just theories. The next twenty years were to test these theories to the full.

Source C

▲ This poster, produced in 1901, shows how Marxists viewed Russian society: the workers – 'we have no freedom'; the capitalists – 'we do the eating'; the army – 'we do the shooting'; the clergy – 'we fool you'; the royal family – 'we rule you'; the Tsar.

Source D

The Workers have nothing to lose but their chains. They have a world to gain. Workers of the world, unite.

▲ Karl Marx, *Manifesto of the Communist Party*, 1848.

QUESTIONS

1. Make a list of all the different groups of people who were against the Tsar. Which group do you think was the most dangerous?
2. Read the section headed **Marxists**. Now explain what Karl Marx meant in Source D.

5.3 The Revolution of 1905

Source A

The Tsar does not have any will power. Though he means well and is quite clever this weakness makes it impossible for him to be emperor of Russia. He alone is to be blamed for the war against Japan.

▲ Adapted from *The Memoirs of Count Witte*, 1912. Witte was a Russian statesman and negotiated peace after the Russo-Japanese War. He was made Prime Minister in October 1905.

Between 1900 and 1904, Russia had a series of bad harvests. Prices went up. This meant that people could not afford to buy the goods produced by Russian industry, so production fell. As a result of all this, peasants rioted and industrial workers went on strike. University students assassinated two government ministers. But these events were not enough to start a revolution. What, then, did?

The Russo-Japanese War 1904–5

In **China** the old empire was collapsing. Both Russia and Japan wanted to move in on two countries in the empire, Korea and Manchuria, because these countries were rich in minerals. In 1904, Japan made a surprise attack on the Russians at **Port Arthur**, and then went on to sink the entire Russian Black Sea fleet. Eventually the war between Russia and Japan was ended by the **Treaty of Portsmouth**. Under the treaty, Japan kept Port Arthur and was allowed more influence in Korea.

Defeat was a tremendous blow to the Russian government. And when the Russian soldiers went home, they told people that there had been a lack of food and guns, and that their commanders did not know what they were doing. More and more angry people began to demand change.

Father Gapon

Father Gapon was a Christian priest who ran a large trade union in St Petersburg. Trade unions were illegal in Russia. But sometimes the **Okhrana** (secret police) allowed a union to be set up and then put in one of their agents to run it. In this way the Okhrana could keep track of any people who were talking about revolution. Father Gapon started off as an Okhrana agent. But gradually he became more concerned about the needs of the workers than about his job as a secret agent.

Source B

▲ Father Gapon, who led the workers' march to the Winter Palace in St Petersburg.

'Bloody Sunday' – 22 January 1905

On 20 December 1904, the biggest industrial works in St Petersburg, **Putilov**, sacked four workers. So Father Gapon called his union out on strike. Factories and workshops all over St Petersburg shut down. By the beginning of January 1905, there were 120,000 workers on strike.

Father Gapon organized a petition asking for better working and living conditions which he wanted to give to Tsar Nicholas. On Sunday 22 January 1905, Father Gapon led 150,000 men, women and children to the Winter Palace in St Petersburg. They were unarmed. Suddenly, the Tsar's troops around the Winter Palace began firing into the crowd. The official figures said that 96 people were killed and 333 injured. But journalists said that this was a cover-up. They put together a list of 4,600 people whom they said had been killed or injured.

Revolution!

1905 was a year of murder and massacre, strikes, riots and risings throughout Russia. There were mutinies in the army and in the navy. In June, the crew of the Russian battleship *Potemkin*, which was moored in Odessa harbour, mutinied and joined striking workers. The trade unions joined together and made up a central committee called the **St Petersburg Soviet**. The situation looked very dangerous. The Tsar was nearly toppled from power as troops struggled to restore law and order.

Source D

I noticed that mounted troops stood drawn up in front of the Winter Palace. All the workers were peaceful and expectant. They wanted the Tsar or one of his ministers to come before the people and take the petition. At first I saw the children who were hit and dragged down from the trees. Then the Cossacks [cavalry] rode right into the crowd and slashed with their sabres like madmen.

▲ An eyewitness, Alexandra Kollontai, remembers what she saw on 'Bloody Sunday'.

Source E

The present ruler has lost absolutely the love of the Russian people. Whatever the future may have in store for the dynasty, the present Tsar will never again be safe in the midst of his people.

▲ Comment made by the US Consul in Odessa, Russia, in 1905.

Source C

◄ 'Execution of the workers in front of the Winter Palace', January 1905, by N. Vladimirov.

Source F

Peasants burned the estates of the landowners, destroying everything they could get their hands on – valuable books, pictures, china and antique furniture.

They did not steal anything, but burned magnificent houses, cattle sheds, barns and granaries. Many landowners fled.

▲ Mary Stolypin-Brock, *Memoirs*, 1953. In 1905 her father was Governor of Saratov Province, and she saw the violence about which she later wrote.

▼ Leon Davidovich Bronstein (1879–1940). He was called *Leon Trotsky*, and was one of the leaders of the St Petersburg Soviet. In 1905, he was sent into exile in Siberia. He managed to escape. He returned in 1917 and became the Bolshevik chairman of the Petrograd Soviet (see page 117).

Source G

The October Manifesto

Tsar Nicholas decided that the only way for him to survive was to give the Liberals (see page 104) what they wanted. In that way, they might just support his regime and defeat the peasants and workers who were trying to destroy it.

The October Manifesto of 1905 gave the Russian people freedom of speech, and the right to form political parties. It said that the Tsar would set up a parliament (a **Duma**), and that all adult males would have the right to vote. But the Duma would not be able to suggest laws itself. It would only be able to say yes or no to laws put forward by the Tsar.

What did the Liberals do?

The October Manifesto split the Liberals. Some Liberals accepted it, saying it was the best they could get at the time. They were called the **Octobrists**. But many other Liberals were deeply suspicious. They realized that the exact powers of the Duma had not been made clear. They simply did not trust Tsar Nicholas.

How did Nicholas get control again?

The workers and peasants were not satisfied. Riots and strikes continued in the cities and the countryside. When winter began, the government acted. It ordered troops to break up the St Petersburg Soviet and the Moscow Soviet. The leaders of the Soviets (one of whom was **Leon Trotsky**) were sent into exile in Siberia. Eventually, by force, Tsar Nicholas's government was back in control.

The first Duma
Tsar Nicholas and his ministers were determined that the Duma should have as little power as possible. In March 1906, people voted to choose the members of the first Duma. Then Nicholas told the members just what they could and could not do. They could reject laws put up by the Tsar. But the Tsar could dismiss the Duma whenever he wanted, and call for fresh elections. The Tsar, too, chose all government ministers, and could rule without the Duma if he wanted to.

The Dumas
The Liberals had always wanted a Duma. They believed that peaceful change could only come about through a Duma.

- Between 1905 and 1917 there were four Dumas.
- In the first two Dumas, peasant farmers made up the largest single group. The Dumas were always asking for reforms. Because of this, Tsar Nicholas dismissed them.
- In 1907, Nicholas changed the rules. From then on, only landowners and town-dwellers could vote.
- The Dumas after 1907 lasted longer and usually agreed with the Tsar.

Source H

▲ A Russian cartoon, drawn in 1905. The giant spectre of a revolutionary tramples over citizens in the streets.

QUESTIONS

1. Read pages 106–7.
   How did the Russo-Japanese war and 'Bloody Sunday' help to bring about the Revolution of 1905?
2. Look carefully at Source H.
   What point do you think the cartoonist was trying to make?
3. Make a list of the groups who were opposed to the Tsar in 1905. Now write beside each what it was they wanted.
   Explain whether the groups who revolted against the Tsar's government achieved what they wanted.

SUMMARY

▶ In 1905 Russia was economically and industrially backward.
▶ In 1905 Russia was ruled by an autocratic Tsar. Most people were poor peasants.
▶ Russia had a large army and secret police force.
▶ Main opposition groups were Liberals, Social Revolutionaries and Marxists.
▶ 1904–5 Russo-Japanese War.
▶ Jan 1905 'Bloody Sunday'.
▶ October Manifesto.
▶ 1906 First Duma met.

5.4 Two important men: Peter Stolypin and Grigori Rasputin

Peter Stolypin
In 1906, Tsar Nicholas made **Peter Stolypin** his Prime Minister. Stolypin had a difficult job because he had to please the people who wanted change as well as those who wanted things to stay just the way they were.

Terrorists
During his first year as Prime Minister, Stolypin had thousands of terrorists tried and executed. Many people hated him. Once, Social Revolutionaries bombed his house. Stolypin was not hurt, but his two children were hurt and 27 adults were injured.

Kulaks
Stolypin wanted to get rid of the fear of revolution. He believed that it was important to keep the peasants loyal to the Tsar. In order to do this, he tried to make them more prosperous. Stolypin thought that well-off peasants (who were called **Kulaks**) would not revolt against the government that had made them wealthy. He therefore scrapped the laws that kept them tied to their villages, and Tsar Nicholas released land for sale. Stolypin and the Tsar hoped that this would help more and more peasants to leave their villages, buy land and set up on their own.

Source A
I must carry out reform.
At the same time I must stop revolution.

▲ Peter Stolypin, 1906.

By 1917, only 10% of all peasant families were making a profit by selling their own produce from their own farms. The rest stayed on the large **communal** farms. These were farms which were worked by all the peasants in a village.

Murder!
In 1911, Stolypin was murdered while he was at the Royal Opera House. The secret police knew about the plot to murder him, but they did nothing to stop it happening.

▼ A group of prosperous peasants and merchants, photographed in 1905.

Source B

Grigori Rasputin

The respect that people had for Tsar Nicholas was weakened by scandals at court. Most of these scandals were connected with **Grigori Rasputin**, a holy man from Siberia.

Alexis and haemophilia

In 1904, the Tsar's wife Alexandra, who was called the **Tsarina**, gave birth to a son, Alexis. The Tsar and Tsarina already had four daughters, but the birth of a son meant that the boy would become Tsar when Nicholas died. However, Alexis had haemophilia, a rare blood disease which meant that his blood would not clot. If he cut himself, he could bleed to death. If he bumped himself he could bleed inside his body for weeks. There was no cure.

Alexis and Rasputin

Rasputin said that he could cure Alexis' haemophilia. So the Tsarina invited him to the Russian court, where Rasputin was at least able to keep Alexis calm. Then the Tsarina came more and more under Rasputin's influence. She and the Tsar began asking him for advice as to how to govern Russia.

Scandals

Rasputin said he believed that a person could only be truly sorry for their sins if those sins were dreadful ones. So he started drinking heavily and going with as many women as he could. His drunken orgies became the talk of St Petersburg. Some people really did believe that Rasputin was a holy man; others were afraid of his power and wanted to keep in with him.

Government

Stolypin was murdered in 1911. The Tsar then sacked all his chief advisers. He took advice on how to govern Russia only from his wife, the Tsarina, and Grigori Rasputin.

Source C

▲ This Russian cartoon shows Grigori Rasputin, the Tsar and the Tsarina.

QUESTIONS

1 Stolypin tried to strengthen the rule of Tsar Nicholas. How did he do this?

2 How did Rasputin affect the popularity of the Tsar and his family?

3 Look at Source C. What point is the cartoonist making?

5.5 What was the impact of the First World War on Russia?

Source A

▲ A painting of a bread shop in Moscow in 1917. The sign in the window says 'No bread will be distributed today'.

Source B

Rising prices and food shortages were worse for townspeople than for people living in villages.

In strike after strike people began shouting 'Down with the Tsar' for the first time.

The First World War 1914–18

In the First World War, Russia fought on the side of the Allies (see page 14). After a successful beginning, things went badly wrong.

- The Russian army was heavily defeated at the battles of **Tannenberg** and the **Masurian Lakes** in 1914.
- In 1915, the Russians were driven out of Poland.
- The Russian government could not keep its army supplied with food and equipment.
- By 1916, thousands of Russian soldiers were deserting.

Agriculture

- Millions of Russian peasants were fighting in the army. This meant they could not work the land back home.
- The number of work horses on the land fell by nearly a third during the war because they were needed by the army.
- There were several bad harvests.
- The collection and distribution of food was badly organized. As a result there were terrible food shortages.

Industry

Industry was not as badly hit as agriculture. Even so, factories found it difficult to get raw materials, and many factory workers were away fighting. Fuel was in short supply, too, which meant that goods often could not be moved to the right place at the right time.

Prices

Between 1914 and 1916, most workers' pay doubled. But the price of basic food went up by between 300% and 500%. Millions of people were close to starvation.

◀ Adapted from L. Kochan, *The Making of Modern Russia*, 1962.

Nicholas takes command of the army

In August 1915, Rasputin advised Tsar Nicholas to take over command of the Russian army. This proved to be a disaster. Nicholas was not a good leader and was not good at military tactics. Worse, as Commander-in-Chief of the army, he could be blamed for everything that went wrong.

Alexandra and Rasputin

With the Tsar away at the Front, Tsarina Alexandra was really the ruler of Russia. She sacked ministers and put Rasputin's friends in their place. Rasputin's advice was the only advice she would listen to. And it was not always good advice.

The death of Rasputin

The Duma, members of the royal family and important people at court begged Alexandra to get rid of Rasputin. But she refused. Finally, a group of noblemen murdered him. However, even after Rasputin's death, Alexandra was influenced by his friends.

Source C

I must give you over a message from Our Friend. He begs you to order an advance near Riga, otherwise the Germans will settle down for the winter.
He says we can and we must.

▲ Part of a letter from Tsarina Alexandra to Tsar Nicholas when he was at the Front. It was written on 28 November 1915. 'Our Friend' was Rasputin.

QUESTIONS

1. Read page 112. How did the First World War affect:
   a Russian agriculture
   b Russian industry?
2. What was the importance of Rasputin?

Source D

▲ This picture of Nicholas blessing his troops was painted in 1917 from a photograph taken in 1915.

5.6 Why was there a Revolution in March 1917?

Revolutions do not happen for just one reason. Sometimes it is easier if you divide the causes of a revolution into long-term causes, short-term causes and the 'triggers' that set the whole thing off.

Long-term causes of revolution in Russia:
- Poor living and working conditions of the people.
- Failure of the Tsarist government to bring about major reforms.

Short-term cause of revolution:
- The effect of the First World War on Russia.

'Triggers':
- The events in St Petersburg in the winter and spring of 1916-17.

The winter of 1916–17
The winter and spring of 1916–17 were the coldest that Russia had known for many years. In the countryside, the ground was frozen solid for weeks. Animals died from cold and starvation. People were hungry, too. Fuel froze. If there was spare food, goods trains could not move it into the towns.

Riots and strikes in Petrograd
During the war, St Petersburg was renamed Petrograd. It was here that the troubles began that were to lead to revolution.

The railways could not get food and fuel into Petrograd. The government kept 340,000 soldiers in Petrograd to guard the Tsarina in case of trouble. But the riots and strikes that had rumbled on since the start of the war got worse.

By 9 March 1917, there were 200,000 people out on strike. There were protest marches, and the protestors chanted slogans like 'Land and Freedom' and 'Down with the Tsar'. On 11 March, troops fired on the protestors. But on the following day, the soldiers joined the protesters, and Petrograd was in the hands of the revolutionaries.

The Provisional Government and the Soviet
Tsar Nicholas ordered that the Duma was to be shut down. But twelve members of the Duma decided to set themselves up as a government. They called themselves the Provisional Government. Meanwhile, the workers were organizing themselves into a Soviet based on the 1905 St Petersburg Soviet (see page 107).

Source A
This is a hooligan movement. Young people run and shout that there is no bread simply to create excitement, along with workers who prevent others from working.

▲ Written by the Tsarina Alexandra in March 1917.

Source B
The workers here are on the verge of despair. It is thought that the slightest explosion will result in uncontrollable riots. The impossibility of finding food and the loss of time through queuing for hours outside shops have become unbearable.

▲ From a secret police report in 1917.

Abdication

Tsar Nicholas hurried back from the Front. But he was told that his army was no longer loyal to him, and **abdicated** immediately.

The Provisional Government took over. Five hundred years of Tsarist rule suddenly came to an end.

> ## QUESTIONS
>
> 1. Sources A and B on page 114 are concerned with the riots and strikes in Petrograd in 1917.
>   a. Why are they so different?
>   b. In what ways would each source be useful to a historian?
> 2. There were many reasons for the Tsar's abdication in 1917.
>   a. List all the reasons you can think of.
>   b. Is any one reason more important than any of the others?
> 3. Was there, in your view, anything the Tsar could have done to keep his throne?

5.7 How did the Bolsheviks gain power?

Source A

▲ It was common, after about April 1917, for peasants to loot and then set fire to their masters' manor houses. This was painted by John Wladimiroff.

The Petrograd Soviet

All over Russia, peasants, soldiers and workers elected committees, called **Soviets**. The most powerful Soviet was the Petrograd Soviet. It controlled the army, railways and factories. In many ways, it was more powerful than the Provisional Government. Most members of the Petrograd Soviet were **Marxists** (see page 105) and were split into two main groups: the **Mensheviks**, who believed that the middle classes should take over power first, and the **Bolsheviks** who wanted the working class to take control (page 105). All through the summer of 1917, the Petrograd Soviet challenged the Provisional Government.

The Provisional Government

Alexander Kerensky became leader of the Provisional Government in July 1917. He was a Menshevik. He promised the people land and elections for a new parliament.

Unpopularity of the Provisional Government

The Provisional Government carried on the war against Germany, even though troops were deserting in their thousands. The Provisional Government did not give the peasants the land they wanted, and it did not set up elections for a new parliament. Thousands of people were still starving. So the Provisional Government was very unpopular.

Lenin and the 'July Days'

Lenin, the leader of the **Bolsheviks**, lived in Switzerland. But as soon as the revolution of March 1917 broke out, he wanted to get back to Russia. The Germans allowed him to cross their land in a sealed train that did not stop at any station on the way to Petrograd. The Germans agreed to this because they knew Lenin wanted to get the Russians out of the war.

Once he was in Petrograd, Lenin said he would give the people **peace**, **land** and **bread**. He wanted to get rid of the Provisional Government. In July, armed mobs took to the streets, shouting slogans in support of Lenin. But the Provisional Government smashed the revolt, and Lenin had to flee to Finland.

General Kornilov's rebellion

General Kornilov, who still supported Tsar Nicholas, turned his troops against the Provisional Government. This meant that Kerensky (the leader of the Provisional Government) had to ask the Soviets for help. Bolshevik soldiers formed an armed Red Guard, and Bolshevik railway workers stopped Kornilov's advance. The Provisional Government was saved, but meanwhile Lenin had slipped back into Russia.

Source B

Until the Revolution in March, the number of deserters from the army was about 3,500 every two weeks.

After the Revolution, this jumped to about 17,000. When troops arrived at the Front, they refused to take up their rifles. 'What for?' they asked. 'We are not going to fight.'

There was a large landowner called Prince Volkonsky. Two months after the Revolution, trouble began. Peasants grazed their cattle on his land and cut down his timber.

When he complained to the authorities, they said that they had lost all control.

▲ Adapted from, L. Kochan, *The Russian Revolution*, 1970.

Source C

We call you to a revolution. We call on you not to die for others but to destroy others, to destroy your class enemies at home. Peace, Land and Bread.

All power to the soviets!.

▲ Vladimir Lenin, in a speech to soldiers, 1917.

The November Revolution 1917

Many people believed that the Bolsheviks had saved Russia from being ruled again by the Tsars. So the Bolsheviks became more and more popular. When **Leon Trotsky** (see page 108) began asking men to join the Red Guard, over 25,000 joined in the first couple of days. Bolsheviks controlled the Moscow and the Petrograd Soviets.

By November, Lenin was ready. Law and order had collapsed. In the countryside, peasants were burning the landowners' estates. Bolshevik ideas were spreading through the army. People did not support Kerensky any more. On the night of 6 November, Trotsky and the Red Guards took over important buildings in Petrograd. Kerensky and his government fled. The Bolsheviks were the new rulers of Russia.

Source D

▲ This painting is the work of a Soviet artist in 1935. It shows a Red Guard in the throne room of the Winter Palace, November 1917. The painting is called *The Inevitable*.

SUMMARY

Events of 1917
- **March** Provisional Government took over power.
- Tsar Nicholas abdicated.
- Soviets were set up throughout Russia.
- Petrograd Soviet challenged the Provisional Government for power.
- Lenin returned to Petrograd. '**July Days**' Bolshevik Revolution failed.
- General Kornilov's rebellion. Provisional Government saved by Bolshevik Red Guard.
- **November** Lenin and the Bolsheviks became the new rulers of Russia.

QUESTIONS

1. Read Source C. Which groups of Russian people would want 'Peace', 'Land' and 'Bread'?

2. Explain how
   a. Kerensky and the Provisional Government
   b. Lenin and the July Days
   c. Trotsky and the Red Guard

   helped to bring about the Bolshevik Revolution.

5.8 How did the Bolsheviks establish themselves in power?

When Lenin and the Bolsheviks seized power in Petrograd, it was by no means certain that they could gain and hold power throughout Russia. Fewer than one Russian in 500 was a Bolshevik. The First World War was still raging. Peasant soldiers were deserting and the people were starving. But by 1924, when Lenin died, the **Soviet Union**, made up of Russia and fourteen other republics, was firmly set up.

Decrees and declarations

Lenin knew that the Provisional Government had failed because it had not given the people what they wanted (see page 116). Between November 1917 and February 1918, the Bolshevik government in Petrograd issued a lot of decrees and declarations and telegraphed them to all the towns and villages in Russia. These told the people what they should do, and what they were to expect from the new government.

Land

One of the first decrees was the **Land Reform Decree**. This took land away from the Church, nobles and large landowners, and gave it to the peasants.

Bread

People in the towns were also short of food, so Lenin sent troops into the countryside to seize grain and other foodstuffs to take to the towns. This hit the peasants living near the towns, leaving them without seed corn to plant for the next year.

Elections

Lenin held elections for the new **Constituent Assembly** (Kerensky had failed to do this in July 1917). But the Bolsheviks only ended up with 175 of the 707 seats. So the Bolsheviks allowed this Constituent Assembly to meet just once. Then they set up their own **Congress of Soviets** to govern the country.

Source A

- Factories, mines, workshops and railways, other industries and transport will be owned by the Workers' and Peasants' State.

- All banks will be owned by the Workers' and Peasants' State.

- All magazines and newspapers opposed to the Workers' and Peasants' State will be closed down.

▲ Some of the decrees and declarations issued between November 1917 and February 1918.

Source B

You may go where you belong, to the rubbish-heap of history!

▲ Trotsky, addressing the Constituent Assembly.

The Communist Party

The Bolsheviks changed their name to the **Communist Party**, and banned all other political parties. The Red Army and the new secret police, the **Cheka**, kept Lenin and the Communist Party in power.

Peace

In March 1918, Lenin signed the **Treaty of Brest-Litovsk** with Germany. This brought peace to Russia, but at an enormous price. The treaty gave Germany 33.3% of Russia's agricultural land, 80% of its coal mines, 50% of its industry and 25% of its railway system.

Civil War 1918–21

Lenin's policies made him many enemies. In August 1918, a terrible Civil War broke out. The Bolsheviks and their supporters, called the Reds, were fighting for their survival. Against them were the Whites – supporters of the Tsar and supporters of the old Provisional Government. The old Allied powers from the First World War fought on the side of the Whites. The fighting was bitter, and there were acts of dreadful cruelty by both sides.

During the civil war the Tsar and his family disappeared. They had been kept under house arrest at Ekaterinburg in the Urals. When the Whites got dangerously close, the Bolsheviks shot the Tsar, Tsarina and all the children.

After three years of bitter fighting, the Bolsheviks won the Civil War and controlled all Russia.

▲ The Civil War in Russia.

▼ Leon Trotsky addressing the Red Army in Moscow in 1917.

Source C

Source D

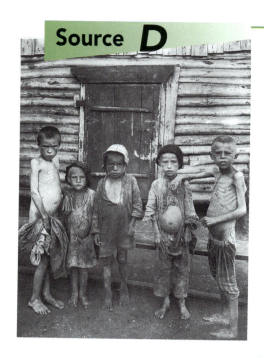

◀ These starving peasant children were photographed at a camp in Samara in October 1921.

War Communism

In order to win the Civil War, Lenin developed a system of government called **War Communism**.

- The government took over factories and said what they were to produce.
- The government stopped all private trade.
- The government introduced food rationing.
- The government sent the Red Army into the countryside to take food from the peasants in order to feed the people in the cities.

By 1921, when the Civil War ended, everything was in great disorder.

- The hard winter of 1920–1 meant that there were food shortages.
- Peasants refused to grow food if the Red Army was simply going to seize it.
- Famine and disease hit the peasants in the countryside, and also people in the towns.
- Sailors mutinied at the **Kronstadt** naval base.

It was clear to Lenin and Trotsky that War Communism would not work once the Civil War was over. They needed to replace War Communism with a system that would work and not arouse rebellion even if it went against their pure communist ideas.

	1913	1922	1925	1927/8
Grain harvest (millions of tons)	80.1	50.3	72.5	73.3
Cattle (million head)	58.9	45.8	62.1	70.5
Pigs (millions of tons)	20.3	12.0	21.8	26.0
Coal (millions of tons)	29.0	9.5	18.1	35.4
Pig iron (millions of tons)	4.2	0.116	1.53	3.2

Not to scale

▶ How industry and agriculture recovered under the NEP.

The New Economic Policy

In 1921, Lenin introduced the **New Economic Policy** (NEP).

- The state controlled only the most important industries.
- People were encouraged to start up shops and small factories, which were allowed to make a profit for their owners.
- Workers were paid in money or food for overtime.
- Peasants were allowed to sell food and make a profit for themselves.

Lenin's New Economic Policy worked. Production increased slowly, and by 1927 it was back to the 1913 level. But by that time the **Union of Socialist Soviet Republics** (USSR), as Russia had become, had a new leader: **Joseph Stalin**.

SUMMARY

- **March 1918** Treaty of Brest-Litovsk between Russia and Germany.
- **1918–20** Civil War between the Reds and the Whites.
- War Communism and the Red Army win Civil War.
- **1921** New Economic Policy.

QUESTIONS

1. Lenin promised the Russian people 'Peace, Land and Bread'. Had he carried out this promise by the time of his death in 1924?
2. a. What was War Communism?
   b. What was the New Economic Policy?
   c. What were the differences between them?

5.9 Who will succeed Lenin?

Source A

During the Civil War Lenin set up the **Politburo** (Political Bureau of the Central Committee of the Communist Party) to govern Russia. Members of the Politburo were the most powerful men in the USSR.

Lenin had a stroke in 1922, from which he never really recovered. From that time, Politburo members argued about which of them would replace Lenin when he finally died. The real struggle was between **Trotsky** and **Stalin**.

◀ Lenin and Stalin in 1922. Lenin (on the left) was recovering from a stroke. Stalin was probably added to the picture some time later.

Trotsky
- Planned the November Revolution in 1917.
- Started the Red Army.
- 1917–20 planned and fought in the Civil War commanding the Red army.
- Popular among ordinary Communist Party members.
- Popular among members of the Red Army.
- Members of the Politburo did not trust him.
- Believed in the idea of **Permanent Revolution**: communism had to spread outside Russia if it was to survive.

Stalin
- Planned the November Revolution in 1917.
- Did routine jobs in the Communist Party and built up support among members.
- In 1922, became a member of the Politburo.
- In 1922, became General Secretary of the Party Central Committee, and put his friends in powerful positions.
- Sided with those who supported the NEP.
- Believed in the idea of **Socialism in One Country**: the USSR could remain communist only if it became a strong, modern country. Communism did not have to spread outside the USSR in order to survive.

Stalin becomes leader
Stalin became leader of the Communist Party by ruthlessly removing those who opposed him. Stalin set about getting them off the Politburo and out of the Communist Party. In 1927, he had Trotsky expelled from the Communist Party. Two years later, he had Trotsky exiled. Trotsky went to Mexico, where he carried on talking and writing about his idea of Permanent Revolution. Because of this, Stalin had Communist agents murder him in 1940.

Stalin then turned on his previous allies and expelled those who supported the NEP. By 1930 there was no opposition to Stalin within the Politburo. He was the leader of the Communists and the USSR.

Source B

25 December 1922
Comrade Stalin has concentrated great power in his hands. I am not certain that he will always handle that power carefully.

Comrade Trotsky, on the other hand, is very able but perhaps too self-confident.

4 January 1923
Stalin is too rude to lead the party. Comrades should think of a way of removing him and appointing another man in his place.

▲ Adapted from Lenin's *Testament*. During his last illness, Lenin wrote notes on the future of the Communist Party and its leading members. Those notes, called Lenin's *Testament*, were read to important Communist Party members after his death.

▶ A painting of Lenin returning to St Petersburg from Switzerland in April 1917. Stalin has been painted standing behind Lenin. In fact, Stalin was never there at all.

Source C

Socialism in One Country

Stalin believed that, sooner or later, the countries of the West would attack the USSR because they hated communism so much. He said that there was only one way in which the USSR could survive this attack. The USSR had to become a strong industrial country – at least as strong as the countries of Western Europe.

But Stalin did not start from a good position. In 1928, the USSR did not have strong and prosperous industries. So Stalin decided to stop Lenin's New Economic Policy (see page 121). In its place, he started a series of **Five Year Plans**. These plans set targets which industry and agriculture had to meet.

Source D

It is sometimes asked whether it is possible to slow down the speed of change a bit. No, comrades, it is not possible!

The speed must not be reduced. To slacken the pace would be to lag behind. Those who lag behind are beaten. We do not want to be beaten.

We are fifty or a hundred years behind the advanced countries. We must catch up within ten years. Either we do it or they crush us.

▲ Stalin, in a speech made in 1931.

QUESTIONS

1. What were the main differences between Trotsky and Stalin?
2. Make a list of the steps by which Stalin became leader of the USSR.
3. Look at Sources A and C. Why do you think they were altered?

5.10 The collectivization of agriculture

Source A

Comrade Editor
If, as you say, the peasants join the kolkhoz because they want to, why do you send soldiers to put peasants in prison if they make any complaint? If you took a vote, you would only find half a percent who joined the kolkhoz of their own accord.

Each one thinks that it is a terrible thing. Each one wants to be a master and not a slave. It is better to hang yourself than join a kolkhoz.

▲ One of many letters sent to a village newspaper, complaining about collectivization.

Agriculture in 1928

In 1928, all land in the USSR was farmed by peasants. Even the **kulaks** (see page 110) were poor compared to farm workers in the West.

The peasants could not farm efficiently. The soil was often too poor to grow crops well, and they could not afford to buy fertilizers. They had very basic farming equipment, too. Some kulaks could afford horses and wooden ploughs. But most dug the ground with wooden spades and hoes, and sowed seed by hand.

The collective farms

In order to improve food production Stalin decided to end private farming. The peasants were asked to join their farms together into large collective farms called **kolkhoz**. These farms would be large enough to use modern machinery, like tractors. They would be worked efficiently. Fewer peasants would be needed to work the land, so thousands could leave and go to work in industry.

How did the kolkhoz system work?

The peasants who stayed on the land were paid wages by the kolkhoz. Every kolkhoz was run by a committee under the local Communist Party. They had to produce what the government wanted, at very low prices.

Source B

▲ This photograph of Russian peasants was published by the government of the USSR in 1931. It was called 'We would like to work together'.

Did the peasants want to work on collective farms?

At first, Stalin wanted to persuade peasants to work in the kolkhoz system. But many refused, especially among the kulaks. They had nothing to gain from joining a kolkhoz. They would have to give up whatever wealth their family had earned in return for an equal share in the profits of a collective farm. Stalin therefore made collectivization compulsory.

Riots and famine

When the peasants realized that they were going to be forced to work on collective farms, there was uproar. Those who did not want to give up their land took desperate measures. They destroyed their crops, burned their farm buildings and killed their animals. Between 1932 and 1933 millions of peasants died from starvation.

The end of the kulaks

Stalin wanted to put a stop to the opposition of the peasants, but still keep food production going. In order to do this, he decided to wipe out the kulaks. He banned them from collective farms, and sent nearly all of them to labour camps. There they were forced to build factories that were needed for Stalin's Five Year Plans. Nearly five million kulaks simply disappeared, never to be seen again.

The effects of collectivization

- By 1935, 95% of the USSR's farmland was in collective farms.
- The Communist Party's control over the countryside was greatly increased.
- More food was sent to the towns.
- The increase in food production was not as great as Stalin had hoped. So as more food was sent away from the countryside, life there got much harsher.
- More food was sold abroad which brought much needed money into the USSR to help build new industries.

Source C

▲ A group of peasants demanding collectivization and the end of the kulaks, 1931.

Agricultural production 1928 and 1933

	1928	1933
Cattle	70.5	38.4
Pigs	26.0	12.1
Sheep and goats (in millions)	146.7	50.2
Grain (in million tonnes)	73.3	68.4

QUESTIONS

1. Why did Stalin decide to make collective farming a law in the USSR?
2. Did the peasants oppose or support Stalin's plans for agriculture?
3. Sources A, B and C are all records from the period. Does this mean that they all give reliable evidence about the collectivization of agriculture? Explain your answer carefully, referring to the evidence in this section.
4. Look at the chart above and read this section. Was Stalin's policy of collectivization successful?

5.11 Five Year Plans for Industry

The first Five Year Plan: targets and achievements

Industry	1927–8	Target	Achieved
Coal	35.4	68.0	64.3
Oil	11.7	19.0	21.4
Pig-iron	3.3	8.0	6.2
Steel	4.0	8.3	5.9
Electricity	5.0	17.0	13.4

(All figures are in millions of tonnes, except electricity, which is in milliard kWh.)

The first Five Year Plan: industrial growth (percentages)

Coal	182%
Oil	183%
Pig-iron	188%
Steel	148%
Electricity	265%

Source A

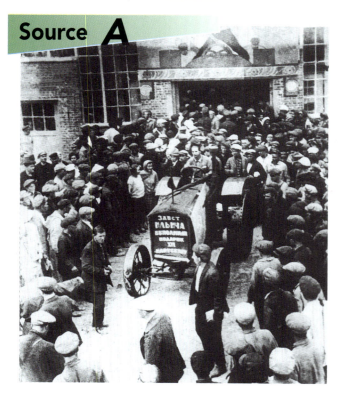

◀ The first tractor to roll out of the Stalingrad tractor works in 1930.

Industry in 1928

The USSR had enormous amounts of natural resources like coal and oil (see page 102). But in spite of this, the USSR was not a great industrial power. The damage caused by the Revolution and Civil War had not been put right. People were not putting money into industry, and nearly all the factories in the USSR were using old-fashioned ways of production.

Five Year Plans

Stalin decided that the USSR had to become a strong industrial power. The communists always believed in state planning as the best way of organizing the country's resources. So Stalin set up Five Year Plans for industry as well as for agriculture.

The first Five Year Plan 1928–32

The first Five Year Plan was not just a list of reforms for industry. It was a list of demands. Targets were set for yearly manufacture of the most important products.

Each factory, refinery, steel works and mine was set its own special target. This said exactly what it had to produce. Managers were punished if these targets were not met. It was a crime not to produce what the state demanded.

Was the first Five Year Plan a success?

In the USSR, industry grew enormously. During the same years, the Depression was hitting the great industrial nations of the world. In the USA, for example, unemployment was rising and industrial output was falling. In the USSR, although only oil reached its production target, every industry had grown by at least 50% in five years.

The second Five Year Plan

Stalin set targets for this plan in 1932. They were probably too high. But even though most of the targets were not met, what mattered was that the USSR's industry grew dramatically.

▲ The government used posters like this one, printed in 1931, to encourage the Soviet people to work together to achieve the Five Year Plans.

The second Five Year Plan

Industry	Original	1934	1937	(as % of 1932 Plan Revision figure)
Coal	250	152.5	128.0	199%
Oil	90	46.8	28.5	133%
Pig-iron	22	16.0	14.5	234%
Steel	17	17.0	17.7	300%
Electricity	100	38.0	36.2	270%

(All figures are in millions of tonnes, except electricity, which is in milliard kWh.)

The third Five Year Plan

By 1938, the USSR's industry had grown a great deal. So Stalin thought it was safe to move into producing consumer goods. This plan aimed to produce luxuries like radios and bicycles. But the plan had to be given up because war with Germany was coming, and the USSR's industry had to produce guns and tanks, uniforms and bullets.

QUESTIONS

1. Read pages 126–7. Why did Stalin think it was important that the USSR became a strong industrial country?
2. Were the Five Year Plans a success? Do you have enough evidence here to enable you to answer the question? Explain your answer carefully.
3. Read pages 124–5. Were Stalin's plans for the modernization of agriculture more successful than his plans for the modernization of industry? Explain your answer.

5.12 What was life like in Stalin's USSR?

Source A

A quarter of a million communists, kulaks, foreigners, convicts and masses of blue-eyed Russian peasants were building the largest steel works in Europe.

In early April everything was still frozen solid. By May the city was swimming in mud. Bubonic plague had broken out ... Sanitary conditions were appalling.

By the middle of May the heat was intolerable. We were consumed by bed bugs and other vermin.

▲ J. Scott, *Beyond the Urals*, 1942. Scott was an American who worked in the new steel works at Magnitogorsk in the Urals.

The Five Year Plans were a success as far as industrial production was concerned. The USSR became a strong industrial power. So when Germany attacked the USSR (see page 166), Stalin's armies were able to resist Hitler. They could do this because they were supplied by factories built during the first and second Five Year Plans. But there was a price to pay.

Peasants on collective farms

Most peasants probably lived better lives on collective farms than before. They had machinery, like tractors, to help them work the land. The collective hospital looked after them when they were ill. The collective school taught their children. They did not have the freedom that they had before, but in those days many of them starved.

Industrial workers

Workers in well-established industrial towns were usually better off. The Five Year Plans meant full employment and more money to spend.

But things were different in the new areas that Stalin was trying to develop. Thousands of peasants poured on to vast building sites to build factories and industrial plants. There was nowhere for them to live, except in overcrowded, run-down buildings with almost no sanitation.

Source B

◀ Volunteers from Komsomol (the Young Communist League) at a construction site in the city of Komsomolsk in 1934. Komsomolsk (in Siberia) and Magnitogorsk (in the Ural mountains) were two new industrial cities built under the Five Year Plans.

Pay

In 1931, Stalin said that skilled workers should earn three times as much as unskilled workers. On top of this, skilled workers were to have generous sick pay and pensions. They were also to have better homes and better food, and could shop in special shops.

Job security

All industrial workers needed government permission before they could change their jobs. They were sacked if they were absent from work, without good reason, for more than one day. The government sent school leavers to places where workers were needed. They had no choice about where they worked, or what work they did.

Religion

Communists did not believe in the existence of God. In 1917 the Bolsheviks took over all the land of the Russian Church because it supported the Tsar. They started persecuting Christians during the Civil War.

From 1929, for example, all factories began working a seventeen-day week. This meant, among other things, that Jewish, Christian and Muslim workers could not worship with their families on holy days.

Christianity

Stalin ordered all schools to teach compulsory lessons in **atheism** (the belief that there is no God). In this way, he hoped that Christianity would simply die out. Government agents arrested people who attended Christian churches, and by 1939 there were only a few hundred Christian churches in the USSR.

Source C

▲ This poster was produced by the communist government in 1931. It says, 'The provision of plenty of crèches, kindergartens, canteens and laundries will ensure the participation of women in socialist construction.'

Source D

Stalin has removed fear from the Soviet Union. No fear of not enough money at the birth of a child. No fear of crippling doctors' fees, school fees or university fees.

No fear of underwork, no fear of overwork. No fear of lack of work in a land where none are unemployed.

▲ Dr Hewlett Johnson, Dean of Canterbury Cathedral, writing in 1939. Dr Johnson was often called the 'Red Dean' because he supported the communist regime in the USSR.

The 1936 constitution
In 1936 Stalin said that the USSR was to have a new constitution.

- One chamber, the **Soviet of the Union** was made up of deputies: one representative for every 300,000 voters.
- The other chamber, the **Soviet of Nationalities**, had an equal number of deputies from each republic of the USSR.
- This two-chamber assembly was called the **Supreme Soviet**.
- This new form of government was meant to show that the USSR was a free and democratic country. Elections were free, but all deputies had to be approved by the Communist Party. And the supreme Soviet only met for few days each year.

The purges
Stalin wanted to make sure there was no opposition within the USSR to his plans for making the country economically strong. To do this, he simply removed everyone who disagreed with what he wanted to do. He did this in a series of 'purges'. He purged the Politburo and the Communist Party, the secret services and the armed forces, factories, schools and universities of everyone who had the courage to speak out against him and his policies. The purges reached their peak between 1936 and 1938. They included not only famous and powerful people, but ordinary men and women, too.

The secret police
Stalin used the secret police to inform on people who disagreed with him. He also used the secret police to persuade people to confess to crimes they had not committed. Famous people had to make their confessions in public at show trials. Those who were found guilty were sent to labour camps or were executed. Soon everyone was afraid of informers and the secret police. Millions of people simply disappeared: hundreds of mass graves have since been found.

Source E

▲ These prisoners at a labour camp are being forced to build the Belomor Canal, which linked the White Sea and the Baltic Sea. The labour camps were known as 'Gulags', after the government department that organized them.

QUESTIONS

1. Compare Sources A and B. What different impressions do they give? Which source is likely to be more reliable?
2. Sources C and D give a very positive picture of the USSR under Stalin. Can you find evidence to support these sources?
3. Read about **the Purges** and **the secret police** and look at Source E on this page. Explain how you think Stalin carried out his plans for the growth of industry.
4. Did life for ordinary men and women improve or worsen under Stalin's regime?

5.13 Exercise

1 The 1905 Revolution and the Revolutions of 1917 were in some ways similar and in some ways very different.
   a Copy the table below and use the information in this chapter to complete it.
   b What were the main differences between the Revolution of 1905 and the Revolutions of 1917?

A comparison of the 1905 and 1917 Revolutions

	1905	March 1917	November 1917
Aims			
Methods			
Outcomes			

2 Why did the rule of the Tsars come to an end?

3 Lenin introduced the New Economic Policy in 1921 (see pages 120–1).
   a Why did he do this?
   b How successful was this economic plan?
   c Why did Stalin abandon this policy? Give as many reasons as you can in your answer.

4 Look back at pages 123–5.
   a What were Stalin's aims when he came to power?
   b How successful had he been, by 1939, in achieving these aims?

5 Stalin modernized the USSR, but the Soviet people suffered greatly in the process. Do you think such suffering was necessary?

6 Stalin has been called by some historians 'The last of the Tsars':

Make two lists, one headed **Similarities** and the other headed **Differences**. Under each heading write down the ways in which Stalin behaved like the Tsars and the ways in which he was quite different.

Now answer the question 'Was Stalin the last of the Tsars?'

BRITAIN 1901–51

By 1901, the government was getting involved in the lives of British people. Parliament had, for example, passed laws about how many hours in a day men and women could work in factories. But when people were out of work or sick, they were very much on their own. The government expected them to have saved enough money when they were in work to help them through hard times. So there was no sickness or unemployment benefit for those who were out of work. There were no state pensions for widows or for the elderly either.

By 1951, all this had changed. The National Health Service gave men, women and children free medical treatment. People had a right to state retirement pensions, sick pay and unemployment benefits.

Source A

I have been to most of the great cities in America and Europe. I have never seen so much dirt or poverty, nor so many sick and hungry people as in the east end of London.

▲ Adapted from a book *England and the English from an American Point of View*, published in 1909, by Prince Collier, an American visiting England.

6.1 What was Britain like in 1901?

Source B

▲ This photograph of slum housing in the East End of London, was taken in 1912.

Living conditions
In 1884, **Charles Booth** began an enquiry into the living conditions of people in London. He published what he discovered in 1902 in 17 books.

Poor people
Charles Booth found out that nearly 33% of all Londoners did not have enough money to buy proper food, shelter and clothing. It was the same in all large British cities.

Middle-class people
Charles Booth reckoned that around one-quarter of all Londoners lived comfortable lives. Shopkeepers, teachers and office managers, for example, earned around £500 a year and could afford to have a maid.

Rich people
Around 2% of all British people earned more than £700 a year. Some were very rich indeed. The Duke of Portland, for example, had a income of several million pounds each year from the coal mines on his land. (See the conversion chart on page 240.)

Who lived longest?
People with money lived longer. This was because they lived in comfortable houses, wore warm clothing, ate good food and could afford to pay for medical treatment if they needed it.

For every thousand babies born in the slums, 33 died before their first birthday. Only four babies in every thousand born to rich parents died before they were one year old.

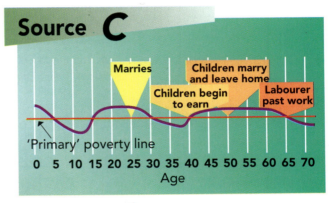

▲ This graph is taken from S. Rowntree, *Poverty, a Study of Town Life*, published in 1901.

▲ This photograph of Park Lane, London, was taken in 1910. Many rich people had apartments in buildings like this.

Source E

Last night we had clear soup with custard shapes, a mousse of ham with a sauce with cherries in it, roast lamb and all kinds of vegetables, partridges, an ice which was made to look like a melon, and mushrooms on toast, and, of course, lots of wine and always champagne.

▲ A guest describes a dinner in a great house at the beginning of the 20th century.

Industry in 1900
- British shipyards produced over half the world's tonnage in shipping.
- British manufacturers handled about one-third of the world's trade.
- Britain's main exports were textiles, coal, machinery, ships and railway engines.

BUT

- Germany and the USA began exporting coal.
- Belgium, Hungary, Russia and Canada were starting up their own industries.
- Japan and India were developing their own textile industries.

All this meant that the countries of the world bought less and less from Britain. They began selling to other countries, too. Britain's share of the world's trade began to drop.

Agriculture
In the 1870s, there was a depression in British agriculture. This meant that farmers earned less and less. Many gave up altogether. Some, however, looked for new markets for what they produced. Dairy farmers sold their milk to the new bottling companies, and to cheese and butter factories. Others turned to new types of farming. They grew vegetables and fruit, and they sold their produce to jam factories, canning factories and greengrocers. In East Anglia, farmers began growing bulbs, like their colleagues in Holland.

Source F

▲ The electrical fitters' shop in the Kodak factory, Harrow, Middlesex in about 1907. There were hundreds of workshops like these in Britain at that time.

Source G

Britain had a complete railway system. Coal and iron had not begun to run short. In lands far away there was an increasing demand for goods that Britain alone could make.

Many people believed that, if they wanted to, Englishmen could afford to relax and take things more easily.

▲ Adapted from a book written by Arthur Marshall, an economist, and published in 1903.

Trade and finance

Dividends

Britain's prosperity depended very much on money invested abroad and on trade. The greatest earnings came from dividends. These were profits which were paid to British people who had invested overseas in enterprises which turned out to be successful. British people invested money in, for example, South African steamship companies, Chinese railways and Sri Lankan tea estates.

Invisible earnings

Next came earnings from the profits made by merchant shipping and insurance companies. These earnings are called 'invisible' because there are no actual goods to be seen.

Goods

Next came profits made on actual goods, from cotton vests to railway engines.

Balance of payments

Every country spends money to buy goods from abroad (imports). It also earns money by selling goods abroad (exports). The difference between the money spent and the money earned is called the **balance of payments**. By 1914, Britain was still earning more from exports than it was paying to buy imports. But many people were worried that 75% of Britain's imports were raw materials and food. Britain was becoming dangerously dependent upon other countries for essential goods necessary for her survival.

▲ The countries of the world in which Britain invested money in 1913.

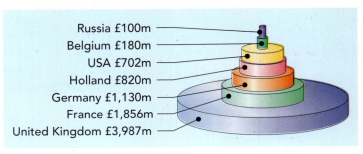

▲ The foreign investment of seven different countries in 1913.

QUESTIONS

1 Read pages 132–133. In what ways were the lives of the rich different from the lives of the poor?

2 Read page 134.
   a What problems did British industry face?
   b What problems did British agriculture face?

3 Look at this page, and explain:
   a Dividends
   b Invisible earnings.

4 Read the section headed **Balance of Payments**. Why was it a problem that 75% of Britain's imports were raw materials and food?

6.2 How did the Liberal Governments attack poverty 1906–14?

Source A

▲ A London County Council doctor examines a boy at Holland Street School in 1911.

Source B

I never realised before on what a gigantic scale the German pension system is conducted.
Nor had I any idea how successfully it works.
And that is not all.
Does the German worker fall ill? State insurance comes to his aid.
Is he permanently unable to work?
Again, he gets a regular grant whether he has reached the pension age or not.

▲ In 1908 Lloyd George visited Germany. This is part of what he said about his visit. It was reported in the *Daily News* on 27 August 1908.

In the 19th century, most well-off people believed that poverty would simply disappear as Britain got richer. But by the beginning of the 20th century, many people were beginning to believe that direct action by the government was the only way to tackle the problem.

In 1906, the Liberal Party won a huge victory in the general election. The new Liberal government set to work to try to wipe out poverty.

The welfare of children

The Liberal government believed that it was very important to make sure that the children of the poor were looked after properly.

- In **1906**, the **School Meals Act** told local authorities to pay for school meals for the poorest children. By 1914, over 150,000 children a year were eating free school meals.
- In **1907**, the government told every local authority that it had to have a **school medical service**. The government paid for school clinics to be set up and run, where treatment was free.
- In **1908**, the **Children and Young Persons' Act** said that parents could be taken to court if they were cruel to their children.
- **Juvenile courts** and **remand homes** were set up to keep young offenders away from older criminals.

Old age pensions

David Lloyd George was Chancellor of the Exchequer in 1908. In his first Budget he set up **old age pensions**:

- Pensions were paid to all old people over the age of 70 who had less than twelve shillings a week income.
- Pensions were paid on a **sliding scale** of between one and five shillings a week, depending on the old person's income.
- The money to pay these pensions came from government funds.

National Insurance Act 1911

This Act gave workers insurance against sickness and unemployment.

Insurance against unemployment
- Workers, employers and the state each contributed 2½d a week.
- Workers could claim 7 shillings a week for a maximum of 15 weeks in any one year.

Insurance against illness
- This was for all workers who earned more than £3 a week.
- Workers paid in 4d a week to the scheme; their employers and the government between them paid 5d per worker.
- When workers became ill, they could claim 10 shillings a week for 26 weeks.

(See conversion table on page 240.)

These laws introduced by the Liberal government were very important. In the past, governments had tried to make sure that poor people were looked after. Now, for the first time, a government was trying to help people so that they would not become poor in the first place.

Source C

▲ This government poster is advertising National Health Insurance. Lloyd George is the 'doctor'.

QUESTIONS

1. How did the reforms of the Liberal governments (1906–14) help the poor?

2. Which reform do you think was likely to help more people over the years?

3. Look back at Source C on page 133. Work out the ages when a person was poorest. Now look at the reforms listed on these pages and decide how far they would have improved those times of poverty.

6.3 How did the government intend to pay for the reforms?

▲ A cartoon called 'The Philanthropic Highwayman', published in the magazine *Punch* in 1909 (philanthropic means kind and helpful).

The People's Budget
The problem
The Liberal reforms cost money. This money had to be found by the government, on top of the money it needed for the routine running of the country. This was a problem because the government also needed money for the Royal Navy, so that it could keep ahead of the German Navy. Lloyd George reckoned that an extra £16 million would have to be raised by the Budget of 1909.

What did the 1909 Budget do?
- Increased taxes on tobacco and alcohol.
- Introduced a licence fee on cars.
- Raised income tax.
- Increased death duties.
- Introduced a new tax on the profit gained from selling land.

Lloyd George called this budget the 'People's Budget'.

Did Parliament agree to the budget?
The Liberal Party had more members in the House of Commons than all the other parties. So the budget was passed by the Commons without any real problems. But it was different in the House of Lords, where, most members (called Peers) were Conservative. Many were also rich and powerful landowners and were naturally very against the measures in the budget. So the House of Lords quickly threw out the People's Budget.

Source B

The real issue is whether the country is to be governed by King and the Peers or by the King and the People.

▲ Said by David Lloyd George in 1911.

The Parliament Act 1911

In the end, the House of Lords passed the People's Budget. But the Liberal government was determined to reduce the power of the House of Lords. To do this, **Herbert Asquith**, the Prime Minister, introduced the Parliament Bill. The House of Lords was determined to reject it.

The King steps in

King George V said that there should be a general election. If the people voted again for a Liberal government, he would know that they wanted the power of the Lords reduced. He would then make a lot of Liberal peers – enough to get the Parliament Bill through the Lords. When the general election happened, a Liberal government was elected again.

The Parliament Bill becomes law

The House of Lords took fright, and passed the Parliament Bill before the King could create any new peers. The Conservatives in the House of Lords did not want there to be enough Liberal peers to outvote them all the time.

How was the power of the House of Lords reduced?

- It could not reject a 'money bill' like a budget.
- It could only reject a Bill twice; the third time the commons sent up a bill, the Lords had to pass it.
- Parliaments could only last for five years, not seven.

Source C

Should 500 men (in the House of Lords) be able to turn down the decisions made by people who work to make the wealth of this country?

Who made 10,000 people owners of the soil, and the rest of us trespassers in the land of our birth?

▲ From the speeches of David Lloyd George, 1910–11.

SUMMARY

- **1906** The Liberal government began a programme of reform.
- **1906** School Meals Act passed
- **1907** School medical service introduced.
- **1908** Juvenile courts set up to keep young offenders away from hardened criminals.
- **1908** Old age pensions introduced.
- **1909** People's Budget to pay for reforms.
- **1911** Parliament Act restricted the power of the House of Lords.
- **1911** National Insurance Act.

QUESTIONS

1. How did the 'People's Budget' help the people?
2. Read Source B. To what was Lloyd George referring what he talked about 'the King and the Peers', and 'the King and the People'?
3. Read Source C and read about the Parliament Act of 1911.
   a. What was Lloyd George's attitude to the House of Lords?
   b. Why did the Liberals want to reduce the power of the House of Lords?
   c. Why were they successful?

6.4 How did the Labour Party begin?

The Independent Labour Party

In 1893, at a conference in Bradford, West Yorkshire, a group of people set up the **Independent Labour Party (ILP)**. Members of this party believed in **socialism** and in **socialist** ideas. They believed that:

- important industries should be owned by the state and run for the good of all people
- the state should help widows, the sick and the old.

The leader of this new political party was **James Keir Hardie**. He was a Scottish miner, and was one of the very few working-class men who was a Member of Parliament.

What support did the Independent Labour Party have?

At the general election in 1895, no ILP candidate was elected. But support for the ILP grew throughout the country. Voters elected ILP members on to local councils, school boards and boards of Poor Law guardians. ILP ideas were spread by special newspapers, like the *Clarion*, and at hundreds of rallies and meetings held up and down the country.

The Labour Representation Committee

Members of trade unions set up the **Labour Representation Committee (LRC)**. The LRC started a fund to pay the election expenses of Labour candidates, and to pay their salaries if they were elected.

In 1900, two ILP candidates were elected: Keir Hardie and Richard Bell.

Source A

The working class cannot represent themselves in Parliament because of the money problem. They have to earn money in order to live, and MPs are not paid salaries or wages.
Working class MPs will depend on the trade unions to raise the money.

▲ Adapted from a Fabian Society article, 1893.

Source B

STRIKE!
ON THE
Taff Vale Railway.

Men's Headquarters,
Cobourn Street,
Cathays.

There has been a strike on the Taff Vale Railway since Monday last. The Management are using every means to decoy men here who they employ for the purpose of black-legging the men on strike.

Drivers, Firemen, Guards, Brakesmen, and SIGNALMEN, are all out.

Are you willing to be known as a **Blackleg?**

If you accept employment on the Taff Vale, that is what you will be known by. On arriving at Cardiff, call at the above address, where you can get information and assistance.

RICHARD BELL,
General Secretary.

◀ A poster printed during the strike on the Taff Vale Railway 1901.

The Taff Vale decision

In 1901, the Taff Vale Railway Company sued a trade union called the Amalgamated Society of Railway Servants, for £23,000. This was because the railway company had lost money when the railway workers went on strike. The court decided that the trade union had acted illegally, and it had to pay up. This meant that no union could strike because its funds would be threatened.

What did the trade unions do?

The trade unions swung their weight behind the Labour Representation Committee. In the 1906 general election the ILP won 29 seats. Then it changed its name to the 'Labour Party', and elected Keir Hardie as its leader.

Trades Dispute Act 1906

The new Labour Party persuaded the Liberal government to support the Trades Dispute Act. This changed the law so that unions were not responsible for any money their employers lost during a strike.

Trade Union Act 1913

This Act said that unions could use their funds for anything legal. This meant that they could use their money to back political parties like the Labour Party.

Source C

What is a Socialist? One who has yearnings
To share equal profits from unequal earnings;
Be he idler, bungler or both, he is willing
To fork out his sixpence and pocket your shilling.

▲ Popular rhyme in the early 1900s.

Source D

FORCED FELLOWSHIP
Suspicious-looking party: 'Any objection to my company, guv'nor? I'm agoin' your way' - (aside) 'and further'.

▲ This cartoon was published in the magazine *Punch* in 1909.

QUESTIONS

1. Read Source A. Why was it difficult for working-class people to become Members of Parliament? Were there any other reasons?
2. How did the trade unions help the Labour Party?
3. What was the importance of the Trade Union Act of 1913?

6.5 Votes for Women?

At the beginning of the 20th century, no woman could vote in a British general election. Most people thought that only men should deal with national politics. But in the years up to 1914, there was a steady and sometimes violent campaign as women tried to change this.

Source A

What a Woman may be, and yet not have the Vote
MAYOR · NURSE · MOTHER · DOCTOR or TEACHER · FACTORY HAND

What a Man may have been, & yet not lose the Vote
CONVICT · LUNATIC · Proprietor of white Slaves · Unfit for Service · DRUNKARD

▲ This postcard was produced in 1912 by a group of women artists called the Suffrage Atelier. Their aim was to make advertisements, banners and decorations promoting the cause of women's right to vote.

Women in 1901

Most men and many women believed that a woman's place was in the home supporting her husband and bringing up their children. But things were slowly changing. Girls' schools were well established; some universities accepted women as students; a few women became doctors; married women could keep the money they brought with them into the marriage.

Local elections

Women could vote in local elections. This was because local councils dealt with local matters which were likely to affect their homes. This was thought to be the proper concern of women.

Source B

Is it right that one half of the human race should be under the control of the other half when the only reason is that men like it?

▲ Adapted from Harriet Taylor Mill, writing in 1851.

Source C

The working woman needs the suffrage in order to obtain better houses, better conditions of living, shorter hours of working, better care for her children.

▲ Written by Mrs Wibaut in *Working Women and the Suffrage*, published in 1900.

The suffragists

Suffragists believed that women would get the vote eventually. All they had to do was to keep on the right side of the law, and do all that they could to persuade the general public and Parliament that women ought to be given the vote.

Who were the suffragists?

In the early days, the suffragists were well-connected, upper- and middle-class women. They tried to use their influence to persuade men in powerful positions to support women's suffrage (suffrage = the right to vote). They were determined to achieve the right to vote by peaceful, legal means.

In 1897, **Millicent Fawcett** organized the **National Union of Women's Suffrage Societies**. Between 1901 and 1914, all kinds of men and women, rich and poor, famous and unknown, joined the suffrage movement. Steadily, they carried on with their quiet campaign of winning over MPs and public figures.

Anti-suffragists

Many people believed strongly that women should not have the vote. In 1908, **Mrs Humphrey Ward**, a novelist and social worker, started the **Women's Anti-Suffrage League**. She believed that a woman's place was in the home. Everything a woman did should be aimed at making her home a better place. According to Mrs Ward, if a woman had any spare time, she should use it in helping those less fortunate than herself. She certainly should not be fighting for what she believed to be her 'rights' alongside men.

Source D

▶ Cyclists came from all over England to attend a rally for women's suffrage in 1913.

QUESTIONS

1 Explain fully what is meant by
   a suffrage
   b suffragists

2 List the arguments used at the time:
   a for giving women the vote in parliamentary elections
   b for **not** giving women the vote in parliamentary elections.

   Use the text and Sources A, B and C.

Source E

Mrs Pankhurst led a small group to see the Prime Minister. They were refused entry at the door of the House of Commons. 'I am firmly resolved to stand here until I am received!' she cried. Inspector Jarvis then began to push her away, and his men laid hands on the other women. Mrs Pankhurst deliberately hit the inspector so that he had to arrest her.
'I know why you did that', he said. He called to his men: 'Take them in.'

▲ Adapted from *The Suffrage Movement* by Sylvia Pankhurst, published in 1931. Here she describes her attempt to talk to the Prime Minister.

The suffragettes

In 1903, Mrs **Emmeline Pankhurst** had had enough of the quiet, responsible approach of the suffragists. Together with her daughters **Christabel** and **Sylvia**, she started the **Women's Social and Political Union (WSPU)**. A newspaper, the *Daily Mail*, nicknamed them the suffragettes, and the nickname stuck. The difference between the suffragists and the suffragettes was that the suffragettes were not afraid to break the law in order to get votes for women.

What did the suffragettes do?

Suffragettes broke up political meetings, slashed paintings and poured acid into pillar boxes. In 1912, they started a massive stone-throwing operation. At 4 p.m. on 1 March, suffragettes broke hundreds of shop windows. The police arrested 219 suffragettes. But the suffragettes did not mind being arrested because it drew attention to their cause.

Hunger strikes

When they were in prison, many suffragettes went on hunger strike to get publicity for their cause. But the prison authorities were afraid that a suffragette might die in prison, and that this would give them even more publicity. So they began **force-feeding**. To force-feed a hunger striker, prison officers pushed a tube down her throat and into her stomach. Then they poured liquid food down this tube. In this way, suffragettes on hunger strike were kept alive.

Source F

▲ A suffragette poster, probably for the 1910 election, showing the force-feeding of a suffragette on hunger strike.

Cat and Mouse Act 1913
In 1913, Parliament passed an Act which has been nicknamed the 'Cat and Mouse' Act. Weak hunger strikers were released from prison. But when they were strong again, they were re-arrested and sent back to prison.

Emily Davison
Emily Davison found a terrible way to publicize women's suffrage. On 4 July 1913, which was Derby Day at Epsom, she stood by the rails watching the main race. As the King's horse, Anmer, rounded Tattenham Corner, she threw herself under his hooves, and she later died from her injuries. Inside her coat were sewn the colours of the WSPU – green, white and purple.

▲ Suffragettes had their own shop in Bow Road, London, where they sold posters, pamphlets, books and their newspaper, *The Suffragette*. In this photograph, taken in 1912, Sylvia Pankhurst is painting the shop front.

Suffragettes and the First World War 1914–18
Britain entered the First World War on 3 August 1914. Immediately, the suffragettes called off their campaign of violence. The government released all suffragettes who were still in prison.

Suffragette leaders toured the country, making speeches and leading rallies. They urged men to fight, and women to back them by working in factories and helping with the war effort.

Suffragists and the First World War 1914–18
Millicent Fawcett and most of the suffragists were in favour of the war effort. They paid for ambulances in northern France and found women to drive them; they organized women's voluntary work too. But they all also carried on talking and writing to politicians about the need to give women the vote.

Source H
Opinion is changing in favour of giving women a vote due to the excellent work they have done for us and the country during the war.

▲ A. C. Morton, in a speech to the House of Commons in 1917.

Attitudes change

Before the First World War, many people were put off by what the suffragettes were doing. They said that the suffragettes were irresponsible, and were simply proving that women were not to be trusted with the vote. Some politicians did not want to give women the vote because it would look like they were giving into violence. And thousands of people still believed that a woman's place was in the home. But the war changed this. Everyone saw that women were working hard and playing a full part in the war effort.

Votes for women!

- 1918: The **Representation of the People Act** gave the vote to all men over the age of 21, and to women over the age of 30. But the women had to own a house, or be married to a householder.
- 1928: The **Equal Franchise Act** gave the vote to all women over the age of 21.

Source I

How could we have carried on the War without women? Wherever we turn we see them doing work which three years ago we would have said was men's work.

After the war we will have to look to rebuilding the country. I find it impossible to withhold from women the power and the right of making their voices heard.

▲ Adapted from a speech in 1917 by Herbert Asquith. When he was Prime Minister before the war, he had been against women's suffrage.

Source J

▶ This drawing was published in the magazine *Punch* in 1918.

AT LAST!

Source K

A member of the House of Commons said, 'If you are extending the franchise (vote) to our brave soldiers, how about our brave munition workers?' That argument was difficult to resist. Then ... 'How about our brave women munition workers?' And, having agreed to the first argument it was impossible to resist the second.

▲ Adapted from the memoirs of Lord Birkenhead, a Conservative politician.

QUESTIONS

1. Look back over section 6.5. What were the main differences between the suffragists and the suffragettes?
2. Read Source E. Why did Mrs Pankhurst hit the policeman?
3. Explain:
   a force-feeding
   b the Cat and Mouse Act 1913.
4. Did women get the vote in 1918 because of
   a the activities of the suffragists
   b the activities of the suffragettes
   c the work women did during the 1914–18 war?

SUMMARY

- **1897** Millicent Fawcett started the National Union of Women's Suffrage Societies.
- **1903** Emmeline Pankhurst started the Women's Social and Political Union (Suffragettes).
- **1913** The 'Cat and Mouse' Act was passed.
- **1914–18** Women took on men's work on the Home Front during the First World War.
- **1918** All women over 30 who owned a house, or were married to a householder, were given the vote.
- **1928** All women over the age of 21 given the vote.

6.6 Why was there a General Strike in 1926?

Miners' grievances

Before the First World War, individual mine owners fixed what they paid miners. During the war, the government told the mine owners that they had to pay the same wages to every miner, no matter which pit he worked in. The miners preferred this system.

But when the war ended, the mine owners were again free to fix miners' pay. The problem was that the price of coal was falling. So the owners cut miners' pay by up to 50%. The cuts varied from pit to pit because some pits made more money than others.

Source A

▲ This photograph, taken down a pit in the 1920s, shows the sort of conditions in which miners worked.

Black Friday

The Miners' Federation, which was the miners' union, decided to protest about the pay cuts. So it called its members out on strike on Friday, 15 April 1921. The Miners' Federation expected that two other big unions – the National Transport Workers' Federation (NTWF) and the National Union of Railwaymen (NUR) – would join them. They had an agreement, called the **Triple Alliance**, which said that this would happen. But at the very last moment, these two unions pulled out, leaving the miners to strike alone. This is why the miners called Friday, 15 April 1921 'Black Friday'. The miners managed to stay out on strike until 1 July, but then they went back to work on the mine owners' terms.

Red Friday

Coal prices went on falling. The mine owners cut miners' pay again, and put an extra hour on the working day. At this point, the government stepped in. It gave the mine owners enough money (a **subsidy**) so that they could keep miners' pay at the old levels for nine months.

The unions called their success 'Red Friday'. But really they had only bought a breathing space. Everyone knew there would be a showdown if the miners and pit owners did not agree about what was to happen when the government subsidy ended on 1 May 1926.

Planning for a General Strike

Every trade union belonged to the **Trades Union Congress** (TUC). The TUC agreed to back the miners. It said that it would call a General Strike if the government did not agree to the miners' demands.

Miners and mine owners

The government subsidy was due to end on 1 May 1926. The mine owners said they could not afford to pay wages at the same level after that date. They said that miners would have to accept another reduction in their pay. But the miners refused to take a pay cut. In the end, the owners tried to force them to accept longer hours and lower pay by locking them out of the pits.

Source B

Yesterday was the heaviest defeat that has happened to the Labour Movement. It is no use trying to say otherwise. We on this paper have said that if organized workers stand together, they would win.
They have not stood together, and they have been beaten.

The National Union of Railwaymen, and the Transport Workers' Federation have called off their strike.
The miners are fighting on.

The owners and the government have delivered a frontal attack upon the worker's standard of life.

▲ This is adapted from part of an article about Black Friday. It was published in the *Daily Herald* on 16 April 1921. The *Daily Herald* was a newspaper paid for by the trade unions.

Source C

Not a minute on the day
Not a penny off the pay.

▲ Miners' slogan, 1924–5.

Strike!

The TUC swung into action. It called workers out, industry by industry. Railwaymen, dockers and builders, workers in the iron and steel industries, in heavy chemicals, gas and electricity all stopped work. Soon 1.5 million workers were on strike. The TUC published a newspaper called *The British Worker*, which explained the TUC's point of view to the British people.

The government acts

The government used the **Emergency Powers Act**. It swore in thousands of special constables. It also asked volunteers to drive buses and trains, and to unload ships in the docks. The army kept the power stations going. In every town there was a strike committee to maintain supplies of food, medicine and fuel. The government published a special official paper, *The British Gazette*, to explain its point of view to the British people. The government said that the General Strike was about political power, and that the unions wanted to take over running Britain.

The strike collapses

After nine days, the General Strike collapsed. The TUC had simply wanted to help the miners. But now it found itself confronting a lawfully elected government, and many people thought Britain was close to revolution. On 12 May, the TUC took its support away from the miners, who were left to struggle on alone.

By November 1926, most mines were working again. Miners had to accept lower wages and longer hours, and their union was penniless.

Source D

▲ Government precautions for the General Strike: a tank in Hyde Park, London on 10 May 1926.

Source E

Neither in fact nor, I believe, in law, is the course adopted by the Trade Unions a strike in the proper sense of the term.
It is an attempted revolution.
If it succeeds, we would be ruled by a small body of extremists.

▲ Lord Grey, writing in the *British Gazette* in May 1926.

Source F

We are entering upon the second week of the general stoppage in support of the mine workers against the attack upon their standard of life by the coalowners. Nothing could be more wonderful than the magnificent response of millions.

▲ From the *British Worker* in May 1926.

Source G

◀ A cartoon, 'The Lever Breaks', published in the magazine *Punch* in May 1926.

The effects of the General Strike

The General Strike left the trade unions in a very weak condition. In 1927, Parliament passed the **Trades Disputes Act**.

- Workers could only strike if their own business or industry was involved in a dispute.
- Workers could not strike in sympathy with workers in other industries. This meant that another General Strike would be illegal.
- Parliament changed the rules about the ways in which unions paid money to the Labour Party. Each union member had to sign a special form allowing their union to do this. This hit hard at Labour Party funds.

QUESTIONS

1. Look at section 6.6.
   a. Why were the miners worried about their pay?
   b. What was Black Friday? Why was it called Black Friday?
   c. What was Red Friday?
2. The government's financial help to mine owners came to an end on May 1 1926. What did **a** the mine owners do? **b** the miners do?
3. Explain the part played by the TUC in the strike of 1926.

SUMMARY

▶ **March 1921** State control of mines ended; miners' wages cut by up to 50% because of the falling price of coal.

▶ **April 1921** Triple Alliance organized strike; 'Black Friday' when NUR and NTWF pulled out, leaving miners to strike alone. After ten weeks, miners returned to work on owners' terms.

▶ **July 1925** 'Red Friday' when government subsidized miners' pay after another attempt by owners to reduce wages because of the falling price of coal.

▶ **May 1926** Government subsidy ended; mine owners tried to force miners to accept longer hours and less pay by locking them out of the pits.

▶ **May 1926** General Strike called by TUC; strike collapsed after nine days because of withdrawal of all unions except the Miners' Federation.

▶ **November 1926** Most miners back at work on owners' terms.

▶ **1927** Trades Disputes Act ended possibility of sympathetic strikes and made union financial support of Labour Party more difficult.

6.7 The Depression: How did industry and government cope?

Problems before the 'Great Depression'
Before the First World War, Britain sold goods like ships, machinery and textiles to countries that had no industries of their own. But after the war, many countries started to set up their own industries. So they did not need to buy British goods any more, and British industry did not need to produce so many ships, machinery and textiles. As a result, workers in these industries lost their jobs.

The effects of the 'Great Depression'
The **Great Depression** of 1930 and the following years (see pages 61–4) put many more people out of work. The four basic industries of coal, cotton, shipbuilding and iron and steel had an unemployment rate twice as high as other industries.

New industries
Some parts of Britain were not so badly hit. New, light industries had developed since the war in the midlands and south-east. These produced, for example, cars, aeroplanes, vacuum cleaners and toasters. These were made in factories powered by electricity, not coal. There was very little unemployment in these industries either before or during the Depression.

▲ Part of Tyneside in the 1930s.

▲ Britain during the 1930s.

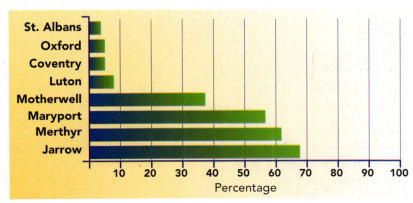

◀ Percentage of insured workers unemployed in 1934.

A Labour government in power

A new Labour government came to power in 1929. The Prime Minister, **Ramsay MacDonald**, promised to tackle the problem of unemployment.

Problems with money

The government had to spend money paying benefit to unemployed people. This money came from the taxes paid by people in work. The problem was that fewer and fewer people were in work, and more and more people were becoming unemployed. So the gap between what the government paid out and what it collected in taxes was growing month by month.

The government's solution

A government committee said:
- Everyone paid by the government should have their pay cut. This would mean cutting the pay of, for example, teachers, soldiers and the police.
- Unemployment benefit should be cut.
- No one should receive unemployment benefit until they had had a **Means Test**. This test would find out how much money was coming into their home.

The government collapses

When these ideas were put to the Cabinet, most ministers refused to agree to them. They thought that people would not accept the cuts, which would lead to a great deal of hardship. The government collapsed.

The National Government

Ramsay MacDonald did not resign. Instead, he formed a new government which was made up of Conservative, Liberal and Labour MPs. It was called the **National Government**. Quickly the government agreed to:

- cut the pay of people it employed – people like teachers, MPs, judges and the police
- cut benefits to the unemployed
- apply a Means Test to the unemployed before they could receive benefits. The government saved a lot of money by these cuts.

▲ This General Election poster of October 1931 is asking voters to support the National Government.

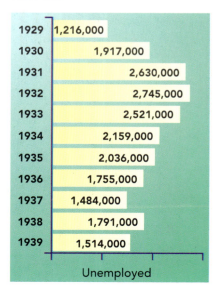

▼ Registered unemployed, 1929–39.

Year	Unemployed
1929	1,216,000
1930	1,917,000
1931	2,630,000
1932	2,745,000
1933	2,521,000
1934	2,159,000
1935	2,036,000
1936	1,755,000
1937	1,484,000
1938	1,791,000
1939	1,514,000

Government action – helping industry

Saving money was one way of fighting the Depression. Another way was to support industry, by creating jobs:

- The **Special Areas Act** (1934) meant that the government could pay for special projects where there was high unemployment. For example, it funded a new steel works at Ebbw Vale in South Wales.
- In 1935, the government loaned money to ship owners so that they could scrap old ships and buy new ones. This made work in the shipyards.

Government action – helping agriculture

Another way of fighting the Depression was to support agriculture, by protecting farmers from cheap foreign imports:

- Farmers who grew wheat were guaranteed a basic price of 10 shillings per hundredweight.
- By 1939, farmers who produced hops, milk, bacon, oats, barley, meat and potatoes were all guaranteed a basic price for their goods.

Government action – getting ready for war?

The help that government gave to industry and to agriculture created hundreds of new jobs. But there was another area of government spending which created work.

In 1933, **Adolf Hitler** came to power in Germany (see pages 88–91). Some British politicians, industrialists and bankers began to fear for the future. So they began equipping and expanding the armed forces. From 1935 to 1939, spending on armaments increased by 300%. Thousands of new jobs were created in steel making, engineering and munitions.

In 1939, however, there were still 1.5 million people out of work.

Source C

'Work at last'

▶ This cartoon, 'Work at last', was printed in the *Daily Express* in 1936.

QUESTIONS

1. Look at the graph on page 151. Why was there so much difference between the unemployment figures in different areas?

2. Look carefully at Source B.
   a. How are the voters being persuaded to vote for the National Government?
   b. Did the National Government deliver what it was promising in the poster?

3. Look at Source C. What point was the cartoonist making? Was he correct?

6.8 The Depression: How did people cope?

Source A

▲ Men from Jarrow on their march to London in 1936.

Unemployment benefit and the 'dole'

Out-of-work people could claim **unemployment benefit** for fifteen weeks. After this, for the next 32 weeks, they could claim **the dole**. During the Depression, the government could not afford to pay benefit and the dole at the old rate. (See pages 151-3). In 1931, the government cut the dole by 10% and made everybody claiming it take a Means Test.

The Means Test

Government officials visited all the people who claimed the dole. They found out exactly how much was earned by everyone living in the house. Even the earnings of a son or daughter doing a paper round were counted. If the officials thought there was enough money coming into the home, they stopped or reduced the father's dole money.

Source B

I was in a transport cafe on the Great North Road, when a young couple came in with a child. They were walking 450 km from South Shields to London because the man understood he could get a job there. They had a baby's feeding bottle with only water in it. The baby had a newspaper nappy on. They picked up another newspaper and put that on for another nappy. I felt anger against the system and I thought somebody ought to do something about it.

▲ Frank Cousins remembers the 1930s in a TV interview in the 1960s. He later became leader of the Transport and General Workers' Union.

The Jarrow March 1936

Some people protested by going on hunger marches to show the rest of Britain, and the government, just how much they were suffering. The most famous of these marches was the one from Jarrow, in the north-east of England. It was organized by the local MP, **Ellen Wilkinson**. Hundreds of unemployed men marched to London. There they presented a petition to the government, asking for help. When they got back home, they found that their dole money had been stopped because they were not available for work while they were on the march.

Better for some?

Even when the Depression was at its worst, 75% of British workers still had a job. Where there were new industries (see page 151), families lived better than before. Wages were higher and, because of birth control, families were smaller. Some people's health improved

Source C

because they could afford to buy modern houses with proper sanitation. They could also afford to buy good food.

In 1900, people had worked for around 55 hours a week. By 1935, people who had a job were expected to work around 45 hours a week. Most workers had holidays with pay too. Many people had time and cash to spend on going to the cinema, dance halls and theatres.

Source D

The 1930s were a wonderful time for me. I went to dances and shows and to the cinema with my latest boyfriend. I worked as a secretary at the recording company HMV in their London office and met lots of stars. The Depression never touched us, though I do remember hanging out of my office window to watch one of the hunger marches. We all felt very sorry for the poor men, but it wasn't anything to do with us, really.

▲ Con Dawson remembers what it was like for her in the 1930s.

◀ This is one of the most famous photographs of the Depression. It was taken in Wigan in 1939. The photographer posed the children and the workman before taking the picture.

Source E

When I was about eleven or twelve, I used to wander through the City. My London was a warm and colourful place with its red buses and trams, advertising placards, the bright Underground stations and coffee stalls.

▲ Louis Heron describes what it was like to be young in London in the 1930s in his book, *Growing up Poor in Britain*. He later became editor of *The Times* newspaper.

QUESTIONS

1. People who were out of work could claim unemployment benefit and 'the dole' by law. Why, then, did they go on hunger marches?

2. How did the Depression affect Frank Cousins (Source B) and Con Dawson (Source D)? How do you explain the difference in their attitudes?

3. We know that Source C is a picture that was created by the photographer. Is it any use as a source of information about the Depression?

4. Choose two sources from pages 151–5 which seem to you to best represent the Depression. Use the information from these pages to explain your choice.

6.9 How did the government plan for peacetime Britain?

Source A

▲ Bombed terraced houses in the Muttley Plain district of Plymouth.

Queen Elizabeth believed that the British people deserved a better life once the Second World War was over. So did the government. It realized that there would be a lot to do when the fighting ended. Many people were homeless because of bombing. Industry would have to start producing peacetime goods. Men and women in the armed forces would need civilian jobs. And many of the problems which had made life so difficult in the 1930s had not been solved.

Source B

I feel quite exhausted after seeing so much sadness, and magnificent spirit. The destruction is so awful and the people so wonderful - they deserve a better world.

▲ Part of a letter written by Queen Elizabeth, wife of King George VI, to her mother-in-law, Queen Mary, in 1940.

The Beveridge Report

In 1941, the government asked **Sir William Beveridge** to suggest ways in which it could help the sick, the unemployed, low-paid workers and retired people. Beveridge produced his report a year later. It was called *Social Insurance and Allied Services*. He said that he had looked at all the problems, as the government had asked him to. He had decided that they were all linked together. And because the problems were linked, Beveridge said that the solutions should be linked as well.

What did Beveridge say should happen?

Beveridge said that people should contribute to an insurance scheme run by the government that would look after them 'from the cradle to the grave'. It would:

- give benefits to the sick, unemployed and disabled
- give benefits to pregnant women
- give allowances to families with children
- give pensions to old people and widows
- give grants to meet the cost of funerals

Source C

Want is one of the five giants we have to attack on the road to reconstruction. The others are Disease, Ignorance, Squalor (dirty, poor conditions) and Idleness.

◀ Adapted from Sir William Beveridge's report, *Social Insurance and Allied Services*, 1942.

But Beveridge said that his scheme he was suggesting would only be successful if the government made sure that everyone had a job.

The Reconstruction Committee

Beveridge's scheme was very popular. Over 100,000 copies of his report were sold in the first month it was published. So the government had to act. It set up the **Reconstruction Committee**, which proposed changes in education, housing, health, employment and social insurance. Education and housing were tackled before the war ended.

Education

In 1944, Parliament passed the **Education Act**. It said that the state had to provide free education for all children, and that children had to be taught in separate primary schools and secondary schools. No one could leave school until they were 15 years old.

Every child took an examination when they were eleven years old. How they did in this examination decided the type of school they went to when they left primary school. Grammar schools gave children an academic education; secondary modern schools taught more practical subjects and technical schools taught technical skills. The idea behind the Act was that every child should have the sort of education which suited them best.

Housing

During the war, plans were made to build whole **new towns**. These were to be built in the countryside, well away from the old cities. But it would take many years to build a whole town, and homeless people needed houses immediately. So the government backed the production of houses that could be put up very quickly. These were nicknamed 'pre-fabs' and were built from sections produced in factories. Workmen could build a pre-fab in a few hours. The first one went up in April 1944, and before long, thousands were built throughout Britain. Pre-fabs were meant to last for about ten years, but many people were still living them in the 1990s.

QUESTIONS

1 a What was the Beveridge Report?

b The Report said that people should be looked after 'from the cradle to the grave'; How did it suggest this should happen?

2 Read Source C.

a What were the 'five giants'?

b The government began planning for the future by concentrating on housing and education. Which of the 'five giants' were these intended to tackle? Explain your answer.

6.10 Why did the Labour Party win the General Election of 1945?

Source A

▲ A Conservative Party election poster.

Source B

▲ A Labour Party election poster.

Source C

On with the forward march!

And let us make sure that the cottage home to which the warrior will return is blessed with modest but solid prosperity, and that Britons may remain free to plan their lives for themselves and those they love.

▲ From an election speech given by Winston Churchill as part of the 1945 campaign.

General Election 1945

During the war the two parties had joined together in a National Government led by Winston Churchill.

Which party would run Britain after the war? Would it be the Conservatives, led by **Winston Churchill**, the great hero of wartime government? Or would it be the Labour Party, led by **Clement Attlee**, a quiet and almost unknown politician? The policies which the Conservatives and Labour put forward during the election campaign were very different. The people clearly preferred what the Labour Party was saying should be done. The result of the election was a landslide victory for the Labour Party. Labour ended up with 393 seats in the House of Commons, the Conservatives 213 and the Liberals 12.

Source D

The nation faces a tremendous overhaul, a great programme of modernisation and re-equipment of its homes, its factories and machinery, its schools, its social services.
All Parties say so – the Labour Party means it.
The Labour party will put the community first and the interest's of private business after.

▲ From *Let us face the future*, the Labour Party manifesto.

Source E

The men and women of this country are asking what kind of life awaits them in peace.
They need good homes, food, clothing, employment and help for accidents, sickness and old age.
For their children they need a good education.

▲ From an election speech given by Clement Attlee on the radio as part of the 1945 election campaign.

Source F

I must tell you that a socialist policy is opposed to British ideas of freedom.
There is to be one State, to which all are to be obedient.
This state, once in power, will tell everyone where they are to work, what they are to work at, where they may go and what they may say.
No socialist system can be established without a political police.
They would have to fall back on some form of Gestapo.

▲ From an election speech given by Winston Churchill on the radio as part of the 1945 election campaign.

QUESTIONS

1. Study Sources A–F.
   How did **a** The Labour Party and **b** the Conservative Party try to persuade people to vote for them?

2. Is there enough evidence here to explain why the Labour Party won the 1945 election?

6.11 How did the Labour government begin rebuilding Britain?

There was much for the new Labour government to do to make Britain a prosperous peacetime country. They faced many problems. These were made worse by:

- a wheat shortage which meant bread had to be rationed.
- a terrible winter in 1947 which hit industrial production.

Nevertheless, the government pressed ahead with its reforms.

Source A

We now have to win the peace. It will take time to replace the wealth wasted in the war.

▲ Clement Attlee, speaking in the House of Commons after winning the 1945 general election.

Source B

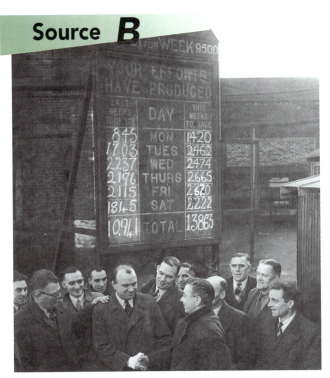

▲ These miners are congratulating themselves on record production at the end of 1946.

Nationalization

Parliament passed laws which nationalized key industries:

- in 1946, the **Bank of England**, **air transport** and **radio**
- in 1947, **roads**, **railways** and **ports**
- in 1947, **electricity** and **gas**
- in 1947, **coal**
- in 1948, **iron** and **steel**.

The idea behind nationalization was that important industries should be run by the state for the good of all the people.

The welfare state

The **Beveridge Report** (page 156) stated that the five 'giant evils' of '**Want**, **Disease**, **Ignorance**, **Squalor** and **Idleness**' had to be dealt with before Britain could provide its people with a good quality of life.

The new Labour government was determined to act on the Beveridge Report and set up a welfare state which would care for people 'from the cradle to the grave'.

- 1946: The **New Towns Act** said that twelve new towns were to be built.
- 1946: The **National Insurance Act** set up a single scheme to cope with everyone's needs, from unemployment benefit to a funeral grant.
- 1946: The **Industrial Injuries Act** insured workers against loss of earnings if they were injured, disabled or killed at work.
- 1946: The **National Health Service Act** gave free medical, dental and eye treatment to all families.

Source C

It was fantastic.
My mother and dad were the first at the dentist. Instead of having just a few teeth out, they had the complete set out and free dentures.
Thought it was wonderful. My sister had had school supply spectacles for ages. As soon as the NHS started she was there at the optician.
Marvellous, NHS spectacles, you know, some style about them.

▲ Clare Bond remembers in 1985 what it was like for her family in Leeds when the National Health Service was introduced.

Source D

◀ This cartoon, published in *Punch* in 1945 was called 'Putting the cart before the horse'.

▼ The percentage of Britain's income used to pay for health, education, housing and other social services, 1900–80

SUMMARY

▶ **1942** The Beveridge Report recommended measures to be taken against want, ignorance, squalor, disease and idleness.

▶ **1944** Education Act set up system of free primary and secondary education for all children.

▶ **1944** The first 'pre-fab' houses built.

▶ **1945** Election of Labour government.

▶ **1946** New Towns Act.

▶ **1946** National Insurance Act; Industrial Injuries Act; National Health Service Act.

▶ **1946** Nationalization of air transport, radio and the Bank of England.

▶ **1947** Nationalization of roads, railways, ports, gas, electricity and coal.

▶ **1948** Nationalization of iron and steel industries.

Early problems
- People who had earlier not been able to afford to see doctors and dentists began to demand treatment on the National Health Service (NHS).
- The government tried to control spending, but long waiting lists began to build up.

However, despite the problems at its beginning, most people supported the NHS and few wanted to return to the 'old' system.

A whole new era of state care, concern and protection was about to begin.

QUESTIONS

1 What is meant by 'nationalization' of industry? Why did the Labour Government want to nationalize key industries?

2 What is meant by a welfare state? How did the Labour Goverenment set about creating a welfare state in Britain?

6.12 Exercise

1 Read section 6.2.

Date	Reform	Who was helped?

  a Draw a table like the one above to show the effects of Liberal reforms, 1906–14.
  b Why did the Liberal Party introduce these reforms?

2 Look back at section 6.5. Now read the following opinions:

Women only gained the vote in 1918 because of the ways in which they worked for their country during the First World War.

Adapted from Robert Rayner, Nineteenth Century England, 1931.

It is often said that 'the war gave women the vote'. It did nothing of the kind. It just speeded up something that was going to happen in any case.

Adapted from Roger Fulford, Votes for Women, 1957.

Explain which opinion you think is correct. Try to find evidence to support your answer.

3 In 1948 Aneurin Bevan (the Labour Minister who set up the National Health Service after the War) said this about the Means Test of the 1930s:

The Means Test. . . . is why no amount of persuasion can take away. . . . a deep hatred for the Tory (Conservative) party. So far as I am concerned, they are lower than vermin.

  a What was the Means Test?
  b Why did the government introduce the Means Test?

4 Read these two views:

There was a great upheaval between 1946 and 1948. As a result of this an entirely new service was introduced.

Adapted from Patrick Benner, The Early Years of the National Health Service, 1989.

The setting up of the welfare state came at the end of years of reform which were gradually building up.

Adapted from Michael Rawcliffe, The Welfare State, 1990.

Which view do you agree with and why? Look back at sections 6.2, 6.9 and 6.11. Remember to give hard evidence which supports why you agree with one view and disagree with the other.

THE SECOND WORLD WAR 1939–45

In 1939, Hitler invaded Poland. Britain and France declared war on Germany and fighting began again in western Europe. By 1941, Germany controlled most of Europe. Only Britain was left to fight Hitler. Then Germany invaded the USSR, which began fighting on the side of the Allies. The Japanese attack on the American base at Pearl Harbor in 1941 brought the USA into the war. The retreat of the Axis powers (Germany, Italy and Japan) from mid-1942 was long and determined. Allied victory finally came in 1945.

7.1 What was the war like in the early years?

Blitzkrieg

On 1 September 1939, Hitler's troops invaded Poland. They used a new technique called **blitzkrieg**. Blitzkrieg means 'lightning war'. First the dive bombers attacked; then the steel-plated tanks from the Panzer division; and finally soldiers on foot. By the end of the month, Poland had surrendered.

Phoney war

Many people in Britain thought that, as soon as war was declared, German bombers would come and destroy their cities. The government issued gas masks to everyone and sent the children away to the countryside so as to keep them safe. The sea defences were made stronger in case Germany invaded by sea. But nothing happened.

People began calling this the 'phoney war' – the war with no fighting.

> **Source A**
>
> The wicked Poles, Hitler said, were treating their German citizens in the most outrageous way. . . . He pretended that German Poles had been killed by the Polish authorities so that he could 'prove to the world' that the Poles had started the war.
>
> ▲ Adapted from R Musman, *Hitler and Mussolini*, 1968.

Battle of the River Plate

There was, however, fighting at sea. On the first day of the war, German submarines sank the British passenger ship *Athenia*. A short time later, German ships sank the British battleship *Royal Oak*. The Battle of the River Plate was one of the first actual sea battles. A New Zealand ship, HMNZS *Achilles*, played an important part in defeating the German battleship *Admiral Graf Spee*.

Winston Churchill

The 'phoney war' ended in April 1940 when German troops occupied Norway and Denmark. Neville Chamberlain, the British Prime Minister, resigned. He was replaced by **Winston Churchill**.

Operation Yellow and the Maginot Line

In May 1940, Hitler started Operaton Yellow. German troops quickly over-ran Holland, Belgium and Luxembourg. German troops simply went round the end of the French defences – the Maginot Line – and attacked France through the Ardennes.

The British Expeditionary Force (BEF)

At the beginning of the war, the BEF crossed to France to help if Germany attacked. But German troops attacked so quickly that British and French soldiers were forced to retreat westwards to the Channel coast. By 21 May 1940, 350,000 British and French soldiers were trapped by the German army in the French port of Dunkirk.

Source B

Reports of 'merciless bombing' by the Germans and 'the hell of Dunkirk' were ridiculous.
I walked along the beaches oand never saw a corpse. There was very little shelling.

▲ Extract from a statement made in 1942 by a British general in command of soldiers at Dunkirk.

Source C

◀ A contemporary painting by Charles Cundall, showing troops being rescued from the beaches of Dunkirk.

Dunkirk and Operation Dynamo

To rescue the troops, the British government launched Operation Dynamo. The navy's large ships could not get close enough to the beaches around Dunkirk. So all sorts of small boats – including fishing boats, sailing dinghies and pleasure steamers – sailed across the Channel to take the British and French soldiers off the beaches. Over 800 small boats helped ferry 338,226 soldiers to Royal Navy ships waiting in deeper water.

The German air force (called the **Luftwaffe**) sank 240 small boats, and 68,000 men were killed in Operation Dynamo. The British left 120,000 vehicles, 90,000 rifles and 2,300 guns on the beaches of northern France. The 'Miracle of Dunkirk' was a great moment in British history, and in reality was a tremendous defeat.

▲ The German conquest of western Europe by July 1940.

Vichy and General Pétain

After Dunkirk the Germans quickly defeated France. Hitler allowed southern France to govern itself from the town of Vichy. He hoped this would stop the French colonies and navy from supporting Britain. The Vichy government was led by General Pétain, but it was really controlled by the Germans.

Source D

We shall defend our island, whatever the cost may be. We shall fight them on the beaches, we shall fight on the landing grounds, we shall fight in the fields and in the streets, we shall fight in the hills; we shall never surrender.

▲ From a speech to the House of Commons, made by Winston Churchill on 4 June 1940.

QUESTIONS

1. Read Source A on page 163. Why do you think that Hitler acted in the way described? Do you think he would have been believed
   a in Germany
   b in Britain?
2. Why did some people refer to the early part of the war as the 'phoney war'?
3. Why have some historians referred to the Dunkirk evacuation as 'one of the great moments in British history'. In your answer explain also the importance of the Dunkirk evacuation in the story of the war.

Operation Sealion and the Battle of Britain

Operation Sealion was Hitler's plan for invading Britain. First he had to defeat the RAF (Royal Airforce). In July 1940, the **Luftwaffe** began attacking RAF bases, aircraft factories and radar installations in Britain. During the summer, the RAF and the Luftwaffe fought the Battle of Britain in the skies over England. In September, Hitler called off Operation Sealion: he did not realize how near the RAF were to defeat and thought that the Luftwaffe could not succeed.

The Blitz

Instead, from September 1940 to May 1941, German bombers attacked British cities. They bombed London; they bombed ports like Liverpool and Hull, and cities like Coventry. They killed over 40,000 people and made more than 2 million people homeless in what was called 'The Blitz'.

The USSR enters

Since the fall of France in 1940, Britain and the Commonwealth had stood alone against Hitler. Then they found an ally when, in June 1941, Hitler launched an attack on the USSR. By November, German troops were close to Moscow. The Soviet troops retreated, burning everything they could not carry with them. This is called a **scorched earth** policy. Soon the Germans were short of supplies as they faced the terrible Soviet winter. So the German advance ground to a halt.

Source E

▲ 'All behind you, Winston', a British cartoon by David Low, dated 14 May 1940.

Source F

Never in the field of human conflict was so much owed by so many to so few.

▲ Winston Churchill commenting in the autumn of 1940 on the important role played by British pilots in preventing a German invasion.

SUMMARY

▶ **Sept 1939** Germany invaded Poland.

▶ **April 1940** Germany invaded Norway and Denmark.

▶ **May 1940** Germany invaded Holland, Belgium, Luxembourg and France. British troops rescued from Dunkirk.

▶ **Aug-Sept 1940** Battle of Britain.

▶ **Sept 1940 - May 1941** The Blitz.

▶ **June 1941** Germany invaded the USSR.

7.2 How important was the fighting in North Africa?

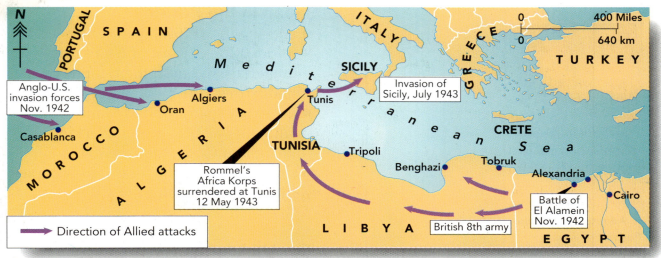

▲ The war in North Africa.

Source A

Never in the field of human conflict have so many surrendered to so few.

▲ A humorous comment made in 1940 after the Allies defeated Mussolini's forces in North Africa.

Rommel

In North Africa, British troops captured Eritrea, Somaliland and Abyssinia. Hitler was afraid that the Allies would soon hold all the coast of North Africa. He therefore sent out one of his top generals, Erwin Rommel, with fresh German troops. Rommel had instructions to capture the Suez Canal (Britain's link with India) and the Middle East oil fields. By July 1942, Rommel had advanced far into Egypt and was threatening the Suez Canal.

Montgomery

The British built up their force in North Africa. In October 1942, General Montgomery started a massive counter-attack. The British were victorious at the **Battle of El Alamein**.

QUESTIONS

1. Source A is about the Allies' victory in North Africa. It also has a hidden meaning. What is it?
2. Why was Montgomery's victory at El Alamein in October 1942 so important to Britain's war effort?

Operation Torch

The American General Eisenhower headed Operation Torch. In November 1942, 100,000 British and American troops landed in Morocco and Algeria. Now Rommel's forces were under attack from both the east and the west. In May 1943, nearly a quarter of a million German soldiers surrendered to the Allies at Tunis. North Africa was now under Allied control. Allied troops could cross the Mediterranean and begin attacking Italy.

7.3 Why did war break out in the Pacific in 1941?

Source A

Japan waited until the Allies in Europe were so weak that they could not interfere in Asia.
Then Japan decided to deal with the USA.

▲ Adapted from Hakome Mielche, *Portrait of Japan*.

Source B

▲ The Japanese attack on 7 December 1941 on the American naval base at Pearl Harbor.

Source C

We have heard from many sources that the Japanese military forces planned, in the event of trouble from the USA, to attempt a surprise mass attack on Pearl Harbor.

◀ Adapted from a report sent home by the American Ambassador in Tokyo in January 1941.

Japan in the Pacific
- During the 1930s, Japan controlled the production of most of Asia's raw materials and used them for its own industries.
- In 1931, Japan invaded Manchuria, and after 1937, it began attacking mainland China (see page 34).
- In July 1941, Japanese troops occupied the former French colony of Indo-China.

The USA in the Pacific
- The USA traded in the Pacific and felt threatened by Japanese strength.
- In 1940, the USA limited its export of oil to Japan.
- In 1941, the USA, Britain and France stopped exporting raw materials to Japan.

Japan and the USA
The Japanese government knew that its oil reserves would last for just two more years. It had to persuade the Allies to drop their trade ban – by force if necessary. Japan and the USA held talks all through the summer and autumn of 1941, but they could not reach agreement. The Japanese decided to try force. They were going to try to defeat the American Pacific Fleet. Then perhaps they could capture the Dutch East Indies, with its supply of oil, and British Malaya, with its supply of rubber.

The attack on Pearl Harbor

At 8 a.m. on Sunday, 7 December 1941, Japanese aircraft swept down on the American base at Pearl Harbor, Hawaii. The attack killed 2,400 Americans, sank 8 battleships and damaged or destroyed 350 planes. This brought America into the war on the side of the Allies and the American fleet was quickly rebuilt.

The fall of Singapore

The Japanese attacked American and British colonies in Asia. By May 1942, they had captured Hong Kong, Guam, Wake, Malaya, the Dutch East Indies, Burma, the Philippines, New Guinea and Singapore. When the Japanese took Singapore, they captured 80,000 British troops. It was Britain's worst defeat in the war.

By mid-1942, Japan controlled most of South-East Asia and was beginning to threaten Australia.

Source D

PEARL HARBOR 'COULD HAVE BEEN AVOIDED'

Japan's entry into the Second World War could have been avoided according to an unpublished report by Britain's Ambassador in Japan at the time. The report says that the attack on Pearl Harbor was not inevitable and could have been prevented by negotiation.

But the British Prime Minister, Winston Churchill, was angry about this report and ordered that it should be destroyed. Churchill said, 'It was a blessing that Japan attacked the United States and thus brought America wholeheartedly into the war.' However, one copy of the report has survived and was recently found by the Ambassador's son.

The report is contained in a new book 'Betrayal at Pearl Harbor' by a British writer and an Australian war-time code-breaker. In it they claim that Churchill had information about the attack on Pearl Harbor, but kept it from the Americans. The two writers state that the British had been breaking the Japanese naval code for years.

▲ Adapted from an article in the British newspaper, *The Guardian*, on 7 December 1992.

◄ The Japanese conquest of South-East Asia.

QUESTIONS

1. Why do you think Japan attacked Pearl Harbor?
2. Do you think that the attack was a surprise to the Americans?
3. How convincing do you find the newspaper extract in Source D?

7.4 What was it like for civilians during the war?

Bombing
Aircraft design had improved since 1918. Planes could now fly long distances to bomb enemy cities. For the first time, thousands of civilians were in real danger. London, for example, was bombed every day for 75 days in the autumn of 1940 (see page 166). From 1942, every German city with more than 100,000 people could be reached by Allied bombers.

Source A

North Evacuees Ask for Chips and Beer

EVACUATED CHILDREN IN THE NORTH RECEPTION AREAS ARE ASKING FOR FISH AND CHIPS, AND BEER OR STOUT.

This declaration was made at the annual meeting in Newcastle yesterday of the Newcastle, Gateshead and district Band of Hope Union by Mr Frank J. Taylor, organising secretary.

Lady Trevelyn, President of the Union, who presided, stated that she was shocked to hear a story concerning an evacuated child in the South of England who, on arrival at the billet, was asked by the hostess: 'Would you like some biscuits dear?'. 'Biscuits?' the boy replied. 'What I want is beer and chips. That's what I get at home.'

▲ An extract from the *Newcastle Evening Chronicle* in 1940.

Blackout
In Britain, the government introduced a blackout so that cities could not be spotted by German bombers. Special curtains stopped light streaming out of windows; street lights were dimmed and so were the lights on buses, lorries and cars.

Anderson shelters
The British government issued people with **Anderson shelters** made from corrugated iron. People put them up in their gardens and sheltered in them when the bombs fell.

Evacuation
In August 1939, thousands of children were sent away from the cities to live with families in the countryside. This was to keep them safe from harm.

Food shortages
In countries occupied by the Germans and Japanese, food was taken from civilians for the soldiers. Some cities, like Leningrad in the USSR, were under siege for many months. This meant that thousands of people died because supplies could not get in. Britain had difficulties getting food from abroad, so the government introduced **rationing**.

Source B

◄ St Paul's cathedral still standing after the bombing of the city of London, October 1940.

Nazi-occupied Europe

The Nazis took raw materials, food supplies, art treasures and even workers back to Germany. But Hitler regarded the people of western Europe as Aryans (see page 92). This meant that they got better treatment from the Nazis than the people of eastern Europe. Hitler regarded people from eastern Europe as **Untermenshen** (subhuman), and the Nazis treated them with great harshness.

Japanese-occupied Asia

In the Far East, the Japanese treated civilians cruelly. This was particularly so if they were Chinese, as in Malaya.

Resistance movements

- From 1940 the **British Special Operations Executive** (**SOE**) sent agents behind enemy lines to help people who were resisting the German occupying forces.
- The French Resistance (the **Maquis**) ran escape routes for allied airmen who had been shot down over enemy territory.
- In the USSR, **partisans** blew up railway bridges and roads.
- In Czechoslovakia, partisans murdered the SS Lieutenant **Reinhard Heydrich**. In retaliation the Nazis wiped out the village of **Lidice**. They shot all 192 men, sent all 82 children to gas chambers and sent all women to concentration camps. Then they burned the village to the ground.

The role of women

As in the First World War, women took over men's jobs in factories and farms, offices and workshops. Thousands also worked at home and overseas as nurses and in the women's units attached to the army, navy and airforce, and the intelligence and supply forces.

Source C

I swear to assist the Red Army by all possible means. I swear that I would rather die in a terrible battle than surrender myself, my family or the Soviet people to Nazi rule.

▲ An oath taken by Soviet partisans.

Source D

▲ German soldiers hanging Soviet civilians.

QUESTIONS

1. Make a list of all the ways in which the civilian people were affected by the war.
2. Which of these do you think would have caused civilians the most hardship?

7.5 The Holocaust

Source A

Then the prison guards opened the doors of the gas chamber and threw the children in.
I said 'I've never seen anything like. It's absolutely terrible.'
My guide said, 'You get used to anything after a while.'

▲ An SS officer describing his reaction to being shown how the Jews were gassed. He was speaking in a television programme in the 1960s.

The Final Solution

Hitler hated the Jews. He believed that the Aryan race was supreme (see page 92). In 1941, the Nazis decided that the Final Solution to the Jewish problem was to kill all the Jews in Europe.

The Holocaust

Between 1941 and 1945, the Nazis killed around six million Jews. Later, this mass killing was called the Holocaust.

The death camps

Most Jews died in specially built death camps run by the SS (see page 95). One of these camps was **Auschwitz** in Poland. Death camps were usually built beside railway lines. This made it easier for the Nazis to transport Jews there. Once in the camps, the Jews were divided into those who were fit to work and those who were not. Those who were not fit to work, like old people, pregnant women and children, were gassed at once. The Jews who could work survived for as long as they were fit. Some Jews were used for medical experiments.

▼ Belsen concentration camp. A picture taken in 1945 when the Allies liberated Germany.

Source B

Gas

The Nazis drove the Jews into huge rooms. Then they sealed the rooms and released Cyclon B gas crystals. When all the Jews were dead, the Nazis took out their gold fillings, shaved off their hair and collected their glasses. Then they burned the bodies or buried them together in huge graves.

Source C

◀ 'Not all guilty', a David Low cartoon, dated 19 April 1945.

Source D

If the Jewish Question is talked about, do not discuss a Final Solution. You can mention that the Jews are being taken to labour camps, but that is all.

▲ From instructions issued on Hitler's command to all Nazi government members, 11 July 1943.

Propaganda

Hitler did not want the German people to know about the death camps. Some people had complained when he had ordered the gassing of 90,000 elderly and handicapped people, and he did not want any trouble over the Jews. He had films made showing the Jews working in good conditions in labour camps.

Finding out

When news of the death camps leaked out, many Germans simply did not believe it. The Allies knew, in 1942, that Jews were being killed. But it was not until 1944 that they knew about places like Auschwitz and the gas chambers. As the Allied armies **liberated** central Europe, they reached the death camps at places like Belsen and Dachau. Gradually they discovered the full horror of the Holocaust.

Source E

So far three million have died. It is the greatest mass killing in recorded history: and it goes on daily, hourly, as regularly as the ticking of your watch. Allied troops don't believe it.

◀ Arthur Koestler, an American journalist, writing in the *New York Times* in January 1944.

QUESTIONS

1. Running the death camps must have been an appalling experience. Why, then, did the SS not refuse to do it?
2. Why did the German people not stop the Nazis from killing the Jews?
3. 'The Nazis must have been ashamed of what was happening in the death camps or they would not have issued the instructions in Source D.' Do you agree with this comment or not?
4. Read Source E. Why do you think the Allied troops did not believe what Arthur Koestler reported?

7.6 How did the Allies defeat Hitler?

The Battle of Stalingrad
By mid-September 1942, the German armies had reached Stalingrad, deep inside the USSR. Both sides fought hard for the city; thousands died. The German commander, **von Paulus**, finally surrendered to the Soviet troops in January 1943.

The siege of Leningrad
Over one million Soviet people died during the siege of Leningrad. Most of them were ordinary men, women and children. They died from starvation because the Germans surrounded the city and would not let in any food.

Germany's retreat fron the USSR
Finally, the Germans gave up the seige of Leningrad. In January 1944, they began the long retreat from the USSR. By the end of 1944, Soviet troops were invading Germany.

Italy
On 9 July 1943, Allied forces landed in Sicily. Then they pushed northwards through Italy and took Rome. In April 1945, the Allies finally took control of the whole of Italy.

The importance of the USA
The USA's entry into the war was vital to the defeat of Hitler. The USA provided fresh troops, ships, planes and tanks in huge numbers.

Operation Overlord
This was the Allies' plan to invade Europe. By June 1944, the Supreme Commander, **General Eisenhower**, had assembled 100,000 men and 4,000 landing craft in southern England. On 6 June 1944 (**D-Day**), Allied troops began landing on the Normandy coast of France. Then they began fighting their way inland.

Source A

> Soviet soldiers had tremendous experience in hand-to-hand fighting. They knew every drain pipe, every manhole cover, every shell-hole and crater.
> Nothing short of a direct hit would knock them out.

▲ A Soviet general's description of the stubborn resistance put up by Soviet troops at Stalingrad in 1943.

▼ German transport bogged down in the Russian snow, winter of 1942.

Source B

Arnhem

Things did not always go smoothly. At Arnhem in Holland, the Allies tried to capture a bridge over the river Rhine. This bridge would have allowed them to advance into Germany. But they failed to capture the bridge, and almost all of the 10,000 men who parachuted in were killed.

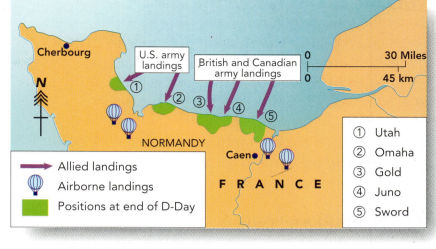

▲ The Allied landings on Normandy, 6 June 1944.

The Germans fought back in southern Belgium at the **Battle of the Bulge**. But they were not successful for long.

Saturation bombing

The RAF and USAF carried out massive bombing raids on German cities like **Dresden**. The raids destroyed a lot of German industry and made the German people feel desperate.

Soviet advances

Soviet troops liberated Poland, Romania, Bulgaria and Yugoslavia. Then they reached the outskirts of Berlin. On 25 April 1945, British and American troops joined up with Soviet troops. The Allies had captured Berlin.

Hitler's suicide

Five days later, Hitler killed himself in his bunker deep under Berlin.

Admiral Dönitz took over and surrendered to the Allies on 7 May 1945.

The war in the west was over.

▲ A cartoon showing Churchill thinking while the army, navy and airforce wait for the date of D-Day.

Why did Germany lose the war?
- In 1940 the British refused to accept Hitler's offers to make peace. After the fall of France in 1940, Britain and the Empire fought on alone until the USA and USSR entered the war in 1941.
- The invasion of the USSR was a disaster for Germany.
- The entry of the USA into the war brought fresh troops and equipment on to the Allies' side.
- Allied forces were stronger in the air and at sea.

The Nuremberg trials
The Allies decided to put leading Nazis on trial. This was to show the world that what the Nazis had done during the war was wrong. However, this raised some difficult moral questions. Soviet troops had treated the Polish people very cruelly before the USSR entered the war on the Allies' side. Some people said, too, that the Allies could hardly accuse the Germans of crimes against humanity, when they killed over half a million innocent civilians in their bombing raids over Germany.

Although, of course, there was nothing to compare with the Nazi slaughter of the Jews in the death camps.

Who was on trial?
The Allies put 21 leading Nazis on trial at Nuremberg in November 1945. **Herman Goering**, **Rudolph Hess** and **Admiral Dönitz** were some of the Nazis who were charged with war crimes. Altogether, three Nazis were found not guilty, seven were put in prison and eleven were sentenced to death. Goering committed suicide before his sentence could be carried out.

Source D
Canada provided nearly a quarter of the air crews under British command. Canadian airmen bombed, fought, photographed and ferried all over the globe except the Japanese and Soviet sector. They dropped parachute troops, dive-bombed, provided air cover and sank submarines.

▲ J. Bartlet Brebner, *Canada: A Modern History*, 1961.

QUESTIONS
1. Draw a timeline setting out the months from July 1943 to May 1945. Record on it the main events of the war, leading up to Germany's surrender in 1945.
2. How does Source D help explain why Germany lost the war?
3. a Why do you think that the allies put leading Nazis on trial?
   b Do you agree that they were right in doing so?

7.7 How was Japan defeated?

By early 1942, the Japanese had captured most of their targets in East Asia. But then the Allies struck back.

Sea battles
In May 1942, the USA navy sank two Japanese aircraft carriers at the **Battle of the Coral Sea**. In June the USA navy sank four Japanese aircraft carriers at the **Battle of Midway**.

Island hopping
'Island hopping' was the American plan for capturing the Pacific. Once the USA captured an important island, US marines built airfields there to support their next attack. The Americans' first success was in August 1942 at **Guadalcanal** in the Solomon Islands. During 1943 and 1944, the Americans captured one Pacific island after another. By February 1945, they had retaken the Philippines.

Problems for the Allies
Allied forces in the Pacific had to cope with the difficulties of **jungle warfare**. Disease from the hot, humid conditions and bad food was frequent.

Japanese soldiers considered surrender to be dishonourable and would fight to the death or commit suicide rather than surrender. This made them difficult to defeat, and casualties were very high.

Bombing and blockading
In 1944, the USAF gained control of the skies over Japan, and began bombing Japanese cities. In March 1945, 80,000 Japanese people died when the Allies dropped **incendiary** bombs on Tokyo. This was more than had died in Britain during the Blitz.

The US navy **blockaded** Japanese ports and so stopped food getting into Japan. Thousands of people were close to starvation.

Source A

▶ US battleship takes on ammunition from a landing ship before firing a further bombardment to aid US ground forces taking Okinawa, June 1945.

Source B

▲ The ruins of Hiroshima after the atomic bomb.

Source C

Dropping the atomic bomb was no 'great decision'.
It was used in the war, and there were more people killed by the fire bombs in Tokyo than there were by the dropping of the atom bombs.
It was merely another powerful weapon in the arsenal of righteousness. The dropping of the two bombs stopped the war and saved millions of lives.

▲ President Truman, addressing students at Columbia University in the USA, in 1959.

Okinawa
In June 1945, the Americans captured the island of Okinawa, 400 miles south of Japan. During the US attack, 2,000 Japanese **kamikaze** pilots died when they deliberately crashed their planes on to American ships. They sank 30 US warships in the process.

Burma
The Japanese were heavily defeated in Burma by the British forces under **General Wingate**.

The atomic bombs and the end of the war
The US President, **Harry S. Truman**, decided to make the Japanese surrender unconditionally. But he had to work out how to invade Japan without ending up with huge numbers of Allied casualties. American scientists gave him the answer.

The Potsdam Declaration
At the Potsdam Conference in July 1945, the Americans told their Allies that they had made, and were ready to use, the **atomic bomb**. On 26 July, the Allies issued the **Potsdam Declaration**. This asked the Japanese to surrender. If they did not, Japan would face 'inevitable and complete destruction' – an atomic bomb would be dropped on Japan. But the Japanese refused to surrender.

Hiroshima
On 6 August 1945, an American bomber, the *Enola Gay*, arrived over the Japanese city of Hiroshima. It dropped just one bomb, which exploded over the city. It destroyed Hiroshima and killed 80,000 people. Thousands more died later from **radiation sickness**.

Nagasaki

Three days later, the Americans dropped another atomic bomb on the Japanese city of Nagasaki.

Surrender

On 14 August 1945, the Japanese government surrendered to the Allies. A number of officers, including the War Minister, General Anami, committed suicide. They were ashamed of their failure to lead Japan to victory. **General Douglas MacArthur** of the USA became Supreme Commander for the Allied Powers for the Occupation and Control of Japan. The Allies governed Japan until 1952.

Over 1 million Japanese soldiers and 600,000 ordinary Japanese men, women and children died in the fighting during the Second World War.

Source D

On 6 August an actress named Midori Naka was in Hiroshima. She was very famous in Japan. The house collapsed around her when the bomb exploded. Before she died on 24 August doctors made careful notes of her sufferings. One doctor noted, 'Almost nothing remained of her beauty'. In the days that followed, her black hair began to fall out..
On 23 August 12 or 13 purple patches, each as big as a pigeon's egg, appeared on her body. A few hours later she was dead.

▲ Description of one death after the bombing of Hiroshima.

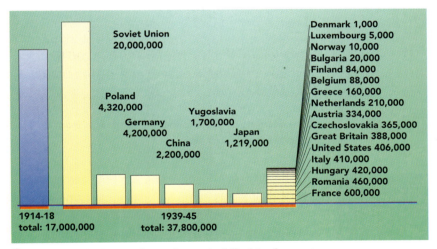

▲ Estimate of the number of people killed in the Second World War.

SUMMARY

- **Dec 1941** Japan attacked Pearl Harbor.
- **Early 1942** Japanese victories throughout Pacific.
- **Mid 1942** Battles of Coral Sea and Midway Island. Americans adopted a policy of 'island hopping'. Fierce Japanese defence of conquered territory.
- **July 1945** Potsdam Declaration.
- **August 1945** Bombing of Hiroshima and Nagasaki.

QUESTIONS

1. Why did the Allies find it so hard to defeat the Japanese?
2. President Truman described the dropping of the atomic bomb on Hiroshima as 'the greatest thing in history'. What do you think he meant?
3. 'The dropping of an atomic bomb on a city full of innocent women and children can never be justified.' Explain whether you agree or disagree with this statement.

7.8 Exercise: The Battle of Stalingrad

Source 1

▲ A Soviet cartoon from the Second World War, showing Hitler ordering his troops to their death.

Source 2

▲ A cartoon by David Low from the *Evening Standard*, the London newspaper, published in November 1942.

Source 3

Every day Rodimstev's men repel twelve to fifteen enemy attacks of tanks and infantry, supported by artillery and aircraft. These soldiers know in their heads and in their hearts that no further retreat is possible. In one day alone they destroyed 2000 Nazis, 18 tanks and 30 vehicles.

▲ Extract fron the Soviet newspaper *Red Star* on 1 October 1942.

Source 4

In April 1942 Hitler ordered his troops to smash what was left of the Soviet armies. Hitler would not think of taking a step backwards – no matter what the cost. The Nazis launched a savage attack on Stalingrad. Stalin ordered his troops to do whatever was needed to defend the city. Hitler ordered General von Paulus never to surrender. Massive numbers on both sides were killed. On 31 January 1943 Von Paulus disobeyed Hitler's orders and surrendered his 100,000 men.

▲ An account of the Stalingrad campaign from a modern school textbook.

1. Take Sources 1, 2 and 3 one at a time and explain what they tell us about the Stalingrad campaign.

2. Would you have a different picture of the Stalingrad campaign if you had only read Source 4?

3. Source 2 was published in a British newspaper on 2 November 1942. Do you think that the cartoonist would really have known what was going on in the Soviet Union at the time?

4. a Do you think Source 3 can be treated as a reliable source? Give reasons with your answer.
   b How valuable is this source to a historian?

5. Some historians have called Hitler's invasion of the Soviet Union a mistake. Do you agree? Use these four sources and your own knowledge to answer the question.

The Battle of Britain

Source 1

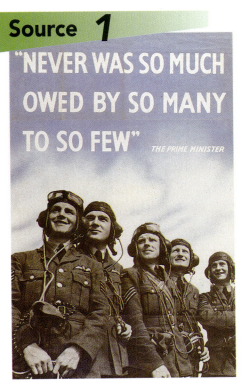

▲ A British poster shortly after the Battle of Britain.

Source 2

No German invasion (of Britain) could succeed until the Germans controlled the skies. Therefore, during August 1940, the Luftwaffe began attacks on RAF airfields in southern England. The resulting aerial battle, the 'Battle of Britain', saw a desperate contest between the Luftwaffe and RAF fighter squadrons. A crucial German error, was to divert effort to air raids on British cities, the Blitz. . . . German invasion plans were delayed in October 1940 and abandoned in January 1941.

▲ Lawrence Butler and Harriet Jones, *Britain in the Twentieth Century: A Documentary Reader, Volume II, 1939-70*, 1995.

Source 3

Without Churchill Britain would have fallen. No other statesman would have inspired the nation to fight on when all seemed lost. Alone, Winston Churchill saved Western civilization from destruction at the hands of the Nazis.

▲ Richard Lamb, *Churchill as War Leader: Right or Wrong?* 1991.

Source 4

Fighters and Bombers lost by the Luftwaffe in the Battle of Britain

Date	Official British figures	Official German figures	Figure agreed after the war
8–23 Aug	755	213	403
24 Aug – 6 Sept	643	243	378
7–30 Sept	846	243	435
Total	2,244	699	1,216

Source 5

Undoubtedly 1940 was Churchill's finest hour. But it is likely that our image of that year owes much to the fact that Churchill published his version of the story before anyone else. . . what happened was what Churchill said had happened. And woe betide (those) who have the nerve to read the papers and then ask awkward questions.

▲ David Reynolds, *Churchill in 1940: The Worst and Finest Hour*, 1993.

1. Why did the Battle of Britain take place?

2. How can the variations in the figures in Source 4 be explained?

3. Why was Source 1 published?

4. a How does Source 3 differ from Source 5 in explaining Churchill's actions in the events of 1940?
   b Why do historians' views of the past change?

5. Look back through Chapter 7. What were a the **short-term** and
   b the **long-term** results of the Battle of Britain?

THE COLD WAR

Source A

◀ This poster was published in France after the war. It gives the French view of the USSR's control of eastern Europe.

From allies to enemies

During the Second World War, the USA and the USSR fought together as allies. When the war ended, the USA and USSR emerged as superpowers. They became bitter enemies in a struggle called the Cold War.

The USA and USSR never fought a direct 'hot war' against each other. But they carried out a dangerous war of words which sometimes spilled over into fighting on a limited scale. Both sides built up huge stockpiles of weapons. It seemed to many people that a third world war was not far away.

8.1 The origins of the Cold War

Fear

The Cold War was based on fear. The USA was afraid that the USSR would try to spread communism throughout the world. The USSR had been invaded by Germany in 1914 and 1941, and was afraid that western powers would try once more to overthrow communism, as they had done during the Russian Civil War.

▶ Joseph Stalin, speaking to a fellow communist, M. Djilas, at the time of the Yalta Conference in 1945.

Source B

Perhaps you think that, because we are allies of the English, we have forgotten who they are and who Churchill is. They find nothing sweeter than to trick their allies.

Capitalist and communist systems

The USA and USSR had different ideas about the importance of the state.

USA (capitalism)
- People owned property, businesses and industry.
- People made profits which they kept for themselves.
- People voted from among several political parties for the party they wanted to govern them.
- People voted for a President, who had to answer to the US Congress for what he did.

USSR (communist)
- All businesses and industries were owned by the state.
- Profits from businesses and industries went to the state.
- People voted in elections, but there was only one political party: the Communist Party.
- The Communist Party leader, **Joseph Stalin**, ruled as a dictator.

Did communism spread in Europe after the war?

The four great powers, Britain, France, the USA and the USSR, met at **Yalta** in February 1945 and at **Potsdam** in July 1945. They were trying to decide what should happen in Europe after Germany was defeated.

At Yalta the great powers agreed that the USSR should be allowed to influence eastern Europe. At Potsdam it was clear that the USSR wanted to control eastern Europe. By 1949, the USSR backed communist governments in Yugloslavia, Albania, Bulgaria, Poland, Romania, Czechoslovakia and Hungary.

What was the 'Iron Curtain'?

In March 1946, Winston Churchill made a speech in which he described what he thought was happening in eastern Europe. He talked about an 'Iron Curtain' falling down across Europe. He clearly thought that communism was cutting eastern Europe off from the rest of the world.

Source C

▲ This British cartoon, called 'Peep under the curtain', was published in the *Daily Mail* in March 1946.

Source D

A shadow has fallen across the scenes so lately lighted by Allied victory.
From the Baltic to the Adriatic, an iron curtain has descended across the continent.
Behind that line lie all the capitals of the ancient states of central and eastern Europe.
Their Communist Parties have been raised to power and are seeking dictatorial control.
This is certainly not the liberated Europe we fought to build up.
Nor is it one which contains the essentials of permanent peace.

▲ Part of a speech Winston Churchill made at Fulton, Missouri, in March 1946.

How did the USA react to the 'Iron Curtain'?

President Truman of the USA agreed with Churchill's speech about the 'Iron Curtain'. He set up the **Central Intelligence Agency** (CIA), which was to work secretly outside the USA. It supported people and governments which were against communism and pro-USA.

The Truman Doctrine

In 1947, President Truman made a speech in which he said that the USA would help people everywhere who were trying to keep their political freedom and who felt threatened by communism. This was called the **Truman Doctrine**. At the time, Truman was really warning the USSR not to take over any more of eastern Europe.

The Marshall Plan

Many American politicians believed that communism gained ground in countries where people were poor and struggling. The Marshall Plan aimed to give millions of American dollars to Europe. The USA hoped that, even if eastern Europe was 'lost' to communism, western European countries would use the money to make themselves strong.

Containment

The Marshall Plan was part of the USA's policy of **containment**. The USA tried to stop communism spreading beyond the countries in which it was already established. (See page 190.)

Cominform

The USSR reacted by setting up **Cominform**. This was an organization to co-ordinate the activities of the Communist Parties in eastern Europe.

SUMMARY

- The USA and USSR were allies during the Second World War.
- After 1945, the USSR supported communist states in eastern Europe.
- In 1946 Winston Churchill said that an 'Iron Curtain' had descended across Europe.
- The USA was afraid that Europe might become communist. The USSR was afraid the western powers wanted to destroy it.
- The Truman Doctrine stated that the USA would support any free country threatened by communism.
- The Marshall Plan gave $17m aid to western Europe.
- The USSR set up Cominform to co-ordinate activities of Communist Parties throughout Europe.

QUESTIONS

1. **a** Look at Source A and read Source B. Do they help you understand why the Cold War began?
   b Were there any other reasons for the Cold War starting?
2. What was **a** the 'Iron Curtain'? **b** the Truman Doctrine and **c** the Marshall Plan?

8.2 The Berlin crisis and the formation of NATO

▲ Germany and Berlin after the Second World War.

Zones of occupation

In 1945, after the defeat of Hitler, the Allies divided Germany into four zones of occupation. British, French, Soviet and American troops occupied one zone each. Berlin, the capital city of Germany, was in the Soviet zone. But Berlin itself was also divided into four zones.

Flashpoint Berlin!

The first crisis of the Cold War took place over Berlin. The three western powers had used Marshall Aid to rebuild their zones of Germany. And then, in 1948, they introduced one new currency, the **Deutschmark** into their zones.

The Soviets were afraid that the western powers were uniting to create a new Germany in the West which would threaten them and their zone. They were also angry that their zone did not qualify for Marshall Aid.

So on 28 June 1948, the Soviets closed the roads, canals and railways that linked the western zones of Berlin to the western zones of Germany. Britain, France, and the USA could not get any supplies into their zones in Berlin.

Would the western powers abandon Berlin?

If the western powers abandoned West Berlin, they would hand two million West Berliners over to communist rule. They would also lose a vital 'listening post' inside the communist world. But was West Berlin worth another war?

Source A

▲ A transport plane being unloaded at Gatow airport, Berlin, in September 1948. The lights of the jeep were needed because power, which came from the Soviet zone, had been cut off.

The Berlin airlift

There was a way to get supplies into West Berlin. The air corridors between West Germany and Berlin could not be blocked. The Americans and British had large enough transport planes to manage an airlift of food, fuel and medicines into West Berlin. If the Russians wanted to stop the airlift, they would have to fire the first shots.

For 318 days, between July 1948 and May 1949, the RAF and the US airforce flew 1.5 million tonnes of supplies into West Berlin. On 12 May 1949, the USSR admitted defeat and lifted the blockade. The western powers could once again reach their zones in Berlin.

Germany divided

In May 1949, the western powers merged their three zones into the **German Federal Republic** (West Germany), which included West Berlin. In October, the USSR set up its zone as the **German Democratic Republic** (East Germany).

NATO

The western powers set up an anti-communist military alliance, the **North Atlantic Treaty Organization** (NATO). In 1949, Belgium, Britain, Canada, Denmark, France, Iceland, Italy, the Netherlands, Norway, Portugal and the USA signed a treaty which said that an attack on any one of the NATO members would be regarded as an attack on them all. Turkey and Greece joined NATO in 1952, and the German Federal Republic in 1955.

The Warsaw Pact

The USSR set up its own military alliance. Albania, Bulgaria, Czechoslovakia, the German Democratic Republic, Hungary, Poland, Romania and the USSR formed the **Warsaw Pact** in May 1955.

▲ The European countries of NATO and the Warsaw Pact.

SUMMARY

▶ **1945** Germany, and Berlin, divided into four zones of occupation.

▶ **June 1948** The USSR closed all routes into the western powers' zones of Berlin.

▶ **July 1948** RAF and USAF began airlift of supplies to Berlin.

▶ **May 1949** Blockade ended by the USSR.

▶ **1949** German Federal Republic and German Democratic Republic established.

▶ **1949** NATO set up.

▶ **1955** Warsaw Pact set up.

Source B

The parties agree that an armed attack against one or more of them in Europe or North America shall be thought of as an attack against them all.
Each will take the action thought to be necessary, including the use of armed force.

▲ Adapted from the document setting up NATO and agreed by the twelve founder members.

QUESTIONS

1 For six years the Allies had been trying to defeat Germany. Why, then, did they try to keep the citizens of Berlin alive by airlifting supplies to them between July 1948 and May 1949?

2 a Why did the Allies form NATO in 1949?
  b How did the Soviets react?

8.2 THE BERLIN CRISIS AND THE FORMATION OF NATO

8.3 War in Korea 1950-53

The Cold War spreads to China
There was a long civil war in China. The USSR backed the communist **Mao Zedong**, and the USA backed **Chiang Kai-shek** and his forces. Finally, in 1949, communist troops took control of mainland China. Chiang Kai-shek fled to **Taiwan**, an offshore island.

The Cold War spreads to Korea
In 1948, there were two separate governments in Korea. The USSR supported the communist leader **Kim Il Sung** in the north, and the USA supported the government of **Syngman Rhee** in the south. In 1950, **North Korea** suddenly invaded **South Korea**. Communist troops captured the capital, Seoul, and very nearly took over the whole country.

The USA reacts
- President Truman said that the Truman Doctrine (see page 184) applied to Asia.
- He ordered US **General MacArthur** the Allied Commander in Japan, to send troops and supplies to South Korea.
- He asked the **United Nations–UN** (see section 8.10) to take action.

The United Nations reacts
- The UN said North Korea was the aggressor.
- It put together an invasion force to protect South Korea. General MacArthur was put in charge of the UN troops, but he took his orders from President Truman not the UN. Although 16 nations sent troops, the UN force was mainly American.

▲ Korea, 1950–53.

Why did the USA invade North Korea?

UN forces quickly pushed North Korean troops out of South Korea. Then President Truman ordered General MacArthur to invade North Korea. In October 1950, US troops crossed the **38th parallel** into North Korea (see map opposite). They said they were liberating the people from communist rule. The UN agreed with American action.

China warns

The Chinese communist leader, **Mao Zedong**, told the USA and the UN that the invasion of North Korea had to stop. If it did not, China would fight on the side of North Korea. But General MacArthur took no notice of the warning. So Chinese troops poured over the border between China and North Korea and they pushed the UN forces back into South Korea.

MacArthur reacts

General MacArthur had ignored the warnings from Mao Zedong. Now he ignored orders from his President. He pushed the Chinese forces back into North Korea and chased them until they were back inside China. Then he demanded a Chinese surrender. President Truman was furious because he had been trying to work out a ceasefire agreement with the Chinese. So he sacked General MacArthur.

War in the air

The USA began bombing North Korea, and the USSR fought back. Soviet pilots flew Soviet planes, but the pilots dressed in Chinese uniforms and the planes had Chinese markings on them. For almost two years the USA and USSR fought each other in the air over Korea. The USA lost 3,500 planes and the USSR 2,800. American and Soviet leaders knew their airforces were fighting each other. But they kept it secret from the press and the people.

Source A

▲ South Korean troops rounding up communists after the American (UN) invasion.

Source B

It seems strangely difficult for some to realize that here in Asia is where the communists have decided to try for world conquest.
If we lose the war with communism in Asia, Europe will fall.
There is no substitute for victory.

▲ General Douglas MacArthur, speech to Congress, 1951.

Who won the war?

Peace talks began in July 1951, but they kept breaking down. However, by mid-1953 both sides wanted peace, and it was agreed that the border between North and South Korea should be the 38th parallel. This is exactly where it was before the war began.

What was 'containment'?

The Korean War made people realize that war in Asia might lead to full scale world war. So the USA developed the policy of **containment**. It would try to stop communism from spreading any further, but it would not challenge communism where it was already established.

The allies of the USA agreed that US bases could be built on their lands. The USSR and its allies built up their armed forces and set up the Warsaw Pact (see page 186).

Source C

It seems to me that the proper approach now would be an ultimatum to Moscow.
This means all-out war.
This is the final chance for the Soviet government to decide whether it wishes to survive or not.

▲ From President Truman's diary in January 1952.

Source D

The best way to make sure of peace and to stop a new war is to organize a system of collective security.
The threat of war as a result of the actions of the western powers means that we have to strengthen the defences of our peace-loving countries.

▲ Adapted from the Soviet Prime Minister's statement about the setting up of the Warsaw Pact. This is from a report in *The Times* in May 1955.

▼ US military bases and alliances in 1960.

SUMMARY

- **1950** North Korea's communist troops invaded South Korea and nearly overran it.
- The USA sent troops to support South Korea.
- The UN supported American action, and troops from other nations joined the US force.
- Communist China supported North Korea in attacking UN forces.
- **1953** The 38th parallel was established as the border between North and South Korea.
- The USA began a policy of 'containment' and set up military bases in 'friendly' countries.

QUESTIONS

1 Read pages 188–9.
   a Draw up a time line of the events of the Korean War.
   b Who won the war in Korea?
2 Read page 190.
   a What was the USA's policy of 'containment'?
   b How does the map on page 190 help to explain how 'containment' was supposed to work?

8.4 Hungary and Suez: two crises in one year

Peaceful co-existence

Between 1955 and 1964, **Nikita Khrushchev** led the USSR. He wanted the USSR to have a more peaceful approach to the West. This was in line with what the USA wanted. The leaders of both countries realized that a full-scale nuclear war would be suicidal.

Khrushchev attacks Stalin

In 1956, Khrushchev made an astounding attack on Joseph Stalin. He announced that Stalin's crimes far outweighed any good he had done. Khrushchev said that, under Stalin's regime, Soviet citizens had 'come to fear their own shadows'. He went on to say that they had been terrorized by 'brutal acts'.

The effect on the communist world

Khrushchev's attack on Stalin had a tremendous effect on the communist world. Communist governments released thousands of political prisoners from gaol. The USSR gave eastern European countries more freedom to run their affairs.

Source A

▶ Crowds pull down a statue of Stalin in Budapest, the capital of Hungary.

Source B

With their heavy 76mm guns, the Soviet tanks had attempted to blast the rebels out of their hiding places, but the incredible youngsters had evolved their own technique for dealing with the mighty 26-ton tanks.

First they would fire on the tanks from upper storey windows, then a small boy would leap out of a doorway, fling a pail of gasoline over the tank's engine compartment and leap back to shelter.

▲ Adapted from 'Five days of Freedom', an article in *Time* magazine on 12 November 1956.

Rebellion in Hungary

In the summer of 1956, there were widespread riots and strikes in Hungary and its capital, Budapest. The communist leader, **Matyas Rakosi**, fled from Budapest. The Communist Party officials who stayed behind were far less extreme. They appointed **Imry Nagy** as Prime Minister. He

- allowed non-communists in his government
- said there were to be free elections
- took Hungary out of the Warsaw Pact
- told the USSR to take its troops out of Hungary.

The USSR reacts

Communist officials were afraid that other countries in eastern Europe would follow Hungary. They were afraid that the Warsaw Pact would break up and that they would have no defences against NATO. On 4 November 1956, Soviet tanks rolled into Budapest.

The West fails to react

The Hungarians fought fiercely. But there was little that poorly armed civilians could do against tanks and machine guns. Hungarian radio stations made desperate appeals to the West for help. The West had encouraged them to rebel. Surely they would send help now. But the West was silent. No help came.

The end of the rebellion

By mid-November, the revolt was over. More than 30,000 Hungarians were dead, and 200,000 had fled. **Janos Kadar** took over from Nagy as leader. Nagy was shot.

Source C

▲ Soviet tanks in the centre of Budapest, November 1956.

Source D

Civilized people of the world!
Our ship is sinking. Light is fading.
The shadows grow darker over the soil of Hungary. Hungary is dying.
Help us.

▲ Extracts from two broadcasts by Radio Budapest to the West in 1956.

The Suez Canal crisis

The West got most of its oil from the Middle East. Hundreds of tankers took oil to industrialized Europe every month. They used the **Suez Canal**, which flowed through Egypt. This meant that the countries of western Europe had to stay on good terms with Egypt's leaders.

The Aswan High Dam

In December 1955, the USA offered Egypt's President, **Gamal Abdel Nasser**, money to build a dam at Aswan on the river Nile. Egypt needed this dam for hydro-electric power and irrigation, so it accepted the offer.

Five months later, Egypt made a military alliance with other Arab countries. The US government thought this alliance was aimed against its ally, Israel. So the USA withdrew the offer of money for the dam. Nasser promptly seized the Suez Canal. He now controlled one of the West's economic lifelines.

Britain, France and Israel attack

British, French and Israeli politicians held a series of secret meetings. On 29 October, the Israeli army suddenly invaded Egypt. Israeli troops swept across the Sinai desert to the Suez Canal. At the same time, British and French troops invaded Egypt from the air and sea. Together they captured the Suez Canal.

The UN and the world react

- The UN, the USSR and the USA demanded that Britain, France and Israel withdraw from Egypt.
- UN troops went into the Canal zone to keep the peace.
- The USSR gave Nasser the money he needed to built the Aswan High Dam.

The Suez crisis was a disaster for Britain and France. It gave the USSR a foothold in the Middle East. It also took people's attention away from what was happening in Hungary.

Source E

▲ President Nasser had the Suez Canal blocked by ordering ships to be sunk at Port Said.

QUESTIONS

1 From the start of the Cold War, official government radio broadcasts from the West encouraged people in communist countries to stand up for their freedoms. Why, then, did the West not support the rebellion in Hungary?

2 Why did the western powers intervene in the Suez crisis when they had not intervened in Hungary?

8.5 Why was the Berlin Wall built?

Why was Berlin important?

In 1945 Berlin was divided into **four zones**. The zones were controlled by the USA, Britain, France and the USSR. Berlin was 160 kilometres inside communist East Germany. The USA, Britain and France used their zones of Berlin to show the Soviets and East Germans just how good life was in the West. The shops were full and there were plenty of jobs for skilled workers. The USA, Britain and France kept spies in their zones of Berlin so they could watch communist East Germany.

In East Germany there was nothing much to buy in the shops. Jobs were hard to get. People travelled from East to West Berlin to work and to shop during their time off. Some people decided to stay in the West. They were called **defectors**.

What did the USSR want?

Khrushchev was the leader of the USSR. He wanted the USA, Britain and France to take their soldiers out of Berlin. He wanted Berlin to belong to East Germany. About 200,000 people a year were leaving East Germany to live in the West. He wanted to keep these people in East Germany so that they could help build up industries and businesses.

The USA, Britain and France did not want to lose West Berlin. In 1961 Khruschev met the new American president, John F. Kennedy. They talked about the problem of Berlin, but nothing was decided.

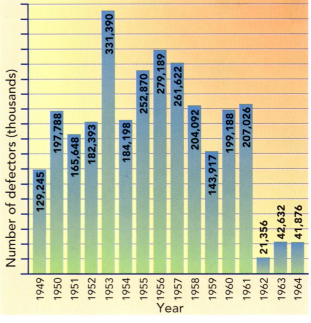

▲ The number of East German defectors crossing to the West via West Berlin or across the West German border, 1949–64.

Source A

▲ East German construction workers building the Berlin Wall in August 1961.

The wall goes up

Thousands of Berliners travelled between East and West Berlin every day. They travelled to work, to shop and to visit friends and relations.

On 13 August 1961 all this changed. East German and Soviet soldiers closed the border between East and West Berlin. They used barbed wire and they were armed with machine-guns. No one could stop them. The soldiers stopped trains running between East and West Berlin. The East Germans who worked in West Berlin were turned back. East and West Berliners were very angry, but there was nothing they could do except shout and jeer and protest. By 20 August 1961 the barbed wire wall had gone. In its place was a high wall built from concrete. Later, the East Germans added watch-towers, floodlights and machine-guns. Many East Germans were killed trying to cross to the West.

Why was the Wall built?

The East German government said that the Wall was built to keep out spies from the West. The Western governments said the Wall had been built to keep East Germans in East Germany. Between 1961 and 1962, 41 people were killed trying to escape across the Wall from East to West Berlin. There was nothing the western governments could do. Berlin remained a divided city until 1989.

Source B

The Berlin Wall is a totally against the right of free circulation throughout the city. It is against the Four Power agreement reached in Paris on June 20 1949.

▲ Dean Rusk, US Secretary of State, speaking in August 1961.

Source C

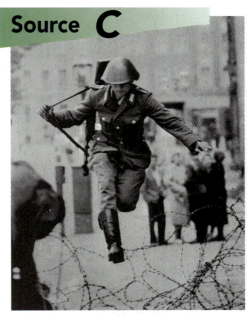

▲ An East German soldier sprinting from East to West Berlin, 15 August 1961.

QUESTIONS

1. Why did the East Germans build the Berlin Wall? Use the sources and information in this unit in your answer.
2. Why did the western allies not just withdraw from West Berlin when the Wall was built?

SUMMARY

▶ **1953** Death of Joseph Stalin marked easier relations of the USSR's attitude towards the West.

▶ **1956** Rebellion in Hungary put down by USSR. No help from the West.

▶ **1956** Nasser took over the Suez Canal. French, British and Israeli troops invaded Egypt to secure the Canal.

▶ **1961** East Germany, backed by the USSR, built the Berlin Wall to separate the western and eastern zones of the city.

8.6 The Cuban missile crisis 1962

Source A

▲ A photograph of a medium-range ballistic missile base in Cuba, taken from an American U-2 spy-plane in 1962. It sparked off a crisis that brought the world to the brink of nuclear war.

Source B

The 1930s taught us a clear lesson. Aggressive behaviour, if not stopped, will lead to war.

We will not lightly risk a world-wide nuclear war. But we will not shrink from the risk if it is to be faced.

▲ Adapted from the broadcast made by President Kennedy to the American people on 22 October 1962, and listened to by millions throughout the world.

The USA and Cuba

The USA controlled most of the Cuban ecoonomy. In 1959, Cuba was taken over by **Fidel Castro**. The US government thought that Castro's ideas were suspiciously communist. So when Castro asked for money for his reforms, the USA refused to give him any.

Cuba and the USSR

In February 1960, Castro signed a trade deal with the USSR. As a result, in January 1961, the USA cut all diplomatic links with Cuba.

The Bay of Pigs

A group of Cubans living in the USA planned to overthrow Castro. The CIA (see page 184) helped them. In April 1961, the exiles invaded Cuba at the Bay of Pigs hoping to spark off a revolution against Castro. They did not. The invaders were quickly defeated and the whole event made the new American President, John F. Kennedy, look very silly.

Spy-planes

On 14 October 1962, US spy-planes took photographs over Cuba. When the photographs were developed, experts said they showed missile sites and Soviet planes on Cuban airfields.

Blockade

President Kennedy decided to send the US navy to **blockade** Cuba. He did not want any more USSR missiles to reach the island. Soviet ships, carrying missiles, steamed towards Cuba. The US navy waited for them. All over the world, people waited for the nuclear holocaust.

Kennedy v. Khrushchev

On 25 October, the US navy stopped a Soviet oil tanker and turned back twelve other ships sailing for Cuba. Khrushchev and Kennedy sent notes to each other:

Note 1: **Khrushchev to Kennedy**
Lift the blockade of Cuba; talk about missile bases separately.

Note 2: **Khrushchev to Kennedy**
Remove US missile bases from Turkey and Italy, and Soviet missiles will go from Cuba.

Note 3: **Kennedy to Khrushchev**
Blockade will be lifted when missiles leave Cuba.

At this point Kennedy's brother, who was the US Attorney General, told the Soviet ambassador that US missiles were soon to be taken out of Turkey and Italy.

Note 4: **Khrushchev to Kennedy**
Agree to remove missiles from Cuba.

The Cuban missile crisis was over.

The results of the crisis
- People believed Kennedy was the natural leader of the western world.
- A **hot-line** was set up between the US White House and the Soviet Kremlin so that the two leaders and their staff could speak to each other direct.
- In August 1963, Britain, the USA and the USSR agreed to stop testing nuclear bombs in the air.

▲ American cities that could be reached by missiles fired from Cuba.

Source C

I have received your message of 27 October. In order to end the conflict which is threatening world peace, the Soviet government has given orders to dismantle the missiles, crate them and return them to the Soviet Union.

▲ Adapted from a message from Khrushchev to Kennedy, 28 October 1962.

QUESTIONS

1. Kennedy called the Soviet missiles on Cuba 'offensive weapons'. Khrushchev called them 'defensive weapons'. Explain which you think they were.
2. Who deserves the credit for avoiding nuclear war: Kennedy or Khrushchev?
3. How did the crisis make the world a safer place?

8.7 Czechoslovakia: The 'Prague Spring' 1968

Source A

We cannot let your country leave the communist path and tear itself away from the communist commonwealth.

▲ Adapted from a statement made by the Communist Parties of the USSR, Bulgaria, Hungary, East Germany and Poland in July 1968.

Source B

When forces inside a communist country that are against communism try to turn that country towards capitalism, then all communist countries must try to stop this happening.

▲ Adapted from a statement made by Leonid Brezhnev, the Soviet leader, in August 1968. This later became known as the 'Brezhnev Doctrine'.

Source C

Let us show them [the occupation soldiers] that they are our enemies today.

▲ From a Czechoslovak radio broadcast in August 1968.

Why were the Czechs discontented?

By 1967, many Czechs felt that their communist leaders were out of touch with the problems facing their country. Trade and industry were doing badly. Most people's standards of living was falling. Anyone who disagreed with the Government was thrown into prison.

What was the 'Prague Spring'?

The Czech communists decided that the time had come for a change. They chose **Alexander Dubček** for their leader. Within a few months he had introduced reforms:

- Government control of industry was relaxed. Many decisions were left to managers and workers.
- Censorship of the press ended.
- Czech people were allowed to travel abroad.
- Czech people were allowed to hold political meetings.

Dubček said his reforms did not mean that Czechoslovakia would leave the Warsaw Pact.

Source D

▲ Czechs use a tree trunk to try to ram a Soviet tank as it moves along the streets of Prague in August 1968.

How did the USSR react?

Leonid Brezhnev, the leader of the USSR, was alarmed, despite what Dubček said.
- In May 1968, he held military exercises near the Czech border.
- In June, he agreed to the Warsaw Pact countries holding military exercises inside Czechoslovakia.
- He held meetings with Dubček.

What did Dubček promise?
- The Communist Party would be in full control inside Czechoslovakia.
- Czechoslovakia would stay in the Warsaw Pact.
- He would stop the Czech press criticizing the USSR.

What did eastern Europe do?

In August 1968, President Ceausescu of Romania and President Tito of Yugoslavia visited Dubček. They gave him their support. This made Brezhnev afraid that other countries in eastern Europe would copy what Dubček was doing, and that the Warsaw Pact would break up.

Brezhnev acts

On 21 August, 500,000 Warsaw Pact troops invaded Czechoslovakia. After fierce street-to-street fighting, they took control of Prague and other important cities. They captured Dubček and sent him to Moscow. He was replaced as leader by **Gustáv Husák**.

Source E

▲ Czech crowds gather for the funeral of Jan Palach. Jan Palach was a student who burned himself to death in Wenceslas Square, Prague, as a protest against the Soviet invasion.

SUMMARY

▶ **April 1961** 'Bay of Pigs' invasion of Cuba failed.

▶ **October 1962** Cuban missile crisis.

▶ Hot-line set up between White House and Kremlin. Ban on nuclear testing agreed 1963.

▶ **August 1968** Warsaw Pact troops invaded Czechoslovakia and deposed Dubček.

QUESTIONS

1. a How do the sources show that the Czechoslovakian people were determined to become independent of the USSR?
   b Why, in the end, were the people not able to achieve what they wanted?

2. Look back to 'Rebellion in Hungary' on page 192. What similarities, and what differences, can you find between the Hungarian and the Czechoslovakian uprisings?

8.8 Vietnam: A struggle for power

▲ Vietnam and the surrounding countries.

A divided country
North Vietnam was run by the communist government of **Ho Chi Minh**. South Vietnam was ruled by **Ngo Dinh Diem**. He was a corrupt anti-communist politician. Many people in South Vietnam hated his regime, particularly the peasants. They sheltered and supported the communist **Vietcong**, who made guerilla attacks on Diem's troops. Ho Chi Minh's communists in North Vietnam supplied the Vietcong with arms and money.

What was the domino theory?
The USA believed that North Vietnam was trying to spread communism into South Vietnam and, eventually, all of South-East Asia. The US government was afraid that country after country in Asia would fall to communism, like a row of dominoes. It was determined to stop this happening. So the US government decided to support Ngo Dinh Diem's regime in South Vietnam.

How did the USA support South Vietnam?
The USA poured armaments and supplies into South Vietnam. The number of American military 'advisers' was increased from 500 to 10,000. However, Diem's regime was so corrupt that the Americans could not work with him and his officials. So the USA encouraged the South Vietnamese army to overthrow Diem's regime. Diem was shot in November 1963 and the generals took over.

A new US President
In the same month that Diem was shot, President Kennedy was assassinated in Dallas, USA. The new President, **Lyndon Johnson**, took a fresh look at US policy in Vietnam.

Source A
The loss of any single country in South-East Asia could lead to the loss of all Asia, finally endangering the security of Europe. You have a row of dominoes set up, you knock over the first one and the last one will go over very quickly.

▲ The domino theory, as set out by Dwight D. Eisenhower, President of the USA, 1952–60.

200 CHAPTER 8 THE COLD WAR

War 1964–8

In August 1964, the North Vietnamese attacked a US destroyer in the Gulf of Tonkin. Johnson made good use of this incident. He persuaded the US Congress to give him the power to direct military operations in Vietnam.

Operation Rolling Thunder

Johnson ordered the US airforce to bomb factories and fuel dumps in North Vietnam. US planes bombed the supply routes from North Vietnam to the Vietcong in the south. They also sprayed chemicals on to the jungles of the south where the Vietcong were hiding. These chemicals stripped the leaves from the trees so that US troops could see the Vietcong. But the chemicals, especially **napalm**, also killed animals and burned people.

Four years later

By 1968, the USA had an army of over half a million men in South Vietnam. Over 36,000 Americans had been killed there. But the aid the USA was giving South Vietnam was matched by the aid which North Vietnam and communist China were giving the Vietcong. It seemed there was no way the USA could win.

Source B

▲ A South Vietnamese mother and her children wade across a river to try to escape from American bombs. The planes were trying to knock out Vietcong snipers who were firing on US marines.

Source C

Let every nation know, whether it wishes us well or ill, that we shall pay any price, bear any burden, meet any hardship, support any friend, oppose any foe, to assure the survival and success of liberty.

▲ From a radio broadcast by John F. Kennedy, President of the USA, 1960–3.

Source D

The American soldier in Vietnam could rely on the latest equipment. Tanks and armoured cars supported any attack and he had the most up-to-date arms – mortars, machine guns, grenade and rocket launchers, and the M16, a fully automatic rifle.
The Americans had bombs of every shape and size, from napalm bombs that roasted their victims alive to cluster bombs whose hundreds of pellets burst out at high speed. They also had electronic instruments and chemical weapons.

◀ An extract from a book on the Vietnam War, written by an American author in 1983.

How did the American people react to the war?

In the 1950s and early 1960s, most American people supported their government's policy in Vietnam. They wanted their government to stop communism spreading. This was because they believed democracy was the best kind of government for all countries.

Reactions change

Americans gradually changed their minds about the fighting in Vietnam.

▲ A rally in Central Park, New York, in April 1967. The rally was held to protest against the war in Vietnam. Young men who had been called up to fight burned their draft (call-up) cards.

- They watched the war on their TV sets every evening. They saw college boys killing women and children. One of the worst massacres was at **My-lai** when American soldiers killed 100 South Vietnamese villagers.
- They read about drug addition among American soldiers.
- Too many soldiers were being killed.

Americans came to realize that they could not win the Vietnam War. Young men who had been called up refused to fight. Public opinion turned against the war.

Vietnamization

Richard Nixon was elected President of the USA in November 1968. He knew that the USA could not win the Vietnam War. He had to find a way of bringing US troops home without losing face. He had to make sure, too, that the South did not fall to the communists.

Nixon decided on a policy of '**Vietnamization**'. He would build up the South Vietnamese army until it was strong enough to fight the communists alone.

Source F

Hey, hey, LBJ, how many kids did you kill today?

 A chant often made by people demonstrating against the Vietnam War. The initials LBJ were those of the US President, Lyndon Baines Johnson.

It took time to build up the South Vietnamese army. While this was happening, the Americans fought on.

- They bombed the Ho Chi Minh trail, along which the Vietcong got their supplies.
- They invaded Cambodia to destroy North Vietnamese bases there. This boosted support for the local communists, the **Khmer Rouge**.
- They invaded Laos to cut the supply routes from Laos to the Vietcong. This boosted support for the local communists, the **Pathet Laos**.

Vietnamization started to work. The South Vietnamese army were managing to defend large areas of their country.

The USA pulls out

In February 1973, North Vietnam, South Vietnam and the Vietcong agreed to a cease fire. By the end of the year, all American troops had left Vietnam. But President Nixon and **Nguyen Van Thieu**, the President of South Vietnam, had a secret agreement. The Americans would send their troops back if the communists broke the cease fire.

By the end of 1975, Thieu's army had collapsed and the USA had broken its promise. The North Vietnamese army and the Vietcong captured Saigon. South Vietnam became a communist country.

▲ American soldiers looking for a sniper.

Source H

You never knew who was enemy and who was friend. They all looked alike. They were all Vietnamese. Some of them were Vietcong. A woman says her husband isn't a Vietcong. She watches your men walk down a trail and get killed by a booby-trap. Maybe she planted it herself. The enemy was all around you.

▲ Captain E. J. Banks, an American marine who fought in the war.

Source I

Two young women who tempted some United States soldiers to lay down their weapons with promises of sex, and then killed them.

A government soldier who deserted to the Vietcong, bringing several stolen documents with him.

An old woman who helped guerillas set up an ambush.

▲ A list of 'heroes' as told by the Vietcong to South Vietnamese villagers during the war.

The effects of the Vietnam War

The war was a disaster for the USA:
- The USA, a strong nuclear power, failed to defeat North Vietnam, a small, non-nuclear power.
- The USA failed to stop South Vietnam turning communist.

The war was a disaster for Vietnam:
- Over two million Vietnamese people died.
- North and South were devastated by American fire-power and their economics ruined.

Source J

By the spring of 1968, American people were convinced that victory in Vietnam was not worth 300 American dead a week and $30,000 million a year.

▲ Adapted from *The Observer* newspaper 28 January 1973.

QUESTIONS

1. Read page 200. Why did America decide to intervene in Vietnam?
2. Study Sources G, H and I. How do those sources help explain why the Americans lost the Vietnam War?
3. Read page 202.
   a. Explain what is meant by the policy of 'Vietnamization'.
   b. Why did President Nixon introduce this policy?

SUMMARY

- **Early 1960s** The USA tried to prevent communism spreading from North to South Vietnam.
- US forces ineffective against Vietcong guerrilla tactics.
- US public turned against the war.
- **1968** 'Vietnamization'.
- **1973** The last US troops leave.
- **1975** Vietnam united under communist rule.

8.9 From arms race to détente 1945–80

Superpower clashes

The two superpowers, the USA and USSR, clashed in many international incidents. Sometimes the clashes were obvious, as in Cuba. Sometimes they were hidden, as in Korea.

What made the clashes even more dangerous was that both sides were piling up deadly nuclear weapons. Each side raced to get more and more deadly ones than the other.

The first nuclear bomb

Only two nuclear bombs have ever been used in war. They were exploded by the USA over the Japanese cities of **Hiroshima** and **Nagasaki**. The world changed from that day. It was now possible for mankind to destroy itself.

The race begins

In 1949, the USSR tested its own nuclear bomb. Now both sides were equal. In November 1952, the USA tested an even more deadly weapon: the hydrogen bomb. The USSR followed in 1953.

What was the 'nuclear deterrent'?
The leaders of the USA and the USSR knew that in a nuclear war there would be no winners. Both sides would be destroyed. But in order to stop a nuclear war, they believed that they should balance each other in the destruction they could cause.

What weapons were developed?
- **Nuclear warheads**, which could be fitted to missiles.
- **Strategic bombers**, which could fly a long way carrying nuclear bombs.
- **Medium range bombers**, which were small and fast and could carry nuclear bombs.
- **ICBMs** (inter-continental ballistic missiles), which were kept underground.
- **SLBMs** (submarine-launched ballistic missiles), which could be launched from submarines anywhere in the world.
- **MIRVs** (multiple independently targeted re-entry vehicles), which could carry up to ten warheads that could be launched at different targets.

Source A

▲ This cartoon was drawn by the British cartoonist, David Low, and published on 9 August 1945.

Source B

It wasn't necessary to hit them with that awful thing.
I hated to see our country to be the first to use it.

▲ Dwight D. Eisenhower was interviewed by an American magazine in 1963. This is part of what he said about dropping the atom bomb on Japan in 1945.

Source C

▶ Many people joined organizations to protest against the bomb. This photograph shows part of a rally in 1959, organized by the Campaign for Nuclear Disarmament (CND) in Britain.

What is 'détente'?

The word **détente** means 'loosening' or 'relaxing'. It is often used when talking about improving strained relationships between the USA and USSR.

Why did the USA and USSR want détente?

By the end of the 1960s, the USSR was spending millions of roubles on the arms race. Yet its ordinary industries were far behind those in the West. **Brezhnev**, the Soviet leader, desperately needed to stop spending money on the arms race and build up Soviet industry.

Nixon became President of the USA in 1969. He desperately needed to get American troops out of Vietnam. But before he did this, he needed to be sure that the USSR would stop supporting North Vietnam. Controlling nuclear arms could be a useful starting point for talks.

Did the USA and USSR achieve détente?

- **Strategic Arms Limitation Talks** (**SALT**) began in November 1969. In 1972, Brezhnev and Nixon signed the SALT I agreement and an anti-ballistic missile treaty. Neither treaty covered MIRVs.
- The USSR recognized West Germany as one country and allowed East Berliners to visit friends and relatives in the West.
- In 1975, Soviet and American astronauts linked up in space.
- In 1975, 35 countries signed the **Helsinki Agreement**. East and West agreed to tell each other when they were going to hold peaceful military manoeuvres and allow the other side to send observers.
- The West recognized Soviet dominance of eastern Europe.
- All countries agreed to respect human rights and basic freedoms.

Source D

▲ This American cartoon, about the reasons for SALT I, was published in 1970.

Source E

The SALT I agreement froze ICBM deployment but not MIRV. Throughout the Nixon administration, the Pentagon added three new warheads a day to the MIRV arsenal. It was a strange way to control the arms race.

▲ Written by Stephen Ambrose in *Rise to Globalism*, 1971.

Détente collapses

Talks for a new SALT agreement began towards the end of 1975. However

- President Carter of the USA criticized the USSR because it imprisoned critics of the Soviet system. Carter said that the USSR was violating human rights.
- Brezhnev said that the poverty in the USA was a violation of human rights.
- In 1979, the USSR invaded Afghanistan.
- President Carter called for a boycott of the Olympic Games in Moscow.

SUMMARY

- **1945** Allies exploded atom bombs above Hiroshima and Nagasaki – first and only time nuclear weapons used in war.
- By **1955** both superpowers had developed atom bombs and hydrogen bombs, and began stockpiling nuclear weapons and delivery systems.
- **1972** By SALT I the superpowers agreed to limit the production of nuclear weapons.
- **1979** Soviet troops invaded Afghanistan; détente was dead.

QUESTIONS

1 Read pages 204–5
  a What was the 'nuclear deterrant'?
  b Why did the USA and USSR carry on developing more and more powerful nuclear weapons?

2 Read pages 206–7
  a What is 'détente'?
  b Why did the USA and USSR want détente?
  c Did they achieve détente?

8.10 The United Nations: another way of keeping the peace?

The United Nations Organization (UNO or UN) was set up as an international peace keeping organization at the end of the Second World War. The UN charter was based on the 'Four Freedoms'; freedom from want, freedom from fear, freeedom of speech, freedom of religion.

The Security council of the UN makes the decisions and has five permanent members: the USA, the former USSR, Britain, France and China. These members have a **veto** (right to stop UN action).

Source A

We, the peoples of the United Nations, are determined to save future generations from the horror of war. Twice in our lifetime war has brought terrible suffering to mankind.

We believe in fundamental human rights, in the dignity and worth of the human person, in the equal rights of men and women and of nations large and small.

▲ Adapted from the UN Charter, 1945.

The UN as peacekeeper

The veto
The UN has often been successful as a peacekeeper only when it has been supported by the Great Powers. Often one of the Great Powers used its **veto** in the Security Council to stop the UN acting. The USSR used its veto many times between 1945 and 1950. Indeed, the UN was only able to act in the Korean War (see page 188) because the USSR had left the Security Council for a short time. The USSR was not the only country to use the veto. In 1956, Britain and France used theirs to try to stop the UN taking action over the Suez crisis (see section 8.4).

Peacekeeping in the Congo 1960
There were terrible riots when the Congo (now Zaire) became independent in 1960. The UN sent in 20,000 troops to keep the peace. The UN also sent in teams of doctors and food experts to help the people.

Peacekeeping in the Gulf War (1991–2)
In 1990, Iraq invaded the tiny oil-rich state of Kuwait. The UN ordered Iraq to withdraw. But Iraq refused. In January 1991, the UN backed the 200,000 Allied troops who took part in **Operation Desert Storm**, which freed Kuwait from Iraq forces.

▲ UN troops in Elizabethville, the Congo, in 1961.

The UN has not always been a successful peacekeeper. For example, in the former Yugoslavia the UN peacekeeping troops become part of the problem as the warring sides ignored it.

Was the UN always involved in important world affairs?
There were many crises where the UN did not take a part. Sometimes the UN could not decide what to do. Sometimes the great powers did what they wanted to do and simply ignored the UN. The UN took no part in the Hungarian rebellion (1956), the Cuban missile crisis (1962), the Vietnam War (1964–8) or the Falklands War (1982).

Source C

I became convinced that the division of the world into rich and poor is much more dangerous, than a division of the world based on differing ideologies [beliefs].

▲ From a book written by U Thant, Secretary-General of the UN, 1962–71.

The UN as a giver of aid

The UN gives help to needy countries and poor people throughout the world. It has many **agencies** which give this help. Here are some examples:

- The **World Health Organization** (WHO) sends teams of doctors and nurses when they are needed in emergencies.
- The **United Nations International Children's Emergency Fund** (UNICEF) works to help children in need in all parts of the world.
- The **International Monetary Fund** (IMF) and the **World Bank** lend money to poorer countries.

The work of all the UN agencies is based on one idea. This is that all people should aim for 'one world' in which mutual support, trust and help will replace inequality, hatred and fear.

Source D

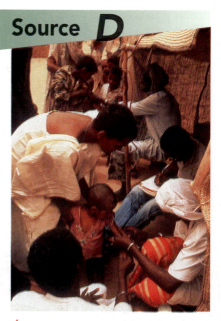

▲ A WHO doctor inoculating a child against smallpox. The disease has now been wiped out.

QUESTIONS

1. In what ways has the UN been successful as a peacekeeper since 1945?
2. Read Source C carefully. Explain whether or not you agree with what U Thant was saying.

8.11 The end of the Cold War

The end of the arms race

In 1980 Ronald Reagan became President of the USA. He was very anti-communist and increased spending on nuclear weapons. The USSR also stepped up its spending on nuclear defence. The situation seemed very grim to many people.

In 1985 Mikhail Gorbachev became leader of the USSR. He was a powerful influence in international relations. He knew that the USSR was nearly bankrupt. He wanted to save money on the arms race and build up the country's economy.

Source A

To many Europeans it appeared that the USA and the USSR had agreed that if war ever came between them, Europe was to be the battleground. There was widespread alarm and good cause for it.

▲ Stephen Ambrose, *Rise to Globalism*, 1985.

Source B

▲ The Berlin Wall being torn down by a happy crowd in November 1989.

In 1985 and 1986 the two leaders met to discuss limiting the production of arms. Finally, in 1987, they agreed to dismantle all nuclear missiles with a range of 300 to 3,400 miles, and build no more.

The arms race was over.

The collapse of the Soviet empire

Under Mikhail Gorbachev the USSR followed a policy of **glasnost**, which means 'more open government'. This had a tremendous effect in eastern Europe. People came out on the streets in their thousands and demanded reform. This time the tanks did not roll in. One by one the governments of the Warsaw Pact fell before the peaceful demands of their citizens. In Berlin, German citizens, helped by the border guards, tore down the Berlin Wall. In Poland, the outlawed trade union, Solidarity, was made legal. In Czechoslovakia, the exiled Prime Minister, Alexander Dubček, returned in triumph.

The end of the Cold War

In December 1989, **George Bush**, the President of the USA, and Mikhail Gorbachev, leader of the USSR, met in Malta to declare that the Cold War was over.

Source C

The new doctrine is in place. Frank Sinatra has a popular song, 'I did it my way'. So Hungary, Poland, any other country has its own way. They decide which road to take.

▲ Gennady Gerasimov, from the Soviet Foreign Office, speaking in 1989.

QUESTIONS

1. What did Gerasimov (Source C) mean by the 'Frank Sinatra doctrine'?
2. Why did the Cold War come to an end?

8.12 Exercise

1 Read section 8.1.
   a Make a list of the causes of conflict between the USSR and the western allies in 1945.
   b Use this list to explain why the Cold War happened.

2 Read section 8.3.
   a What was the 'domino theory'?
   b What was the policy of 'containment'?
   c Why did the USA stop basing its policy on the domino theory and begin the policy of containment?

3 Look carefully at this cartoon (Source 1), drawn in 1945. It is called 'History doesn't repeat itself'.

▲ 'History doesn't repeat itself'. Cartoon by David Low, 1945.

   a Look back at Section 2.3 on the League of Nations and Section 8.10 on the United Nations. What 'message' was the cartoonist trying to get across?
   b Did events between 1945 and 1991 carry out the hope expressed in the cartoon?

4 Read section 8.9.
   a Describe the developments of the 1970s which are called 'détente'.
   b How important was détente to (a) the USA and (b) the USSR?

5 Read the following opinions about the Soviet Union:

View 1
As soon as it was clear the Nazis were going to be defeated, the Soviet Union dropped its policy of co-operation with its wartime allies. Soviet leaders began to plan the spread of communism and the takeover of other countries.

View 2
For years Western leaders believed the Soviet Union was waiting to attack them. The West thought that the only reason why this did not happen was the fact that it possessed the atomic bomb. However, these beliefs about the Soviet Union were not based on fact, but came from the imaginations of western politicians.

   a Both these views are based on hard evidence. Find the evidence in this chapter to support each view.
   b With which view do you agree, and why?

SOUTH AFRICA

Modern South Africa

South Africa is a **multiracial** society. It is made up of four separate racial groups:

- **Blacks**: make up 75% of the population. They speak mainly Bantu and are descended from people who lived in South Africa thousands of years ago.
- **Coloureds**: make up 8% of the population and are of mixed race.
- **Asians**: make up 3% of the population. They are descended from labourers who came to South Africa in the 19th century
- **Whites**: make up 14% of the population and are descended from Dutch and British settlers.

Apartheid

In 1948 the government introduced the policy of **apartheid**. The Blacks were separated from the Whites and had very few political rights. Between 1948 and 1994, Blacks, together with some people from the other racial groups, struggled to bring an end to apartheid.

▼ South Africa in 1910.

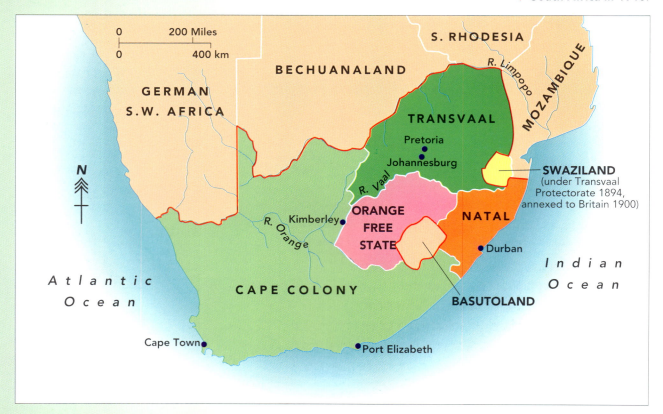

9.1 How did the Whites first settle in South Africa?

The Dutch (Afrikaners)
These were the first white colonists. They arrived in South Africa in 1652 and settled at Table Bay in the Cape. They had strong religious beliefs. One of these beliefs was that they were superior to the native black Africans. The Afrikaners often used black Africans as slaves on their farms.

The British
In the 19th century, the British took control of the Cape. They gave black Africans the vote, tried to abolish slavery and taxed the Afrikaners.

The Great Trek
The Afrikaners did not like what the British were doing. They made the **Great Trek** north and set up two states of their own: **Transvaal** and the **Orange Free State**. But, after the **Boer War** (1899–1902), the British took control of the Transvaal and the Orange Free State, and the Afrikaners became British citizens.

Self-government
In 1910, the British decided to let South Africa govern itself. They joined Cape Colony, Natal, Transvaal and the Orange Free State into the **Union of South Africa**. The government of South Africa then passed a series of laws which were meant to strengthen the position of white people:

- **1913 Native Land Act** forbade black Africans from owning land in 90% of South Africa. They could only buy land in the **native areas**, where the land was poor.
- **Pass Laws** meant that all black Africans had to carry special passes before they were allowed to enter areas which were specially for the Whites.
- **1926 Mines and Works Act** meant that only Whites could hold skilled jobs with the best pay.
- **1932 Immorality Act** forbade marriages between Blacks and Whites.

Source A
It is the placing of black Africans on an equal footing with Christians, contrary to the natural distinction of race and religion that has made us leave.

▲ An Afrikaner woman explains the reason for the Great Trek.

Source B
We beg the Government to give us land where we can set up our homes. The Government governs Black and White and should shelter and protect all its subjects without regard for their colour.

▲ Adapted from a petition from Blacks to government officials, 1914.

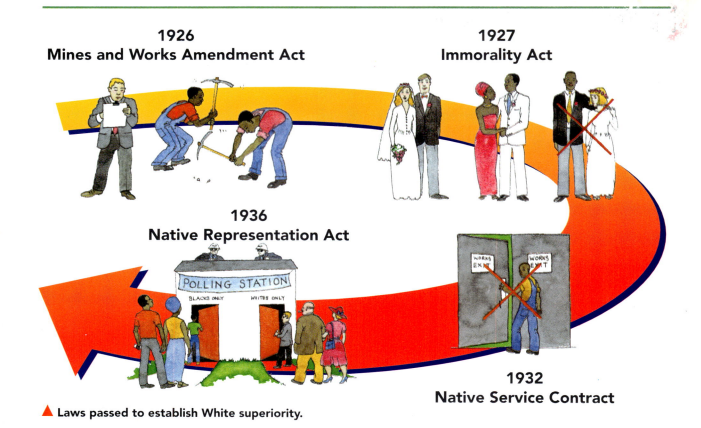

▲ Laws passed to establish White superiority.

- **1936 Native Representation Act** said that white Africans had to vote for their own Members of Parliament and black Africans for theirs. But all MPs had to be white.

It was very difficult for the black Africans to protest about what was happening to them. They had very little political influence and many were dependent upon white employers for a living.

Broederbond (Band of Brothers)

This was a secret organization of Afrikaners. Its members had to be white and Protestant. The Broederbond was strongly opposed to communism and to rights for black Africans. Its members played an important part in persuading the South African government to set up apartheid after the Second World War.

Source C

Total separation must be brought in at once by the state.
It must buy suitable land on which the natives can live.
There they can develop their own political, economic, educational, religious and cultural lives.
A native can go into white areas to work, but cannot take his family.

▲ The Broederbond's ideas about the way in which South Africa should be organized.

QUESTIONS

1 Read pages 213 and 214. How did the Whites strengthen their position in South Africa after 1924?

2 Why were the black Africans unable to prevent the Whites dominating their country?

9.2 The Second World War

South Africa enters the war
In 1939, South Africa entered the war on the side of the Allies. But many South Africans thought that their country should stay neutral. Some Afrikaners hoped Germany would win the war because they approved of Hitler's racial views.

Blacks and Whites
About 200,000 white South Africans fought the war in Africa and Italy. Blacks were not allowed weapons, but 125,000 black Africans went to the Front as labourers and drivers. With so many Whites away fighting, more Blacks were needed to work in mines and factories. So the Prime Minister of South Africa, **Jan Smuts**, had to relax the Pass Laws and laws which stopped Blacks doing certain jobs.

The African National Congress (ANC)
Black Africans hoped that, by the end of the war, their position in South Africa would improve. The **Atlantic Charter** (1941), put together by Roosevelt and Churchill, said that all people had the right to choose their own government. More Blacks also had skilled jobs in towns. In 1943, the ANC began campaigning for the abolition of the Pass Laws and all laws which discriminated against non-Whites.

It was beginning to look as if Blacks would be able to have a better life in South Africa once the war was over.

Source A

▲ A picture of South Africans in the Second World War.

QUESTIONS

1. Why did many South Africans not want their country to fight on the side of the Allies?
2. Why do you think black South Africans not allowed to carry weapons in the war?
3. What led Blacks to believe they would have a better life in South Africa after the war?

9.3 How was the policy of apartheid established in South Africa?

Source A

A revolutionary change is taking place as the native peoples of South Africa move from the country to the towns. Separation tried to stop it. It has not.
You might as well try to sweep the ocean back with a broom.

▲ Extract from a speech made by Prime Minister Smuts in 1942.

Source B

Both Whites and non-Whites will benefit from apartheid.
The non-white people can develop according to their own characteristics.

It is the Christian duty of the Whites to look after the non-white races until they can look after their own affairs.

▲ The theory of apartheid, adapted from a resolution to the Congress of the People in Bloemfontein in 1944.

The Fagan Report

This was published by the South African government in 1948. It said that keeping Blacks away from Whites and forcing them into reserves did not work. The report suggested that Blacks should be encouraged to settle on the edges of cities.

The Sauer Report

This was published by the opposition **Nationalist Party** in 1948. It said that black and white communities should develop separately, and that Blacks should be kept to reserves. They should only be allowed into white areas to work, and even then they should be tightly controlled.

General election, 1948

The voters preferred the Nationalist Party's message. In 1948, they voted Jan Smuts and the United Party out of office. The Nationalist Party formed the government, with **Dr Daniel F. Malan** as Prime Minister.

Apartheid

In earlier years, most Afrikaners had felt threatened by the British (look back to page 213 to remind yourself why). Immediately after the Second World War they felt threatened again, by the United Party's relaxed attitude to Blacks. Poorer Afrikaners were competing for jobs with Blacks, and it looked as if white supremacy might be ending.

The election of the Nationalist Party to government in 1948 made sure that apartheid was government policy. It took about ten years before the whole system was in place. But by 1959, most Afrikaners felt that their position in South Africa was secure.

The Establishment of Apartheid

1949 — Prohibition of Mixed Marriages
No marriages allowed between Blacks, Whites, Coloureds or Asians.

1950 — Population Registration Act
Every person in South Africa was to be classified as belonging to a particular race. Apartheid could then be based on these divisons. Difficult to administer due to existing 'mixes', every year hundreds 'changed race'.

1950 — Group Areas Act
Non-Whites could not live in or own land in white areas, (87% of the country). Thousands of non-Whites were forcibly rehoused to reserves.

1950 — Suppression of Communism Act
This banned the tiny Communist Party and was used by the authorities to arrest and imprison any opponent of the government.

1952 — Passbook Act
All black men (and later women) had to have a pass (identity) book with them at all times. Black workers in white areas hated them – many were arrested every year for passbook offences.

1953 — Bantu Education Act
Strict rules for black children's education. A limited syllabus taught in their own language meant black children were really being trained for manual work. Black teachers were paid much less than white teachers.

1953 — Separate Amenities Act
Public services – transport, cinemas, theatres, post offices, restaurants and even some beaches – were made 'Whites only' or non-White.

1959 — Bantu Self-Government Act
All black Africans (Bantu) were divided into eight reserves or Bantustans which acted as homelands for the black tribes. Independence was promised but did not become a working reality.

9.4 Who opposed apartheid?

Source A

Separate development is designed for the happiness and stability provided by their own language and administration both for the Bantu and the Whites.

▲ Henrik Verwoerd, speaking to the South African people on his election as Prime Minister in 1958.

The African National Congress

Throughout the 1950s, the **ANC** organized a whole series of strikes and demonstrations to protest against apartheid. There were also some special events. In June 1950, it ran a **National Day of Protest** which asked Blacks, Coloureds, Indians and Europeans to take part in a strike to show their opposition to apartheid. In 1952, it organized a **Defiance Campaign**, where black Africans deliberately ignored 'Whites only' signs. Thousands of Blacks were arrested, which drew the world's attention to their plight. Membership of the ANC increased from 7,000 to 100,000.

Chief Albert Luthuli

Chief Albert Luthuli was the black President of the ANC. He believed in non-violent opposition to apartheid. This earned him the respect of many Whites as well as Blacks. In 1961 he was given the Nobel Peace Prize.

Source B

▲ A cartoon which appeared in the *Cape Times*, a South African newspaper, in 1959.

Father Trevor Huddleston

Father Trevor Huddleston was a white priest who worked in a black **township** outside Johannesburg between 1944 and 1956. Townships were areas on the edges of cities where black workers lived in appalling conditions. Huddleston fought fearlessly for black rights, and because he was so outspoken he was in constant conflict with the government and the police. He wrote a book about his experiences called *Naught for your Comfort*, which brought what was happening in South Africa to the attention of the world.

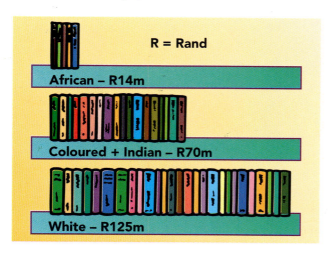

◂ Government spending on school education 1959–60.

The Freedom Charter

People of all races met in a 'Congress of the People' near Johannesburg in June 1955. There they drew up a **Freedom Charter**. The South African government tried to get hold of the Charter, but the Congress had sent it all round the country. The police, acting on government orders, arrested 150 members of Congress.

Treason trials

- **Chief Albert Luthuli**, the President of the ANC, was arrested and tried for treason in 1953.
- **Walter Sisulu**, the Secretary of the ANC, spent 1963-89 in prison.
- **Nelson Mandela**, a black lawyer, was in prison 1964-1990.
- **Oliver Tambo**, the President of the ANC after Albert Luthuli, was forced into exile in 1960.

Women

Black and white women played an important part in opposing apartheid. **Albertina Sisulu**, wife of Walter Sisulu, was put in prison for leading demonstrations against the government. **Margaret Ballinger** and **Helen Suzman** were two white women who worked tirelessly against apartheid. **Lillian Ngoyi** and **Helen Joseph** organized a rally against apartheid, which 20,000 women joined. Lillian Ngoyi and Helen Joseph were arrested and put in prison.

The Sharpeville massacre

On 21 March 1960, thousands of people gathered outside a police station in Sharpeville, a black township. They were protesting against the Pass Laws. In a moment of panic, police opened fire on the crowd. They shot dead 67 Africans and wounded 186, including eight children. Press photographers and reporters were there. The next morning, the whole world read about the massacre and saw pictures of it in their newspapers.

Source C

Every man and woman shall have the right to vote.

No one shall be imprisoned, deported or restricted without a fair trial.

The law shall guarantee to all the right to speak, to organize, to meet together, to publish, to preach, to worship and to educate their children.

All shall be free to form trade unions.

Education shall be free, compulsory, universal and equal for all children.

▲ The Freedom Charter 1955.

Source D

We want equal political rights.
Without them we will always be inferior.
This will sound revolutionary to the Whites because black voters will be in the majority.
But this is the only solution which will guarantee racial peace and freedom for all.

▲ Adapted from a statement made by Nelson Mandela shortly before his imprisonment in 1964.

Source E

▲ Black township outside Johannesburg.

The government acts

The South African government decided to make sure there were no more demonstrations against apartheid. On 18 April 1960, it banned the African National Congress. It also declared a **state of emergency**. This meant that the police could detain suspects without trial for up to 180 days.

The police act

Between 1963 and 1985, 69 people died as a result of police interrogation. The world listened in horror as prisoners died 'naturally'.

The ANC acts

The ANC immediately gave up its policy of non-violence. Its members became involved in sabotage and violence.

QUESTIONS

1 Read Source A and Source D. How did Henrick Verwoerd and Nelson Mandela differ about how Blacks and Whites should live in South Africa?

2 Read pages 218–19. How did **a** The African National Congress **b** Chief Albert Luthuli **c** Father Trevor Huddleston help fight apartheid?

SUMMARY

- **1910** Union of South Africa.
- **1922** Pass Laws introduced.
- **1923** ANC founded.
- **1926–36** Laws restricting Blacks. Broederbond formed.
- **1945** Apartheid officially adopted by Nationalist Party.
- **1948–54** Apartheid laws passed.
- **1955** Freedom Charter.
- **1960** Sharpeville massacre. State of emergency.

9.5 How did the rest of the world react to apartheid?

Source A

▲ A cartoon printed in the *Daily Mirror* in March 1961. The cartoonist is responding to Verwoerd's claim at the Commonwealth Conference that 'Apartheid is better described as a policy of good neighbours.'

The Commonwealth

In 1960, the British Prime Minister, Harold Macmillan, told the South African government that it must not ignore the rights of black Africans. Many members of the Commonwealth wanted to expel South Africa because of apartheid. In October 1960, South Africa decided to become a republic. This meant that its head of state was no longer the Queen, but an elected president. In March 1961, Prime Minister Verwoerd took South Africa out of the Commonwealth.

The Organization for African Unity

By the mid-1960s, many African countries had gained their independence. In 1963, the black nations of Africa formed the Organization for African Unity. One of its major aims was to destroy apartheid.

Rhodesia

The British government, under Prime Minister Harold Wilson, wanted to give independence to Rhodesia. Wilson's government wanted black Rhodesians to have as much political power as Whites. But the Rhodesian Prime Minister, Ian Smith, was determined to keep white supremacy. So in 1963, he declared Rhodesia independent of Britain.

Source B

▲ An anti-apartheid demonstration from the 1960s.

Source C

All states should take whatever action they believe right, and which is in agreement with the UN Charter, to bring about the ending of apartheid policies.

▲ A United Nations resolution passed in 1960.

Source D

I went in straight to the counter and ordered five bottles of Coke and Fanta. Without saying a word a man serving picked up an empty bottle and the next thing I felt was a thud on my head.
I fell on the ground and fainted . . .
My friends told me that a 'deranged' white man had come out of the restaurant shouting that 'no Black had ever entered his shop through the front door'.
Local Africans, who had by now gathered round, pointed to a side window through which Blacks purchased food from that restaurant.

▲ A black South African journalist recalls trying to buy drink from a restaurant in the late 1960s.

The United Nations acts

The United Nations imposed **economic sanctions** on Rhodesia. But South Africa took no notice. It carried on trading with Rhodesia and even sent police to help Ian Smith deal with black **guerrilla** forces. Guerrillas are small groups of irregular fighters.

Namibia

South Africa had run South-West Africa (called Namibia by black Africans) since 1919. After the Second World War, the South African government hoped to be able to take over Namibia completely. But the United Nations would not let this happen because of South Africa's apartheid policy.

Inside Namibia, black Africans formed the **South West Africa People's Organization** (SWAPO), which was a powerful guerrilla group.

Sanctions

In 1962, the United Nations said that no country should trade with South Africa. The UN hoped this would force the South African government to give up apartheid. But South Africa was rich in gold and diamonds, so many countries ignored the UN and carried on trading. By 1970, Whites in South Africa had the highest standard of living of any people in the world. This prosperity brought more jobs and higher wages for Blacks, but it did not bring them political freedom.

▲ Headings from *The Times* of 18 and 25 September 1968.

In response to pressure from their own people, some foreign governments began cutting sporting links with South Africa. Sport, in particular cricket and rugby, was very important to the white community in South Africa. In 1968 a South African-born coloured

Sport

Sport, especially cricket and rugby, was very important to many white South Africans. Some foreign governments began cutting their sporting links with South Africa to try to bring about an end to apartheid.

In 1968, an African-born coloured cricketer called **Basil d'Oliveira** was chosen as a member of the England team to tour South Africa. But the South Africans refused to let him play against their all-white team. So the British government cancelled the tour. No cricket matches were played between England and South Africa between 1968 and 1993. Other Commonwealth countries did the same as Britain.

SUMMARY

- **1960–1** South Africa became a republic and left the Commonwealth.
- **1962** UN imposed trade boycott – had little effect.
- **1968** d'Oliveira refused entry.
- South Africa ignored UN and continued to govern Namibia.

QUESTIONS

1. Why did South Africa leave the Commonwealth in 1961?
2. What steps were taken by other countries to oppose apartheid? How effective were these measures?

9.6 Apartheid under pressure

Source A

In the whole of the continent only in South Africa did White supremacy still seem possible after 1980.

To many people South Africa was breaking the principle of equality and liberty and should be isolated.

▲ *An Illustrated History of Modern Britain 1783–1980*, D Richards and J W Hunt 1983.

African countries become independent

- In 1975, Angola and Mozambique became independent. They had black governments which hated apartheid.
- In 1980, Rhodesia became independent and was renamed Zimbabwe. Robert Mugabe was the first black Prime Minister of the country.

South Africa was now surrounded by states which were hostile to apartheid and ruled by black governments. The South African government was afraid that guerrillas from these neighbouring states would cross into South Africa to help the people there who were trying to end apartheid. So the government strengthened border patrols.

▲ South Africa and her neighbours in 1975.

▲ South Africa and her neighbours, 1975–85.

Black Consciousness movement

In South Africa, opposition to apartheid grew in the 1970s and the Black Consciousness movement was established. This movement was led by a young Black called Steve Biko. His death in 1977 horrified the rest of the world and was one of the better known incidents of the government's campaign of repression and arrests after the Sharpeville massacre (see page 219). He was arrested in good health in August 1977 and died one month later having 'hit his head against a wall' (see Source C). The Black Consciousness Movement tried to teach Blacks to celebrate their blackness and not to be ashamed of it.

Schools

In 1976, the South African government said that half of school lessons had to be taught in Afrikaans. Afrikaans was the language of the Afrikaners, and no one outside South Africa spoke it. The Blacks saw this as a way of making sure that they spoke the language of their masters. Blacks rioted for months.

Soweto

Soweto was an African township (see page 218). On 16 June 1976, 15,000 pupils in Soweto demonstrated against the government's decision that half their lessons had to be in Afrikaans. But police stopped their march with tear gas and live bullets. Many children were killed and far more were wounded. The police did not allow journalists to count the bodies, and they took the film from most photographers' cameras. Blacks reacted angrily. A wave of violent demonstrations swept through South Africa. The police arrested 6,000 people and banned the Black Consciousness movement.

Winnie Mandela

Winnie Mandela, the wife of **Nelson Mandela** (look back to page 219), helped set up the Black Parents' Committee. This committee helped parents whose children had been killed. Winnie Mandela played a very important part in keeping the protests against apartheid alive while her husband was in prison.

Prime Ministers of South Africa 1924–94	
1924–39	Hertzog
1939–48	Smuts
1948–54	Malan
1954–58	Stijdom
1958–66	Verwoerd
1966–78	Vorster
1978–89	Botha
1989–94	de Klerk
1994–	Mandela

Source B

▲ A child killed by flying bullets on 16 June 1976 in Soweto.

Source C

Steve Biko was questioned for three weeks in Port Elizabeth.
He was then driven, naked and almost unconscious, on a 700 mile journey to prison in Pretoria.
He died there the next day: 12 September 1977.

▲ Adapted from Mary Benson, *Nelson Mandela*, 1986. Steve Biko was the 46th political prisoner to die in police custody. The official statement was that Biko had had a fall.

QUESTIONS

1. Look back over this section.
   a. List the ways in which people opposed apartheid.
   b. How did the government react?

9.7 Why did the reforms of P. W. Botha fail?

Enemies of South Africa
P.W. Botha became Prime Minister in 1978. He believed that communists were trying to destroy South Africa. South Africa was being attacked by guerrilla forces from the countries surrounding it, and Botha believed that the USSR, China and Cuba were financing these guerrillas.

Total strategy
Botha decided that South Africa needed a 'total strategy' against its enemies, both inside and outside the country. He first increased the strength of the armed forces and the security forces. The South African army helped groups fighting against black governments in Africa. It tried to destroy ANC bases in Zimbabwe, Zambia, Lesotho, Mozambique and Botswana. It also sent assassins to murder people who did not believe in apartheid. South African agents murdered about 300 ANC activists.

Botha needs Black support
Botha also wanted to keep peace inside South Africa. To do this he needed the support of young, black Africans who were beginning to fill the new skilled jobs in industry. But these young Blacks were totally against apartheid. So Botha decided to make some changes.

▼ The strengthening of South Africa's armed forces, 1961–85.

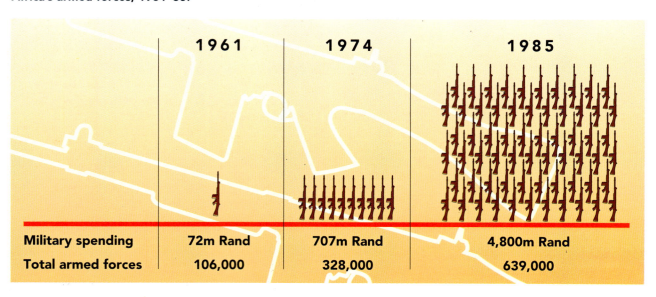

	1961	1974	1985
Military spending	72m Rand	707m Rand	4,800m Rand
Total armed forces	106,000	328,000	639,000

Botha's reforms

Botha introduced some reforms which he hoped would persuade young, skilled Blacks to support his government.

- Blacks who had been allowed into white areas to work were now allowed to buy houses there.
- Blacks could join trade unions, which would help them to improve their working and living conditions.
- The government spent more than before on black education, so that more Blacks could become skilled workers.
- Factories and offices did not have to have separate dining rooms and toilets for Blacks, Coloureds and Whites.
- The government allowed some theatres, restaurants and hotels to become multiracial.
- In 1985, the government abolished the Mixed Marriages Act.
- In 1986, the government abolished the Pass Laws.

Constitutional reforms

Botha wanted to divide the non-white opposition to apartheid. So his constitutional reforms (look at the diagram on this page) gave some power to Coloureds and Indians. But very few of them voted in the 1984 elections. They did not believe that they had any power to change things.

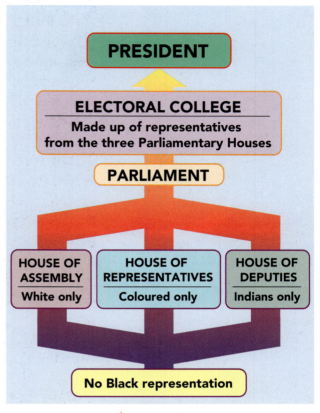

▲ P. W. Botha's new constitution.

Source A

We want *all* rights, not just a few token handouts which the government sees fit to give ...
and we want all of South Africa's people to have their rights, not just a few Coloureds or Indians.

We have been waiting so long, we have been struggling for so long. We have pleaded, cried, petitioned too long now.
We have been jailed, exiled, killed for too long. *Now* is the time.

▲ The Reverend Allan Boesak, addressing the first meeting of the United Democratic Front in 1983.

▲ Archbishop Desmond Tutu.

▼ Eugene Terre Blanche.

Attitudes to reform
Botha had tried to win the support of non-Whites. But he failed.

The United Democratic Front (UDF)
Members of the UDF were Black, White, Coloured and Indian. They came from all sorts of organizations. Some were old ANC members; some were members of Christian women's groups. **Archbishop Desmond Tutu** played a leading part in the UDF.

Not surprisingly, the government began to arrest and imprison members of the UDF.

Blacks divided
Chief Mangosuthu Buthelezi was chief minister of the KwaZulu black homeland. He led the **Inkatha Party**. This party supported **Nelson Mandela** (see page 219), but was very critical of the ANC.

White opposition
Botha had raised taxes on Whites to pay for the reforms which he hoped would persuade the Blacks to support his government. This made some Whites angry because their standard of living was falling.

Afrikaner Resistance Movement
This was set up in 1984 to fight for white supremacy. Its leader was **Eugene Terre Blanche**.

Source B

▲ Demonstration after the killings at Uitenhage.

The breakdown of Botha's reforms

- In **Uitenhage**, the police shot dead nineteen black demonstrators in March 1985.
- Black tenants refused to pay their rents.
- There was a series of 'necklace' killings. Blacks suspected of working with the government were killed by other Blacks. They had a burning tyre put round their necks. The tyre was supposed to be the 'necklace'.

State of emergency

In 1985 Botha declared a **state of emergency**. This meant that he could increase police powers. Pictures of police brutality appeared on television, and many countries became worried about what was happening inside South Africa. Botha expelled foreign journalists to stop them reporting the troubles.

Sanctions

Many foreign nations began to call for sanctions against South Africa. This was supported by most African leaders. But it was opposed by the British Prime Minister, **Margaret Thatcher**. She said sanctions would harm Blacks more than Whites because the Blacks would lose their jobs. In 1986 the USA started sanctions against South Africa. The Commonwealth wanted to do the same. But Mrs Thatcher's opposition meant that the sanctions did not really work.

Source C

The Prime Minister was opposed to economic sanctions against South Africa.
'The threat of sanctions would simply enable the South African Government to rally support against foreign interference. ...
Economic sanctions would be a tremendous slap in the face for all those there who are working for change.'

▲ Margaret Thatcher speaking at the Commonwealth leaders' debate in Nassau, 19 October 1985. A report from *The Times* newspaper.

9.7 THE REFORMS OF P. W. BOTHA

Source D

▶ Police attacking demonstrators in a black township.

Botha's dilemma

Botha could get the support of the Black Africans and the rest of the world if he introduced reforms. However, if he did this, he would lose the support of his own political party, the Nationalist Party.

SUMMARY

- **1978** P.W. Botha became President. Introduced policy of 'total strategy'.
- Abolition of some aspects of apartheid.
- Constitutional reforms to Parliament.
- **1983** United Democratic Front (UDF) formed.
- **1984** Afrikaner Resistance Movement set up.
- **1985** Violence broke out across the country. State of Emergency declared.

QUESTIONS

1 Read pages 226–7.
  a What reforms did Botha introduce?
  b Why did he introduce them?
2 Read Source A on page 227.
  Write one sentence to sum up what Allan Boesak was saying.

9.8 The end of apartheid

F. W. de Klerk
In 1989, **F. W. de Klerk** took over from P. W. Botha as President of South Africa and leader of the Nationalist Party. He began to make changes:

- He released **Walter Sisulu** from prison.
- He allowed Blacks to demonstrate.
- In 1990, he ended the ban on the ANC.
- He told black leaders he wanted to talk to them about votes for all.
- In 1990, he released **Nelson Mandela** from prison.

Black violence
Nelson Mandela immediately called off the ANC's campaign of violence against apartheid. But he could not stop the violence between the ANC and Chief Buthelezi's Inkatha group. Mandela suspected government interference (see Source A).

Source A

* Those responsible for the violence are never caught by the police.

* When the police have been called to stop violence, they have joined in the fighting.

* These acts of violence coincide with ANC campaigns.

▲ Adapted from a letter sent by Nelson Mandela to President de Klerk in April 1991.

Convention for a Democratic South Africa (Codesa)
At the end of 1991, leaders from nineteen different political organizations met in Johannesburg. They wrote a new constitution based on 'one man, one vote'.

Opposition to Codesa
The Afrikaner Resistance Movement threatened to resist any government which gave power to the Blacks.

Referendum
In 1992, de Klerk held a referendum of Whites. About 70% said they agreed with his reforms.

▼ The new South African flag.

Record of Understanding

Mandela and de Klerk met to draw up a basis for future talks. They agreed that all political prisoners should be released, and talked about ways of ending political violence. They then went on to decide that there should be:

- An elected assembly which would draft a new constitution
- An interim government which would run the country until the new constitution was ready.

27 April 1994

Free elections were held in South Africa for the first time on 27 April 1994. Nelson Mandela was elected President. He and de Klerk worked together, leading the interim government until the new constitution was in place.

Nobel Peace Prize

In September 1994, F. W. de Klerk and Nelson Mandela were jointly awarded the Nobel Peace Prize for the part they played in destroying apartheid and bringing peace to South Africa.

▲ The new South African government structure. (World Factfile)

SUMMARY

- **1989** F.W. de Klerk became President. Walter Sisulu released.
- **1990** End of the ban on the ANC. Release of Nelson Mandela from prison. First talks between de Klerk and ANC delegation on the future.
- **1991** Codesa launched.
- **1992** Referendum among Whites showed de Klerk had their support for his reforms.

Record of Understanding.

- **1994** General election throughout South Africa.

Nelson Mandela became President.

QUESTIONS

1 Explain the following:
  a The decision of F. W. de Klerk to end the ban on the ANC.
  b The opposition of some Whites to 'one man, one vote'.
  c The release of Nelson Mandela from prison.
2 What had F. W. de Klerk and Nelson Mandela done to deserve the Nobel Peace Prize?

Nelson Mandela

Nelson Mandela was 72 years old when he was released from prison in February 1990. He had been in prison since 1962 and was expecting to stay there for the rest of his life.

Nelson Mandela was born in 1918. His uncle was a chief, and Mandela remembers how the Blacks lived peacefully in South Africa before white domination.

When Mandela left school, he trained as a lawyer. He joined the ANC and was elected to the ANC executive. The executive was the committee which ran the organization. When the government banned the ANC in 1961, Mandela stayed on the executive committee, but secretly.

In 1962, Mandela was arrested and imprisoned for five years for his work in trying to bring about an end to apartheid. In 1964, he was tried for sabotage and sentenced to life imprisonment. His wife, Winnie Mandela, carried on his work, although he did not always agree with everything she did.

Many people throughout the world wanted Mandela released from prison. When de Klerk became President of South Africa, it was clear that freedom for Mandela and political power for Blacks were not far away.

▲ On 11 February 1990, Nelson Mandela was released from Victor Vorster prison, Cape Town. He had been in prison for 27 years.

▶ Apartheid in action.

9.9 Exercise: The Sharpeville Massacre

▲ Dead and wounded after the police opened fire on demonstraters at Sharpeville.

Source 2

The disturbances resulted from planned demonstrations of about 20,000 natives. The demonstrators attacked the police with assorted weapons, including firearms. The demonstrators shot first and the police were forced to fire in self-defence.

▲ Statement issued by the South African Embassy in London on 26 March 1960.

Source 3

The witnesses said that the crowd was no more than 4000 strong. White witnesses to the shooting supported this figure.

All statements agree that the crowd was not armed, not even with sticks.... and that the police did not give a warning before opening fire.

Nearly all those being treated at the hospital had been wounded in the back.

▲ From a statement made a few days after the shootings by the Bishop of Johannesburg.

Source 4

The native mentality does not allow Africans to gather for peaceful demonstrations. For them to gather means violence. I do not know how many we shot. It all started when hordes of natives surrounded the police station. If they do these things they must learn their lessons the hard way.

▶ Comments made by the commander of the Sharpeville police shortly after the shootings.

1. What impression do you have of events at Sharpeville from studying Source 2?

2. What impression do you have of events at Sharpeville from studying Source 3?

3. Is there any reason to doubt the reliability of what is said in either Source 2 or Source 3? Use the sources and your own knowledge to answer this question.

4. 'Source 3 is an account from an Archbishop, so it must be telling the truth'. Do you agree with this statement?

5. What do you think happened at Sharpeville? Use your knowledge of events in South Africa and Sources 1–4 to explain your answer.

234 CHAPTER 9 SOUTH AFRICA

INDEX

Aaland Islands 31
Abyssinia 36-7, 167
Admiral Graf Spee 38, 164
Afghanistan 207
Africa 36
Afrikaners 213-17
  and Great Trek 213
  and Resistance Movement 228, 231
Albania 183,186
Al Capone 59-60
Alexandra, Tsarina of Russia 103, 111, 113
Alsace and Lorraine 25
ANC (African National Congress) 215, 218-9, 220, 226, 228, 231, 232-3
Ango-German Naval Agreement 38
Anschluss 39
Apartheid 212, 214, 216-233
Appeasement, policy of 40-1
Arnhem 175
Aryan race 93, 99, 171, 172
Asquith, Herbert 139, 146
Atomic Bomb 178-9, 204
Attlee, Clement 158-9
Auschwitz 172-3
Austria 26, 27, 32, 36, 39, 41, 85
Austria-Hungary 4, 6-7, 14, 15, 21, 23, 25, 26-7
Australia 169
Autarky 97

Battle of Britain 166
Bay of Pigs 196
BEF (British Expeditionary Force) 9, 164-5
Belgium 8, 13, 25, 85, 164, 175, 186
Belsen 173
Benes, President 42
Berlin 175, 206
Berlin Airlift 185-6

Berlin Wall 194-5, 210
Beveridge Report 156-7, 159
Biko, Steve 224-5
Blitz 166, 170
Blitzkrieg 163,
'Bloody Sunday' 107
Boer War 213
Bolsheviks 105, 115, 116-120, 129
Bonus army 66
Booth, Charles 132-3
Botha, P.W. 226-231
Brest-Litovsk, Treaty of 1918 25, 119
Brezhnev, Leonid 198-9, 206-7
Broederbond 214
Bulgaria 6, 21, 23, 32, 175, 183, 186
Bulge, Battle of 175
Burma 178
Bush, George 210
Buthelezi, Chief Mangosuthu 228, 231

Cambodia 200, 203
Canada 186
Capitalism 183
Caporetto, battle of 14
Carnegie, Andrew 57
Carter, Jimmy 207
Castro, Fidel 196
Ceausescu, President 199
Chamberlain, Neville 39, 41-5, 164
Children and Young Persons Act, 1908 136
China 34-5, 74, 188-89, 201, 206
Churchill, Sir Winston 44, 158-9, 164, 165, 166, 175, 183
CIA (Central Intelligence Agency) 184
Clemenceau, Georges 24

CND (Campaign for Nuclear Disarmament) 205
Cold War 182-211
Cominform 184
Communism, theory of 105, 122
  spread of 182-5, 188-90, 191-2, 196, 198-9, 200-4, 226
Communist Party (German) 89-90
Communist Party (Russian) 115, 119, 122, 125, 130, 191, 192, 199
Concentration camps 95, 100, 101, 172-3
Conscientious objectors 19
Containment , policy of 190
Coral Sea, Battle of 177
Corfu 32
Cuba 196-7, 208
Czechoslovakia 27, 41-5, 85, 171, 183, 186, 198-9, 210

D-Day 174
Dachau 95, 173
Daladier, Edouard 42, 45
Danzig 25
Dawes Plan 51, 84
Denmark 164, 186
Détente 206-7
Diem, Ngo Dinh 200
Disarmament Conference 32
Dönitz, Admiral 175, 176
'Domino theory' 200
DORA (Defence of the Realm Act) 1914 18,
Dresden 175
Dubček, Alexander 198-9, 210
Dunkirk 164-5

Education Act, 1944 157
Egypt 167, 193
Eisenhower Dwight D., 167, 174

El Alamein, battle of 167
Enabling Act, 1933 91, 94
Eritrea 167
Erzberger, Matthias 82
Eupen and Malmedy 25

Fagan Report, 1948 216
First World War 4-23, 40, 49, 66, 114, 118, 145, 151
France 4, 5, 20-1, 24, 26, 30, 44-5, 74, 84-5, 182-3, 185-6, 193, 208
   and First World War 7-14
   inter-war years and League of Nations 35-41
   Second World War 163-6, 174-6
Franco, General Francisco 39
Freedom Charter 219

Gallipoli campaign 15
Gapon, Father 106-7
Geneva Peace Conference 51
George V, King 139
Germany 23, 24-7, 30-3, 36-46, 51-2, 74, 78-101, 114, 116, 119, 128, 152, 168, 170, 171, 174-6, 182-3, 185-6
   Jews 100-1, 172-3
   Nazi Party 86-9
   Reparations 26, 81
   Second World War 163-7
   Treaty of Versailles 78-81, 85
   Weimar Republic 80-1
German Democratic Republic (East Germany) 186, 194-5
German Federal Republic (West Germany) 186, 194-5
German Labour Front (DAF) 97
Gestapo 95
Glasnost 210
Goebbels, Joseph 87, 96
Goering, Hermann 88, 95, 97, 176
Gorbachev, Mikhail 209-210
Great Britain 4-7, 9-13, 15-21, 24-6, 35, 36-7, 51, 74, 84-5, 101, 132-161, 169-171, 182-3, 193, 197, 205, 208
   Berlin crisis 185-6
   The Blitz 170-171
   Defeat of Germany 174-6
   General Strike, 1926 147-9, 150

Independent Labour Party 140-1
Labour Party 141, 150, 152, 158-9, 160-1
League of Nations 29, 30, 32-3
Liberal Party 136-9, 158
National Government 152-3
Nationalization 160
Policy of Appeasement 38-45
Second World War 163-7
Welfare State 160-1
Great Depression 40, 49, 61-8, 88-9, 151-3, 154-5
Greece 27, 32, 186
Guadalcanal 177
Gulf War 208

Haile Selassie, Emperor of Abyssinia 36-7
Helsinki Agreement, 1975 206
Hess, Rudolf 176
Heydrich, Reynhard 95
Himmler, Heinrich 95
Hindenburg, Paul von 89-90, 91
Hiroshima 178
Hitler, Adolf 35, 38-46, 83, 84, 86-100, 163-7, 171, 172, 174-6
Ho Chi Minh 200
Ho Chi Minh Trail 200-03
Hoare-Laval Pact 37
Holland 164
Hoover, Herbert 63, 66-7
Hungary 27, 183-4, 186, 192, 208

Iceland 186
Inkatha Party 228, 231
International Labour Organization (ILO) 29
Iron Curtain 183
Israel 193, 208
Italy 4, 14, 27, 30, 32, 36-7, 52, 85, 163, 167, 174, 186, 197

Japan 15, 30, 32-3, 34-5, 52, 74, 106-7, 168-9, 171, 177-9, 188,
Jews 86, 93, 95, 98, 100-1, 172-3, 176

Johnson, Lyndon Baines 200-2
Jutland, battle of 17

Kapp putch 82-3
Kaiser, Wilhelm II 5, 17
Kellog, Frank 33
Kellog-Briand Pact 33
Kennedy, John F 194-7, 200
Kerensky, Alexander 115-8
Keir Hardie, James 140-1
Khrushchev, Nikita 191, 194, 197
Kitchener, Lord 12, 15
Klerk, F.W. de 231-3
Korea 106, 188-90
Kornilov, General 116-7
Krystallnacht 101
Ku Klux Klan 58

League of Nations 23-6, 28-37, 38, 49-50, 52, 85
Lebensraum 38, 92
Lend-lease 74
Lenin, Vladimir 105, 116-121, 123
Leningrad, seige of 174
Lidice 171
Liebknecht, Karl 82
Lithuania 32
Lloyd-George, David 17, 24, 136-9
Locarno Pact 85, 92
Lubbe, Marianus van de 90-1
Luftwaffe 38, 165-6
Luthuli, Chief Albert 218-9
Luxembourg 164
Luxemburg, Rosa 82

MacArthur, General Douglas 179, 188-9
Maginot line 164
Manchuria 33-5, 106, 168, 179
Mandates 26
Mandela, Nelson 219-220, 228, 231-3
Mandela, Winnie 225
Marshall Plan 184-5
Mao Zedong 188-9
Maquis 171
Marx, Karl 105
Masurian Lakes, battle of 112
Mein Kampf 87, 92
Mensheviks 105, 115
Memel 25, 32

Midway Island, battle of 177
Mugabe, Robert 223
Munich Conference 42-5
Munich Putsch 83, 87
Mussolini, Benito 36-7
My Lai 202

Nagasaki 179
Nasser, Gamal Abdel 193
National Insurance Act, 1911 137
NATO (North Atlantic Treaty Organization) 1949 186-7
Nazis 45, 86-101, 171-3, 176
Nazi-Soviet Pact, 1939 45
Neuilly, Treaty of 27
Nicholas II, Tsar of Russia 103, 107-11, 113-5, 119
Night of the Long Knives 94
Nixon, Richard 202-3, 206
North Africa, war in 167
Norway 164, 186
Nuclear missiles 196-7, 204-6, 209
Nuremberg Laws 100
Nuremberg trials 176

October Manifesto 108-9
Octobrists 108
Okhrana 103, 106-7
Okinawa 178
d'Oliveira, Basil 233
Oranienburg 95
Operation Desert Storm 208
Operation Dynamo 165
Operation Overlord 174
Operation Rolling Thunder 201
Operation Sealion 166
Operation Torch 167
Operation Yellow 164
Orange Free State 213

Pankhurst, Emmeline 144
Parliament Act, 1911 139
Pearl Harbor 49, 74, 163, 168-9
People's Budget, 1909 138
Petain, General 165
Petrograd Soviet 115, 117
'Phoney War' 163-4
Poland 25, 27, 31-2, 45, 85, 92, 163, 175, 176, 183-4, 186, 210

Polish Corridor 25
Portsmouth, Treaty of, 1905 106
Portugal 186
Potemkin, battleship 107
Potsdam Conference 1945, 183
Potsdam Declaration 178
Prague 198-9
Prague Spring 198-9

Rasputin, Grigori 111, 113
Rathenau, Walther 82
Reagan, Ronald 209
Reichstag 80-2, 87-91, 100
Reparations 26, 32, 81, 84
Rhineland 26, 39
Rhodesia (Zimbabwe) 221-3
River Plate, battle of 164
Röhm, Ernst 94
Romania 6, 27, 175, 183-4, 186, 199
Rome-Berlin Axis 37
Rommel, Erwin 167
Roosevelt, Franklin D. 49, 66-74
    Alphabet Agencies 68-70
Rowntree, Seebohm 133
RAF (Royal Airforce) 166, 175, 186
Russia 14, 15, 20, 23, 25, 53, 92, 102-131
    Civil war 119-120
    Dumas 104, 108-9, 113, 114
    First World War 4-8
    Provisional Government 114-6, 118-9
    Red Army 116-7, 119, 122, 192
    Soviets 115, 117, 118
    Tsar 102-4, 115
    Russo-Japanese War 34, 106-7
    (see also USSR)

Saar coalfields 25, 38
SA (*Sturm Abteilung*) 83, 87-91, 94-5, 100
St Germain, Treaty of 27
St Petersburg Soviet 107-8
St Valentine's Day Massacre 60
SALT (Strategic Arms Limitation Talks) 206-7
Sauer Report, 1948 216
Schacht, Hjalmar 97
School Meals Act, 1906 136

Schlieffen Plan 7
Second Book (of Hitler) 92
Second World War 74, 102, 128, 156, 163-179, 204
Serbia 6, 7
Sèvres, Treaty of 27
Seyss - Inquart 39
Sharpeville Massacre 219
Singapore 169
Sisulu Walter 219, 231
Smith, Ian 221-3
Smuts, Jan 215, 216
Solidarity 210
Somaliland 36-7, 167
Somme, battle of 11, 21
South Africa 26, 212-233
    Codesa 231
    Nationalist Party 216, 230, 231
    Native Land Act, 1913 213
    Pass Laws 213, 215, 227
    Republic 221
    Sanctions 229
    Sport 212-13
    Treason Trials 219
    Union of, 1910 212-3
    United Party 216
South America 51
Soviet Union (see USSR)
South West Africa (Namibia) 222
SWAPO (South West African People's Organization) 222
Soweto riots 225, 226
Spain 39
Spartacus League 82
Speakeasies 59
Special Areas Act, 1934 153
SS (Schutzstaffel) 88-91, 94-5, 171
Stalin, Joseph 121-130, 174, 183, 191
Stalingrad, battle of 174
Stolypin, Peter 110-11
Stresemann, Gustav 84-5, 87
Sudetenland 41, 42
Suez Canal 36, 167, 193, 208
Suffragettes 19, 144-6
Suffragists 143, 145

Tambo, Oliver 219
Tannenberg, battle of 112
Terre Blanche, Eugene 228
Tito, President 199

Trades Disputes Act, 1906 141
Trades Disputes Act, 1927 150
Trade Union Act, 1913 141
Transvaal 213
Triple Alliance 4, 15
Triple Entente 4
Trench Warfare 12-13
Trotsky, Leon 108, 117, 118-120, 122
Truman, Harry S. 178, 184, 188-90
Turkey 23, 27, 186, 197
Tutu, Archbishop Desmond 228

Uitenhage demonstration 229
UDF (United Democratic Front) 228
United Nations 188-189, 193, 207-9, 221-222
USA 4, 14, 17, 21, 23, 24, 29, 32, 34, 48-77, 84, 88, 101, 152, 163, 193, 194-5
and
  arms race 204-7, 209
  atomic bomb 178-9
  Cold War 182-91
  Cuban crisis 196-7
  Democratic Party 66
  Depression 65-7
  'Golden Age' 52-6
  Indians 56
  Isolationism 30, 49-52, 74
  Korean War 188-190
  New Deal 49, 67, 69-74
  Prohibition 59-60
  Republican Party 66
  Second World War 168-9, 174-9
  Wall Street Crash 61-4, 88
  Vietnam 200-4

USSR 45, 102, 121-131, 175-6
and
  Cold War 182-199, 200-211
  Five Year Plans 123, 125, 126-9
  League of Nations 30
  New Economic Policy 121-3
  Politburo 121, 122, 130
  Second World War 163, 166, 171, 172-6

Versailles, Treaty of 22, 23-28, 30, 38-40, 44, 49-50, 85, 89, 92, 93, 96, 98
Verwoerd, Henrik 221
Vichy 165
Vietcong 200-203
Vietnam 200-204, 208
Vietnamization 202-3
Vilna 32

Vittorio Veneto 15
War Guilt Clause 26
Warsaw Pact, 1955 186, 190, 192, 198-9, 210
Washington Naval Agreements 51
Weimar Republic 80-2, 86-7, 89, 91
Western Front 9-13, 20-22
Wilson, Woodrow 23, 24, 28, 30, 49, 50
  and fourteen points 23, 28, 49
Women, votes for 142-6
World Economic Conference 51

Yalta Conference, 1945 182-3
Young Plan 51
Ypres, battle of 10
Yugoslavia 27, 175, 183-4, 199

Zimbabwe (Rhodesia) 223

CONVERSION CHART
British Currency

Old currency: 1 penny (1*d*) x 12 = 1 shilling (1*s*) x 20 = 1 pound (£)
Modern currency: 1 penny (1p) x 100 = 1 pound (£)

1*d* = about ½p	2*s*6*d* = 12½p
1*s* = 5p	5*s* = 25p
1*s*6*d* = 7½p	10*s* = 50p
2*s* = 10p	15*s* = 75p

Acknowledgements

The authors and publishers would like to thank the following for permission to reproduce photographs:

Advertising Archives 54;
A.K.G. London:94, 95 top;
Associated Press: 33, 44, 64 above, 195, 196, 225;
Associated Press/ Star Newspapers/ Johannesburg: 204;
Bridgeman Art Gallery: 104;
Gunn Brinson: 100 above;
The British Library: 78;
Camera Press: 209;
Cape Times: 218;
Cartoon International, Rana R. Lurie: 206;
Centre for the study of Cartoons and Caricature, University of Kent: 18, 61, 166, 175 below, 173, 205 top / David Low/ Associated Press: 33 above/ Solo Syndication: 180, 211;
Cephas/M.J. Kielty: 10;
Culver Picture Inc.: 53, 56, 57, 65, 66;
E.T. Archives: 6 below;
Mary Evans Picture Library: 138, 141, 142, 144, 146, 150;
Daily Express: 153
Daily Mirror: 221;
Greater London Record Offce: 136;
David Hall Collection: 86;
Hulton-Deutsch Collection: 6 top, 37, 40, 82, 84, 94, 106, 110, 113, 120, 132, 133, 137, 143, 145, 147, 149, 151, 152, 154, 155, 174, 186, 189, 194, 205 below;
Imperial War Museum: 10 top, 22, 164, 171, 177, 181;
David King Collection: 109, 111, 123, 124, 125, 127, 130;
Kodak: 134;
Labour Party Museum: 158 right;
Magnum Photo Ltd: 198/Magnum/René Burri: 210;
Mansell Collection: 112, 115;
National Air and Space Museum, Smithsonian Institute: 178;
Novosti: 105, 107, 121, 126, 128;
Peter Newark's Pictures: 68;
Photo Press Library: 156;
Popperfoto: 61, 90, 95 below, 103, 108, 119, 168, 170, 191, 193, 202, 208, 215, 234, 221 below, 228, 233, 234;
Punch Library: 47, 50,73;
Range Bettmann: 56, 58, 59, 64 below;
Range Bettmann/UPI: 201;
Franklin D. Roosevelt Library Collection: 75;
Rex Features Limited: 229;
Frank Spooner Pictures © Gamma: 220, 223;
Society for Cooperation in Russian and Soviet Studies: 117;
Suddentscher Verlag: 83, 89, 96, 99, 100 below;
Tennessee Valley Authority: 71, 76;
Topham Picture Point: 43, 45, top, 76, 93, 129, 160, 172 below, 192, 199, 203;
Ullstein Bilderdienst: 93;

The publishers have made every effort to trace copyright holders of material in this book. Any omissions will be rectified in subsequent printings if notice is given to the publisher.

Cover photo: 'The Road To Ypres' by Christopher Richard Wynne Nevinson. Reproduced by permission of Bridgeman Art Library/The Fine Art Society, London.

The publishers would like to thank Barbara Morphew, Learning Support Teacher, St. Joseph's School, Swindon for her advice in the preparation of this book.

The authors and publishers gratefully acknowledge the following publications from which written sources in the book are drawn. In some sources the wording or sentence structure has been simplified.

Written Sources

Paul Addison, *Now The War is Over*, Jonathan Cape, 1985: 6.11C
Stephen Ambrose, *Rise to Globalism*, Allen Lane, 1971: 8.9E, 8.11A
Patrick Benner, *The Early Years of the National Health Service*, 1989: 6.12
Mary Benson, *Nelson Mandela*, Penguin, 1986: 9.4D, 9.6C
Lord Birkenhead, *Memoirs*
R W Breach, *Documentation and Description in European History 1915-1939*, OUP, 1966: 2.5B, 2.5C
J Bartlett Brebner, *Canada, a Modern History*, University of Michigan Press/AnnArbor, 1960: 7.6D
Malcolm Brown T*ommy Goes to War*, J M Dent, 1972: 1.2C, 1.3B, 1.9-3
Lawrence Butler and Harriet Jones, eds. B*ritain in the Twentieth Century, A Documentary reader, vol. II 1939-70*, Heinemann, 1995: 7.8-2
Brian Catchpole, *A Map History of the Modern World*, Heinemann, 1968: 2.4F, 2.6-2
John Charmley, *Chamberlain and the Lost Peace*, Hodder & Stoughton, 1989: 2.50
G Craig, *Germany 1866-1945*, OUP, 1978: 1.3D, 1.6A
Christopher Culpin, *Making History*, Collins, 1984: 5.7C, 5.8A, 5.8B, 8.1A, 8.2B
Christopher Culpin and P Szvscikiewicz, *The Era of the Second World War*, Collins, 1993: 7.4C
B Engel, *Five Sisters: Women against the Tsar*, Weidenfeld and Nicholson, 1976: 5.2A
Barbara Evans Clements, *Bolshevik Feminist*, Bloomington Indiana University Press, 1979: 5.3D
M Ferro, *Nicholas II, Last of the Tsars*, Viking, 1990: 5.6A
S R Gibbons and P Morican, *The League of Nations*, Longman, 1983: 2.2A
F A Golder, *Documents of Russian History 1914-17*, New York, 1927: 5.5C
Lord Grey, *British Gazette*, 1926: 6.6E
Jon Halliday, *Secret War of the Top Guns*, 1992: 8.3B, 8.3C
S William Halpern, *Germany tried Democracy*, New York, 1965: 4.1B
Hansard, Parliamentary Debates, House of Commons, 1914, Series Vol. 65, HMSO: 1.1E
S Harris, *South Africa*, Dryad Press, 1988: 9.1B, 9.3B
David Harrison, *The White Tribes of Africa*, BBC Publications, 1981: 9.1A
S M Harrison, *World Conflict in theTwentieth Century*, Macmillan, 1987: 1.1A, 1.4C, 1.5A, 2.1B, 7.6A, 8.8H
Adolf Hitler, *Second Book*, New York, 1962: 4.7A
Adolf Hitler, *Mein Kampf*, trans. R Mannheim, Sentry paperbacks, 1943: 4.8A
W Hoffer, trans. C Fox, *Der Nationalsozialismus*, Frankfurt, 1957: 4.8A

House of Representatives 72nd Congress, *Unemployment in the United States*, Hearings before a sub-committee on Labor, 1932: 3.9E

F A Holt (trans.), *An Ambassadors Memoirs*, Hutchinson, 1973: 1.4A

K Jeffreys, *The Attlee Government 1945-51*, Longman, 1992: 6.10D

L Kochan, *The Making of Modern Russia*, Jonathan Cape, 1962: 5.5B, 5.7B

L Kochan, *Russia in Revolution 1890-1918*, Weidenfeld and Nicholson, 1966: 5.3E

Richard Lamb, *Churchill as War Leader: Right or Wrong?*, Bloomsbury, 1993: 7.8-3

W Luchtenburg, *Franklin D Roosevelt and The New Deal*, Harper and Row, 1963, 3.12-7

Nigel Kelly, *The First World War*, Heinemann, 1989: 1.2A

Nigel Kelly, *The Second World War*, Heinemann, 1989: 7.8-3

John Maynard Keynes, T*he Economic Consequences of the Peace*, Macmillan, 1919: 4.3B

Karl Marx, *Manifesto of the Communist Party*, Penguin Edition, 1967: 5.2D

M McCauley (ed.), T*he Russian Revolution and the Soviet State 1917-21*, MacMillan, London, 1975: 5.9B

Hakone Mielche, *Portrait of Japan*, Herbert Jenkins, 1965: 7.3A

Harry Mills, *Twentieth Century World History in Focus*, Macmillan, 1984: 5.10A

Modern History Review vol. no. 1, *Hindsight GCSE*, Sept 1990: 2.2B

R Musman, *Hitler and Mussolini*, Chatto & Windus, 1968: 7.1A

A J Nicholls, *Weimar and the Rise of Hitler*, 1968: 4.2C

J Noakes and G Pridham (eds.), *Documents on Nazism 1919-1945*, 1974: 4.9B

D B O'Callaghan, *Roosevelt and the US*, Longman, 1966: 3.6B

The Poems of Wilfred Owen, ed. Edmund Blunden, Chatto and Windus, 1966: 1.2E

Sylvia Pankhurst, *The Suffrage Movement*, Longmans & Co, 1931: 6.5E

R Pipes, *The Russian Revolution*, Edward Arnold, 1990: 5.6B

Price Collier, *England and the English from an American Point of View*, Scribners Sons, 1909: 6.1A

Robert Rayner, *Nineteenth Century England 1815-1914*, Longman & Co, 1927: 6.12-3

Michael Rawcliffe, *The Welfare State*, Dryad Press, 1990: 6.12-6

Donald Read, *Edwardian England*, Harrap, 1972: 6.3B, C, 6.4A, C

A David Reynolds, *Churchill in 1940: The Worst and Finest Hour*, 1993: 7.8-5

D Richards and J W Hunt, I*llustrated History of Modern Britain, 1783-1980*, Longman, 1983: 9.6A

Martin Roberts, *A History of South Africa*, Longman, 1990: 9.1C, 9.3A, 9.4A

The Russian Review, Vol 12, no 3, *Stolypin – Brock Memoirs*, 1953: 5.3F

Schools Council General Studies Project, *Nazi Education*, Longman, 1972: 4.10C

A Schlesinger, H Israel, *History of the American Presidential Elections*, 3.1A

J Scott, *The World Since 1914*, Heinemann, 1989: 8.8C

John Scott, *Beyond the Urals*, Secker & Warburg, 1942: 5.12A

William L Shirer, *The Rise and Fall of Adolf Hitler*, Secker & Warburg, 1960: 2.5A

J Simkin, *Contemporary Accounts of the First World War*, Tressell, 1981: 1.2G

D Snowman, *America since 1920, the Effects of the Depression*, Heinemann, 1968: 3.8D

Frances Stevenson and A J P Taylor (eds.), *Lloyd George – A Diary*, Hutchinson, 1971: 2.1C

L L Snyder, *The Weimar Republic*, Van Nostrand, 1966: 4.2A

The Spiro Institute for the Study of Jewish History and Culture © 7.5D

Harriet Taylor Mill, *The Enfranchisement of Women*, 1851: 6.5B

Harriet Ward, *World Powers in the Twentieth Century*, Heinemann, 1978: 3.3A

David Warnes, *Russia*, 5.5B

Mrs Wibant, *Working Women and the Suffrage*, 1900: 6.5C

Woodrow Wilson, *The Public Papers of Woodrow Wilson*, vol.1, Harper and Bros, New York, 1927: 2.1A

R Wright, *Black Boy*, Harper & Row, 1947: 3.4B

Heinemann Educational,
Halley Court, Jordan Hill, Oxford OX2 8EJ

A division of Reed Educational and Professional Publishing Ltd

MELBOURNE AUCKLAND FLORENCE PRAGUE MADRID ATHENS SINGAPORE TOKYO SAO PAULO CHICAGO PORTSMOUTH NH MEXICO IBADAN GABORONE JOHANNESBURG KAMPALA NAIROBI

© Rosemary Rees 1996
The moral right of the proprietor has been asserted.

First published 1996

99 98 97 96
10 9 8 7 6 5 4 3 2 1

British Library Cataloguing in Publication Data is available from the British Library on request.

ISBN 0 435 30869 6

Produced by Visual Image, Street, Somerset
Illustrated by Visual Image, Jane Watkins
Printed by Mateu Cromo in Spain